THE LORE OF THE

Old Testament

THE LORE OF THE
Old Testament

by

JOSEPH GAER

Little, Brown and Company · Boston

1952

Published simultaneously
in Canada by McClelland and Stewart Limited

PRINTED IN THE UNITED STATES OF AMERICA
BY THE HADDON CRAFTSMEN, INC., SCRANTON, PA.

 1

To

F AY

Contents

Part I: In the Beginning

Part II: The Patriarchs

Part III: In the Days of Moses

Part IV: The Promised Land

THE LORE OF THE

Old Testament

The Bible in Folk Imagination

I

People of every age and every nation have asked the same questions about the origin of the world and all that is in it. They wanted to know how man came to be and what his life means or ought to mean. From the very beginning man has wanted to know who created the universe and for what purpose; who created the seasons, and all the laws of nature, and why; where good and evil come from; why there is pain and sorrow in the world; whether everything was created for man, or each thing exists for its own sake; the meaning of one man's life, or the life of a generation, or an entire nation; and whether it is possible that the stars are in the firmament, that the wild beasts roam, that the eagle swoops down, that the great mountains rise up and that the rivers keep flowing into the sea all without reason — and that all the days of man are without purpose.

These, and a myriad other questions like these, the people tried to answer in their own way. They looked with searching eyes, listened with attentive ears, and then expressed their thoughts in proverb and precept, in parable and fable, in song and in myth, in fairy tale and anecdote. And when the vast oral lore which the people remembered was preserved in writing, we were made the inheritors of the treasury of folk wisdom.

All the nations of the earth had asked and had answered; and they created their own lore. The Jews were, in that respect, no exception. Like all ancient peoples, they were troubled by the even then age-old questions and developed their own folklore. But practically all their lore was built around characters and events, teachings and doctrines, as found in what is known as the Torah, a word that means "instruction" and was originally used only for the Five

Books of Moses but later applied to the entire of the Old Testament.

In the folklore of the Old Testament the Jews have preserved, with great creative talent, their estimate of the Bible as a history of a nation and as a way of life. They have asked and they have answered so that by their answers men might live to know honor in their own eyes, and die undefeated.

There is a marked difference between the epic Old Testament, which is generally presented with startling simplicity and inspiring starkness, and the lore, which is often lavish in descriptive detail. Yet the folklore, like the book that inspired it, is vivid in realistic imagery, full of promise and fulfillment. There is in it very little concern with such questions as how the rabbit got his rabbit skin or why the flash lightning is wavy and forked. We find very little in their lore about animals, crops, or the common phenomena of nature, although in the early days of their history the Jews were nomads and later they were farmers for many generations. The primary concern in their lore, as far back as it can be traced, is with the relation of the individual to his group, and how a man should live to be found worthy in the eyes of his Creator. It expresses the conviction that the world was created with peace and is ruled with justice.

II

Biblical folklore among the folklores of the nations is, in sheer volume, a "triton among the minnows." The flow of this lore began long before the days of the Judges and the Kings, and the spring is not yet dry.

But the reasons why the Bible was such a rich and fruitful source of folklore and continues to nurture the creative imagination of the people to this day cannot be accounted for by its antiquity alone. They lie rather in the nature of the Bible itself.

The Jews accepted the Five Books of Moses (the Pentateuch) as the Holy Law and the Word of God. And they accepted the Prophets and the rest of the Old Testament as inspired by the Lord. In these Sacred Writings, they believe, are to be found all the wisdom to guide man through the problems of life, from the cradle to the grave. They believe there is nothing new under the sun that is not already revealed in the Bible. Locked in the Bible is the Eternal Truth, coming directly or indirectly from God; but the Truth is locked and requires a key.

A key is required to unlock the very language of the Old Testament. For, in the original Hebrew, the Bible is full of words that have many meanings, called homonyms, which lend themselves to diverse and often conflicting interpretations.

In the very first chapter of Genesis we encounter the statement: "And God said: Let us make man in our image, after our likeness." The Hebrew word for "after our image" is bezalmenu, and the word for "after our likeness" is kidmosenu, and both are homonyms. Both of these words could be interpreted to mean an identical representation, such as a reflection in a mirror. From this might be concluded that man, in shape, in figure, and in bodily structure resembles God; and, inversely, that God looks like man and has shape, figure, and body — a conclusion reached by many theologians. If this interpretation is accepted, a great amount of speculation would arise in folk imagination about God's abode, His raiment, His throne, and the angels ministering to Him. And Biblical folklore testifies to this intriguing speculation.

But some scholars conclude that, as used in Genesis, the terms "image" and "likeness" mean only "intellectual perception"; and this interpretation, too, resulted in considerable folk speculation.

What is true of "image" and "likeness" is true of a great number of words and phrases in the Old Testament. The word for "gods" is Elohim. But this homonym also means, "angels," "judges," "princes" and "rulers." Similarly, the Hebrew words for "brother" and "sister," "male" and "female," "good" and "bad," "up" and "down," and many others are homonymic and their diverse interpretations resulted in a vast number of beliefs and legends.

In addition to the homonyms, the language of some parts of the Old Testament, particularly the language of the Prophets, was not intended to be taken literally. When the Prophet Isaiah, for example, predicted the destruction of the Babylonian empire, and said that on that day "the earth shall reel to and fro like a drunkard" and "the moon shall be confounded, and the sun ashamed" (Isa. 24:20 and 23), obviously he did not mean the words literally.

But if there is danger in taking every word in the Old Testament *literally, there is equal danger in taking it figuratively — as the many diverse interpretations in Biblical folklore would indicate.*

Another reason for the nature and vastness of Old Testament folklore is to be found in a sequence of historic events.

As early as 722 B.C. the Northern Kingdom of Israel, comprising the Ten Tribes, was conquered by the Assyrians and the people taken captive. Like so many historical minorities, the captives melted into the majority leaving not a trace behind them.

One hundred and thirty-six years later (587 B.C.) the remaining Kingdom of Judea was invaded and the people taken captive into Babylonia. Among the captives lived the Prophet Ezekiel, who well remembered the end of the Ten Tribes and was determined that the same obliterating fate should not befall the vanquished Judea. Ezekiel gathered about him the elders of his nation in captivity and, together, they decided to rally their people around their sacred teachings, written and oral, to surround them, "by a burning faith as by a frontier of fire." Ezekiel and his followers collected the Five Books of Moses, some of the Prophets, some of the Psalms and many other works, a number of which were later lost. These works were placed in Houses of Assembly, where the leaders and the teachers read them to the congregations, studied them, explained them and expounded them in a system of learning known as the Oral Law.

The loss of Jerusalem and the Temple, the loss of their Kingdom and even their independence, were offset by the imperishable treasure they had rescued, their Scriptures. These became their Holy City and their Temple, their Kingdom and their Country, within whose unconquerable boundaries they learned how to live and be strong.

Under the whip of persecution, the people looked back upon their past as their Golden Era, and clothed the Biblical characters in garments of scarlet and gold. The harder their lives in exile, the richer became their lore of the days of the Patriarchs, the Judges, the Kings and the Prophets. The Pentateuch became their rock and their salvation, as well as the foundation for the rules of their civil life. The leaders began to organize into orders and treatises all the religious ritual and civil rules, based entirely upon interpretation of the Mosaic Law.

In interpreting the Law, teachers used anecdotes, stories, parables, fables and every other conceivable literary device which could elucidate a general principle or moral concept to a people uprooted, transplanted and held in captivity. In their nostalgic recollection of Biblical times, the preachers often went far beyond anything implied in scriptural narrative. And the more romanticized the stories, the better the people liked them.

Since most of the people were illiterate, the teachings were also given in the form of aphorisms and maxims, proverbs and precepts readily understood and easily remembered.

This narrative lore, used originally as exposition, grew rapidly into a body of learning known as Haggadah, meaning "legends." The Law and the ritual, firmly fixed upon Mosaic Law, became more rigid with the passing of time. But the lore of the captive people was less exclusive and came under the influence of the beliefs and superstitions of their new environment. The Jews of Babylonia, building a fortress out of the Law to protect them from Babylonian (and, later, Greek and Roman) influences, at the same time absorbed into their lore many of the beliefs which had been alien and unacceptable to them as long as they had remained upon their own soil.

It should be noted here that nothing is less exclusive than superstition; and nothing travels faster and further than the folk tale. Whenever one encounters a good folk story, it is certain that it can be found, in one form or another, the world over, changed in each locality to suit the circumstances and the times.

Early Biblical folklore exerted a great influence on the lore of other nations; and, in turn, was influenced by the lore existing in those days. A good example of an early Biblical legend which found its way into the folklore of many nations is given in the story about The Rod in Jethro's Garden (see Chapter IX, Story 10).

In turn, we find traces of beliefs and legends in Biblical lore imported from places remote from Judea. The symbolism of sacred trees belongs to primitive nature worship and is clearly alien to Judaism. Egyptian influences are discernible in such stories as The Heart of a Fox (see Chapter III, Story 13). Even Hindu beliefs are to be found in Biblical folklore. In spite of the great distance between India and Judea, there is evidence that King

Solomon imported more than "gold and silver, ivory, apes and peacocks" from India, called Ophir in the Bible. With them, and with the precious stones and almug wood, came beliefs and legends. As the gold found its way into the treasuries of Solomon, the imported lore found its way into the more permanent treasury of Biblical folklore.

During the Babylonian period the Jews accepted and expanded for the first time the belief in a complex system of angels and demons, and began to delve into the mystery and power of names and numbers which, much later, was to develop into a complete mystic system of amulets and exorcism, resulting in a basic revision of Primitive Judaism. But in appropriating beliefs from whatever source, the Jews invested them with their own religious convictions and made them serve to demonstrate the Eternal Truth as they saw it.

In due time the codes and the lore were collected into many books. Though the exact time when the various collections were made and committed to writing remains in dispute, their order and relationship to each other, as we shall see further on, is well established.

The collected works, in turn, became subject to many interpretations. Each commentator added something of his own, or his times, in his interpretation of the Law and the presentation of the lore. And as long as the Bible continued to be a fortress and a refuge for the dispersed people, Biblical lore continued to grow.

III

A large body of Biblical lore also came into existence or was preserved through a series of circumstances and events outside the immediate experience of the Jewish people.

To begin with, there was a king in Egypt nearly three centuries before the Christian Era whose name was Ptolemy Philadelphus and who, according to legend, was a bibliophile. He had heard of the Hebrew Scriptures and ordered his librarian, Demetrius Phalerus, to have them translated into Greek. Eleazar, High Priest of Judea, was consulted and, again according to legend, he selected one man of each of the Twelve Tribes of Israel for each day in the week, six times twelve he chose them, and sent the seventy-two men to Egypt to translate the Bible into Greek for Ptolemy Philadelphus.

The legend goes on to tell that the seventy-two scribes were all exactly seventy-two inches tall and seventy-two years old. They went to Egypt and worked separately exactly seventy-two days; and at the end of that time each had completed the translation of the Scriptures independently, yet when the seventy-two translations were compared, they were identical to the last period.

A number of elaborate researches have been made into the origin of the concept of the Seventy (or rather seventy-two) translators. The famed Letter of Aristeas, *which claims that he was the emissary for Philadelphus to the High Priest Eleazar in Jerusalem to arrange for the translation of the Scriptures, is now generally regarded as a myth. In those days the Jews of Egypt numbered close to a million and Alexandria was the seat of intense Jewish learning. Since the language of the Jews of Egypt in that day was Greek, it is assumed that some of the Scriptures were translated into Greek for their own use, even before the days of Philadelphus.*

But whatever the facts behind the legend, this much we know with certainty: a complete translation of the Old Testament into Greek was made in Alexandria, Egypt, shortly before the Christian Era, and this work is known as the Septuagint, *symbolized by the Roman numeral for seventy, LXX. The Septuagint in time gave rise to many versions such as the Old Latin, Syriac, Ethiopic, Coptic, Sahidic, Armenian, Georgian, Gothic, Slavonic and Arabic. And each incorporated changes in order, numeration or inclusion, so that they all differed from each other to a greater or lesser degree.*

With the advent of Christianity, the Septuagint (later translated and revised after the Hebrew original by St. Jerome into Latin, and known as the Vulgate), *along with the New Testament, were accepted as the Bible of the Christians. But while the early Christians accepted as unquestioned all the books in the Septuagint, the Jews decided to exclude fourteen of them.*

During the two centuries preceding the Christian Era there existed an extensive number of works, some of high literary quality and many of them claiming to be prophetic revelations, all ascrib-

ing their authorship to the Patriarchs or the Prophets, or Kings David and Solomon. A number of these books were considered by some religious leaders of lesser, or little, value and of disputed origin. But no authority existed to exclude them from the Sacred Writings. Some of these were works of fiction which had found favor with the people; some were popular dissertations on faith or disillusion; others were historical records; and still others were collections of maxims written in poetry and wisdom literature. Their place alongside the Five Books of Moses, the Prophets and the Psalms was gravely questioned.

Was the story of the brawling and undisciplined Samson of divine origin? Did the lusty and, in the original Hebrew, orectic nuptial Song of Solomon belong among Sacred Writings? Was Solomon really the author of Ecclesiastes — that work preaching disillusion and that all is vanity? Were not the beliefs expressed in the story of Tobit of Persian or Egyptian origin and utterly foreign to Jewish lore? These and many other questions were asked. And the time arrived for them to be answered and settled for all time.

In the year 90 A.D., soon after the destruction of the Second Temple of Jerusalem, the famed Rabbi Akiba called together the Synod of the College of Jabneh to establish an approved list of the Sacred Books, to be known as the Canon. Each work included had to pass a rigid test as to its divine origin, its authorship, and, above all, its value as a guide and a rule of divine authority.

After lengthy debate the Canon of the Jewish Scripture was agreed upon; but the Canon excluded some of the books included in the Septuagint. The Protestants, many centuries later, named these excluded works Apocrypha.

Today the Greek Church (officially known as the Holy Oriental Orthodox Catholic Church) recognizes the Septuagint version of the Old Testament; and the Roman Catholic Church recognizes the Vulgate (which differs in a number of important respects from the Septuagint) version of the Old Testament. But the Bible of the Protestants, like the Hebrew Bible, excludes from the Old Testament the following:

Esdras (1 and 2); Tobit; Judith; Esther (last part); Wisdom of Solomon; Ecclesiasticus; Baruch; Song of the Three Holy Children;

History of Susanna; Bel and the Dragon; Prayer of Manasses; Maccabees *(1 and 2)*.

From the Apocrypha the door opens into a large area marked by the forbidding inscription: Pseudepigrapha. *This covers a vast number of works, dealing with Biblical characters and events, visions and adventures, which both Christians and Jews rejected, though some have been included among the Apocrypha by certain Christian sects.*

Some of the best known examples of these works are: The Letter of Aristeas; *the* Book of Jubilees; Maccabees *(3, 4 and 5)*; Enoch *(1 and 2)*; Esdras *(3 and 4)*; *the* Sibylline Oracles; *the* Book of Adam and Eve; *the* Assumption of Moses; *the* Martyrdom of Isaiah; Baruch *(2 and 3)*; Pseudo-Philo's Book; The Story of Ahikar; *and* The Twelve Patriarchs.

With the growth and dispersal of Christianty, a vast number of similar extracanonical works were gathered by the early Greek, Roman, Armenian, Coptic and Syriac Church Fathers. Some of these books are often referred to as "secret"; and some of them are designated The Lost Books of the Old Testament. *They are called "lost" because in many instances we have nothing more than a paraphrase of the work, or a mere fragment of the original, to prove its reality in the past; and Biblical scholars are divided as to how these works should be classified.*

But whether apocryphal or pseudepigraphic, the material is rich in lore, rewarding in imaginative plot and satisfying in moral principle. And all the legendary elements of this material are obviously part of the great lore of the Old Testament.

IV

Another source of Biblical folklore was opened up with the rise of another religion in the East, which accepted the Bible as the basis for its Articles of Faith.

About 570 A.D., a boy was born in Mecca to the rich merchant Abdullah, of the priestly tribe of Koreish, and he was named Mohammed. According to one Islamic legend, the mountains began to dance when Mohammed was born and they sang:

"There is no god but Allah!"

*And the trees whispered happily to each other and responded:
"And Mohammed is his Prophet!"*

*Fifty-two years later Mohammed was ready to declare himself
the Prophet of Prophets and started to convert his people to the
religion we know as Islam or Mohammedanism, and the followers
of this religion are known as Mohammedans or Moslems.*

*Mohammed was conversant with both Judaism and Christianity
and claimed that his people were direct descendants of Abraham's
first born son, Ishmael. In the Koran, the Sacred Scriptures of the
Moslems, a prominent place is given to the Old Testament characters, from Adam to Jonah, and many concepts found in the Bible
are incorporated in it, as well as concepts gleaned from the Talmud
and the many Apocrypha. But, of course, all these are used to
establish Mohammed's Articles of Faith.*

*The Arabs have developed almost a complete lore pertaining to
the characters and events in the Old Testament, beginning with
Creation and down to Elijah and the other prophets. Certain
Biblical heroes in particular have captured their fertile imagination
and they have lavished upon them their most ornate costumes and
romantic adventures, with great tenderness. Adam, Enoch, Noah
and Abraham, Joseph, Saul, David and Solomon have been glorified
in this lore. But none received the adulation accorded Moses, whom
they call Moussa, the Messenger of Allah. He and his kin, and the
servants in Pharaoh's court who recognized Moses as the messenger
of God, are all fully described and generously rewarded with
everlasting blessings in the Garden of Eden.*

*Most of the Islamic stories are patterned after Hebraic tales; but
they also contain many innovations and original observations, and
constitute an estimable contribution to Biblical folklore.*

V

*Toward the end of the Middle Ages (around the 13th or 14th
century), when the great Talmudic works were completed; the
many pseudepigrapha fought over; the addenda to the Talmud,
called Tosafta, gathered; when even the vast and rich exegetical
works on the Old Testament, from the early Midrashim to Rashi,
were all down in black and white, and the sources of Biblical folk-*

lore seemed completely explored and exhausted, there arose a new mystic movement called Cabbalah.

The followers of this movement claimed that in the Old Testament there was indeed locked all the wisdom and all the knowledge of the universe throughout eternity. But, said they, not only was the language of the Scriptures not to be taken literally, it was equally dangerous to take it figuratively. The key to all the mysteries and secrets of the universe could be obtained only by breaking down each word of the Scriptures into its component letters and discovering the true meaning of each letter. Or, the letters could be converted into numbers and their meaning interpreted.

"Woe unto the fools who look no further when they see an elegant robe! More valuable than the garment is the body which carries it; and more valuable than the body is the soul which animates it. Fools see only the garment of the Law; the intelligent see the body; and the wise see the Soul." So it is written in a controversial commentary on the Pentateuch called Zohar or Sepher Ha 'Zohar al Ha 'Torah: The Book of Splendor on the Torah. This book, in Hebrew and Aramaic, was published in the 13th century in Spain by Moses Shem-Tov de Leon, who attributes the entire work to Rabbi Shimon ben Yohai, who lived eleven centuries earlier.

The dispute about the origin and authorship of this work does not detract from its value; nor did it prevent the work from becoming the "Bible" to a large number of followers. And the mystic seeds, planted in the Talmud and the Midrashim many centuries earlier, flowered into full bloom among the Zohar disciples called Cabbalists.

These mystics worked out a triple system of interpretation:

The first is known as Gematria. This is the cryptographic system in which a word or a phrase is translated into its numerical equivalent and the number used to discover the hidden meaning. For instance, by reducing to numbers the phrase "and lo three men stood near him" (Gen. 18:2), the Cabbalists discovered that the total was equal to the total of the numbers of the words "these are Michael, Gabriel and Raphael" — and the mystery as to the identity of the angels that visited Abraham was cleared up. It requires little imagination to see what can be done with Gematria when applied to the Old Testament.

Another system, known as Notarikon, *assumes that the entire of the Old Testament was written symbolically, so that each word must be broken down to its letters, each of which represents the initial of another word.* Adam, *according to* Notarikon, *really should be read: "Adam, David and Messiah." From which the conclusion was drawn that with the creation of Adam the coming of the Messiah was foretold, and that the Messiah would be a descendant of King David. (Another mystic group concluded that Adam stood for: Anatole, Dysis, Arktos, and Mesebria, meaning: "East, West, North and South." From which quite different conclusions were drawn, although the same system was used.)*

The third Cabbalistic system is a little more difficult. It is called Temurah *and deals with permutation. This requires that each word in the Scripture be rewritten and each letter replaced with the letter preceding or the letter following in the alphabet. The results were truly amazing.*

In addition to these three key systems, the Cabbalists also assigned great value to the accenting in the reading of the words. The written word, to them, was basically only a symbol of the spoken word. And its oral value or meaning was hidden in the way it was pronounced.

Anyone can readily see that equipped with Gematria, Notarikon *and* Temurah *(properly enunciated) the mystics, metaphorically, had struck oil.*

The Cabbalists found adherents among both Jews and Christians, and ultimately broke up into a number of sects, all agreeing on the basic concept of the supremacy of the human soul over the invisible powers of evil, but disagreeing on the approach to the mastery of that power.

It was not long before a new accumulation of Biblical folklore, full of mysticism and symbolism, made its appearance.

One of the Cabbalistic sects made its appearance in Eastern Europe late in the 18th century. It flourished until World War I, and some remnants are still in existence in parts of Europe and in Israel. This sect was founded by the Polish Rabbi Israel ben Eleazer who is called by his followers the Basht, *which, in the* Notarikon *system, stands for* Baal Shem Tov, *meaning: "Owner of the Good Name."* The followers are known as Chassidim, meaning: *"The Pious."*

The Chassidic movement differed from their Cabbalistic predecessors in that: (1) they placed faith above learning; and learning above action; (2) they emphasized the value of prayer, which, they maintained, unites the human soul with the soul of the universe; and (3) they taught that it is the duty of every man always to be calm and joyful, believing that "tears may open the gates, but joy will tear down the very walls."

The Chassidim, living through one of the darkest periods of exclusion and oppression in Eastern Europe, retreated into their fortress and refuge, the Old Testament, and either created new legends about those wonderful Biblical times, or gave existing legends a new and joyful twist. The result was an added treasury of Biblical lore.

The quality of this Chassidic lore is almost impossible to communicate because to the Chassidim it served not as exposition but as the very essence of living.

Something of its mystic intensity might be gathered from the following example in the author's personal experience:

When I was very young, my grandmother, who belonged to the Chassidic sect, instructed us, her grandchildren, in the beliefs of our people. Once, when I was about six years old, she told us that he who thoroughly understood the meaning of the Name of God had the key to all of knowledge and the clue to all hidden mysteries. For he who clearly knew the mystical and symbolical meaning of the Name of the Creator, understood both Being and Becoming — a topic on which my grandmother expounded with great simplicity and without embarrassment. To her the fear of God was literally the beginning of wisdom, and the understanding of His Name, the core and essence of Knowledge.

Next to the Name of God, Grandmother told us, came the Ten Commandments, written by the Lord with red fire on black fire long before the world was created. The Ten Commandments, she maintained, were written in roshe tovoth, or the beginnings of words. Anyone who could reconstruct the complete meaning of the Ten Commandments correctly would at once place himself beyond the power of evil and corruption. Such a person could even *make himself invisible. He could see without being seen; he could hear without being heard; he would know the future of every event to the end of time. And the Angel of Death would have no power over him.*

These, and hundreds of beliefs like these, Grandmother recounted, often illustrating them with fables and stories related to Biblical characters. And whatever she told us was something she had heard and remembered, not something she had read. For my grandmother, although she lived to the age of ninety-three, had never learned to read and write.

I can still recall the excitement with which we listened to some of her stories about the hidden meaning of words and ritual acts, about how we could make ourselves invisible, and invincible to the powers of Satan and the many-eyed Angel of Death.

One more source of Biblical lore should be described, a source which has found little favor with most Biblical folklorists: the Pentateuch and Books of Supplications written in Yiddish exclusively for Jewish women.

During the 13th century many German Jews migrated eastward, mostly to Poland. They carried with them the language they spoke, namely German, but they wrote it with Hebrew letters and incorporated into it many Hebrew words. In time this dialect of Hebrew-German developed into a distinct language, Yiddish, which was spoken by all East-European Jews. Before long literary works began to appear in Yiddish, addressed mainly to the Jewish woman, who was exempt and excluded from the study of the Bible and its lore, yet yearned to know what the Hebrew and Aramaic books contained. Most of the early Yiddish books were anonymous, the writers often signing their works: "Author for Pious Women."

In the year 1620, Rabbi Jacob ben Isaac Ashkenazi published in Poland a work in Yiddish called Tzeneh-u-Renoh, *meaning: "Let Us Go Out and See." This work is a strange paraphrase of the Pentateuch with profuse commentaries drawn from practically all Biblical folklore sources. Though it does not rank high as a work of literature, its success was immediate and its influence on generation after generation of Jewish women can hardly be estimated.*

Before long a number of editions of this book appeared, each editor taking liberties with the folklore elements of the work. Var-

ious running commentaries were added, such as: The Examples of the Fathers, *the* Tents of Jacob, *the* Great Deeds *and especially those moral stories known as* The Valuable Jewels. *In succeeding editions the books of Ruth, Esther, Ecclesiastes, The Song of Songs, some Psalms, all of* The Sayings of the Fathers *(a tractate of the* Mishnah*), the apocryphal Judith, and other works were added.*

At about the same period there also began to appear a large number of Books of Supplications for Women which combined (particularly in areas where Chassidism thrived) religion with stories of the supernatural. They were written in Yiddish and enjoyed the popularity of mystery and adventure literature the world over.

These Women's Bibles and Books of Supplications contain little original Biblical folklore. Practically all their legends are derived from earlier sources, either Rabbinic or apocryphal. But the lore is written differently than in any of the sources from which it is derived. Though they speak of Biblical places, Biblical characters and Biblical events, the descriptions are often strangely in terms of their Lithuanian, Bessarabian, Polish or Hungarian surroundings, as the case may be. The remote events of the Bible are subtly used to express current woes and joys, hopes and aspirations. The writing is at once naïve and cunning, reverent and playful, unquestioning in faith and yet full of implied doubt; and, while squeamish at times, the writing is without inhibition or restraint.

It is living folklore.

The many sources of Biblical folklore may explain the vastness and the perpetuation of the lore. But for its greatness we must turn to the Old Testament itself.

In the entire range of world literature there is not another book like it. Apart from its historical value and even greater religious significance, it is the supreme literary work (or rather collection of works), containing the world's best in storytelling, drama, proverbs, and, above all, the most inspired epic poetry. For there is no other work to compare with it in acuteness of observation; in the understanding of human frailty and man's ambition; in the vision of the eye and the mind and the heart; and in the broad knowledge of the laws of life.

Great poets and storytellers, from Dante to Milton, from Bunyan to Goethe, from Tolstoy to Mann, have gone to the Old Testament for themes and inspiration.

It is not surprising then that the storytellers and commentators on the Bible were inspired with its grandeur; and whatever greatness is found in the lore belongs to the Book that kindled it.

The vastness, diversity and complexity of existing Biblical folklore presents nettling problems to one who undertakes to excerpt and glean from it a unified whole.

To begin with, some of the material can be traced back to the days of the Judges or even earlier, whereas some was, figuratively, born yesterday. Again, a given story may be found in a great number of variants, but often equally reliable sources give quite contradictory accounts.

The ages of characters and the time of events, unless fixed by the Old Testament in a way that is not subject to diverse interpretations, rarely agree in the different versions in folklore. Job, for instance, is presented as a contemporary of Moses, in one source; he is supposed to have lived in the days of the Judges, according to another source; still another makes him a contemporary of Solomon; while in a different source he is placed in the days of Esther and Ahasuerus; and still another assures us that Job lived long after the Babylonian captivity and founded a college in Tiberias. The historians seem certain that Job was a contemporary of Abraham. Whereas some Talmudic Rabbis insist that Job never existed and that the Book of Job was written by Moses to strengthen Israel's faith.

Or take the question of the "forbidden fruit." The fruit of the Tree of Knowledge is not identified in Genesis. In the lore it has been variously named as: the fig; the Apple of Paradise; wheat (grown on stalks as tall as the cedars of Lebanon); the nut, which produces sexual desire. One apocryphal work argues in favor of the grape; and another, in favor of the apple. Each identification is deduced from a statement in the text, freely interpreted. Whereas some Rabbinic sources imply that it is forbidden to speculate on the identity of the fruit, the argument being that it is deliberately not named in the Scriptures so that man shall not come to hate it for having brought death to the world.

Sometimes a story is ascribed to one person, in one source, and to another, in a different source. There are, for example, several stories about Elijah that are elsewhere ascribed to Elisha.

In the case of legends well known through the Bible itself, if the lore varies too little from the Bible story, the casual reader may take it as a paraphrase from the Scriptures rather than a folk tale; but if the lore differs to an extreme from the generally accepted, the reader's credulity may be strained, as in the case of Isaac's age, when he was taken by his father to be sacrificed on Mount Moriah. In many legends his age at that time is given as thirty-seven; though most people acquainted with the Biblical story think of him as a very young boy at the time of this event, and he is usually so represented in Biblical illustrations or paintings.

Some of the legends may appear to the reader in a light and almost irreverent vein, as, for example, the story about God's failure in the creation of Woman (see Chapter II, Story 11). Yet such stories give a deeper insight into the folk concept of their Creator than the pietic passages.

Upon reflection, the reader will find the seemingly irreverent legends in accord with the spirit of the Bible, in which Man may challenge God to a debate about divine injustice as in Job; and may even scold Him, as given so boldly in the exchange between God and Moses, after the Jews fashioned the Golden Calf. The Bible records that "the Lord said unto Moses: I have seen this people and, behold, it is a stiff-necked people. Now, therefore, let me alone that my wrath may wax hot against them, and that I may consume them."

Moses angrily responds by asking whether God wants the Egyptians to say that He had delivered Israel from Egyptian slavery "to slay them in the mountains and to consume them from the face of the earth." And he adds: "Turn from Thy fierce wrath, and repent of this evil against Thy people." (Exodus 32.)

In no religion preceding Judaism is the Creator conceived of so much as the Father, rather than the all-powerful God; and in no religious lore is the Creator treated so intimately, as the Head of the family, who may sometimes be questioned, sometimes chided, and sometimes even scolded, as in the case of Moses.

The most nettling problem of all was that of condensation. In the attempt to present as many legends as possible within the confines of one book, it was often necessary to select only one story on a given event, where there were many; and, just as often, the story had to be abridged. And the folk tale, like the porcupine, does not take to confinement.

In this book will be found only a very small measure of the folklore of the Old Testament. But even this shadow at noon, it is hoped, will suffice to indicate the majesty and grandeur of the mountain it represents.

The Plan Followed

The chronology in this book follows the Old Testament to achieve a continuity and unity which would be lacking if the legends were arranged topically.

The stories were selected to include, as far as possible, a cross section of all available sources, following the lore and not the logic. But the material selected was not merely transcribed. It should be clear that though everything included is the same, everything is different.

Every story, every incident, every description, every concept, and every precept in this book is taken from an authentic folklore source. Yet this is not merely a compilation of material from diverse sources. Often several legends have been combined under a single heading; and all the legends have been restated and recreated.

To obviate footnotes, the sources and explanatory notes have been relegated to the Notes on Sources. The reader wishing to know where each story comes from, or what variants exist and where they may be found, will obtain that information in the Notes.

If the reader is puzzled when he finds that quotations from the Old Testament sometimes tally with the Authorized King James Version and sometimes differ from it, that is explained by the fact that the Authorized Version was used because it is, generally, still the best; and the Revised Version was consulted for its superior poetic passages. And in passages where the original Hebrew seemed clearer in thought and sharper in image, the author did not hesitate to render his own translation.

The Douay Version was also consulted but nowhere directly quoted because, whatever its merits may be in more accurate translation of many passages, it does not equal the King James Version as literature.

Each legend included was selected on its own merit as a story, as well as for its relation to the book as a whole, and was judged twice: first, for the concept of truth or the observation of reality it portrayed; and then on how it combined with all the others to reveal a rounded presentation of a way of life.

The Purpose

The preparation of this book is based on the conviction that in the Bible can be found the understanding whereby men of all times may live with dignity and purpose. The key to this understanding does not lie in symbolism or mystic permutations.

There is no key. For there is no lock.

The truths of peace and justice are there for anyone willing to discover them. But the Book, though still universally revered, is increasingly neglected. The Bible, and Biblical lore, have become to many legendary and obsolete, on the assumption that they contain nothing for us today.

This assumption is wrong and the loss is entirely ours.

This collection of folklore, if it succeeds in its purpose, should rekindle the incentive to renew acquaintance with the Bible itself. The purpose therefore is not to present a folklorated story of the Bible, but rather to present a progression of concepts, as revealed in legend and precept, that have occupied the mind of man since the beginning of time and that have never been dealt with more nobly than in the Bible.

PART I
In the Beginning

The first eleven short chapters of Genesis record over two thousand years of Biblical history — from Creation to Abraham (4004–1996 B.C.). And at that, almost a third of the space is given to a repetition of the story of Creation and two detailed genealogies, from Adam to Terah. Yet the events in this brief section of the Old Testament — the stirring day-by-day description of Creation; man's fall and punishment; the first terrible murder; the giants in the earth and their wickedness; the great deluge; the Tower of Babel and the confusion of tongues — have inspired many books and an immeasurable volume of legends.

Out of this vast treasury of extra-Biblical lore about the days when the world was very young the following stories were selected.

CHAPTER ONE

The Week of Creation

1. *The First Day of Creation*

Ten things were created on the First Day: *Heaven* and *Earth;*
Tohu (chaos) and *Bohu* (emptiness); *Light* and *Darkness; Wind*
and *Water; Day* and *Night.*

Heaven and Earth: The same instant that God created heaven
He created earth; and with the same principle He created both. He
stretched out His right hand and the heavens appeared; He
stretched out His left hand and the earth was founded.

There are seven different names for heaven in the Bible, which
proves that there are seven heavens. The first heaven, nearest to
the earth, is a curtain which covers the face of the sun in the evening
and withdraws at daybreak. The second heaven is the dwelling
place of the sun, the moon and the stars. In the third heaven the
food for the righteous is prepared and it is from there that the
manna fell. The fourth heaven is devoted to the Celestial City of
Jerusalem and the Celestial Temple, presided over by Michael,
Prince of Angels. The fifth heaven is filled with ministering angels
who sing all night but are silent all day. In the sixth heaven are
stored the treasuries of snow and rain, hail and dew, the chambers
of the whirlwind and the storm, the balls of fire and the caverns
of smoke. In the seventh heaven reside the souls of the unborn.
There, also, are the ministering angels, called the *Seraphim,* who
surround the two Thrones of Glory.

Since there are also seven different names for earth in the
Bible, we know that the earth consists of seven distinct layers,
each with its own preordained treasuries. The seven earths lie flat
one upon the other, and all of them are supported by great pillars.
The pillars stand on water; the water rests upon mountains; the

mountains rest upon wind; the wind rests upon the storm; and the storm is suspended upon the mighty arm of God.

There is a difference of opinion about the number of pillars on which the earth rests: some sages maintain that the number is twelve, one for each of the Tribes of Israel; others say the number is seven, one for each day in the week; some say five, one for each of the Five Books of Moses; some say three, one for each of the Patriarchs Abraham, Isaac and Jacob; and some are certain that only one solitary pillar supports the entire earth and its name is The Righteous, since it is written: *"The Righteous One is the foundation of the world."*

The dimensions of the heavens are immeasurable. The dimensions of the earth, unlike the dimensions of the heavens, are very clearly given: the seven layers of earth are exactly one thousand cubits thick. And the surface area, east and west and north and south, is measurable as follows: Egypt, which is 400 parasangs long (a parasang is about 3½ miles) and 400 parasangs wide, is one sixtieth the size of Cush; and Cush is one sixtieth the size of the world. Therefore the surface of the earth must be 400 × 400 × 60 × 60 parasangs, or 576 million square parasangs.

However different their dimensions may be in length, in width and in depth, heaven and earth are made out of the same materials. God took two coils, one of fire and the other of ice, wove them into a single coil, as a symbol of peace, and with it he made both heaven and earth.

Tohu and Bohu: After the earth was formed, *Tohu* (chaos) and *Bohu* (emptiness) were created. *Tohu* was a green light that surrounded the entire earth and from it issued darkness; *Bohu* turned into slime-covered stones in the depths of the earth, from which issued water.

Light and Darkness: Though the sun and the moon were not created until the Fourth Day, God created light on the First Day. Unlike the light of the sun or the moon was that first light. It was seven times stronger than the light of the sun and, if it shone today, would enable a man to see the world from end to end, without hurting his eyes. It emanated from the center of the earth, where the City of Jerusalem was to be built, out of the exact spot where the Holy of Holies was to be in the Temple. That light will be rekindled when the Messiah appears on Mount Moriah. And only then will men have clear vision.

Darkness was not just the absence of light on the First Day, but a created substance which issued upon the world from the north. And that darkness, too, was unlike the darkness of night. When God wishes to punish the world for its wickedness, He plagues it with the darkness created on the First Day — as He did in the days of Moses in Egypt.

Wind and Water: The winds had to be created the First Day, for without wind the world cannot survive. "Four winds blow every day, and the north wind blows with them all," it is written. Were it not so, the world could not exist for even a single hour. Each wind brings its own fortune or misfortune. The east wind stirs up the world like a demon; the north wind creates drought; the south wind brings rain and stormy weather. The north wind is good in the summer and harmful in the winter. The south wind is harmful in the summer and beneficial in the winter. The east wind is always beneficial. The west wind is always harmful. That is the way God made them the very First Day of Creation.

The water that was created the First Day was unlike the water upon which the Spirit of God moved. The earlier water was water within water, and the ultimate origin of all the elements. After creating the winds, God created the water of the earth and the water of the sky, and out of the same source He created both. Sometimes the water of the sky comes down to become water of the earth. The clouds, like huge vessels, receive the water poured into them from the sky. When lightning strikes and shatters the clouds, the water pours down in rain. And when a strong wind blows across the mouths of the empty clouds, we hear a great rumbling sound which is thunder. Thunder results also when the water from the upper clouds surges over into clouds near the earth.

Day and Night: The last thing to be created on the First Day was *time*. Before the creation of the world, time did not exist, for in the Eternal time is neither a dimension nor a measure. But once the Universe was created, time was needed. Time was divided into two equal measures, called Day and Night. Day and Night were created before there was a sun or a moon.

Before the Universe could be established, three elements were needed: Water, Fire and Wind. Water conceived and bore darkness; Fire conceived and bore Light; Wind conceived and bore Wisdom. Yet Time was needed for these elements to become the essence of the world. For nothing in the world can be judged by its own attributes and dimensions, unless the dimension of Time is added.

2. *The Second Day of Creation*

The Second Day began with the division of the waters of the earth from the waters of the sky. When God asked the waters to separate, the waters of the earth complained.

"O, Lord! Why should we be down here below and the other waters near You? We, too, want to be up in heaven."

God admonished them: "Water will be needed for the purifications and the sacrifices and those waters will be as near to Me as any in the firmaments."

The waters of the earth still grumbled.

And God said again: "Cleanliness is next to godliness. Without water the earth cannot for long remain clean."

The waters of the earth were finally pacified.

The quarrel of the waters marred the Second Day of Creation. That is why on all the days of Creation it is said: "*And God saw that it was good.*" But it is not said at the end of the Second Day. Because of the quarrels of the waters, discord came to the world. Discord leads to contention; contention leads to hostility; hostility leads to aggression; and aggression leads to war. The Creator would not pronounce as "good" either war, or anything that leads to war.

The quarrel of the waters on the Second Day of Creation is remembered to this day, and no task or enterprise is begun on a Monday, for it is a bad omen to begin any task on the one day when God did not say "*it was good.*"

3. *The Third Day of Creation*

On Tuesday, on the First Tuesday, God created the soil, the oceans, and all vegetation. He clothed the earth in grass, herbs, fragrant shrubs, grain of every kind, vegetables and fruit trees, wood-yielding trees and shade-yielding trees, bulrushes and coriander, the gopherwood for Noah's ark and the vines of Sodom bearing the grapes of gall; and all' the other kinds of plants on earth; including the crocus, the myrtle, the mallows, the lily and the rose of Sharon. All were in bloom when they were created, and the fruit trees were laden with fruit. And the air was filled with their fragrance.

Among the plants created on the Third Day there was one stranger than any in all creation. It looked like a man; it walked on two feet; when hurt, it wept and when happy, it laughed; and it could even speak. Yet it was only a plant. It was attached to the ground by a long stem which had roots in the ground and it gained its sustenance that way. In two ways the *Adneh Sadeh* could be clearly distinguished from man: its blood was green; and it had no free will. But what really made it a plant was the fact that it knew no temptation, nor could it ever be righteous.

When the great deluge came, ten generations after Adam, the Adneh Sadeh perished along with many other exotic plants created on the First Tuesday, and has not been seen since.

Because on Tuesday God saw what he did and *twice* pronounced it "good," Tuesday is an especially lucky day to start an enterprise, lay a cornerstone, start a voyage, begin school, or get married.

4. *The Fourth Day of Creation*

To avoid any jealousy between heaven and earth, God worked one day on the earth and the next on the heavens above. Since on Tuesday He created the herbs, the berries and the fruits bearing their own seed, Wednesday was devoted to the completion of heaven.

The Sun and the Moon: First God created two great lights,

the sun and the moon. They were equally bright, and the same in every other respect. The day and the night were already established in time and there was no need to distinguish between them in light. The moon was created to make the measure of time easier, and to keep men from becoming sun worshipers.

But the moon grew jealous of the sun and complained:

"O, Lord! Why can't You make me just a little brighter so that men will know us apart?"

And God said: "You foolish moon! Because of your discontent, I shall partly grant your wish. One of you shall be the lesser. It shall be you. And you shall henceforth receive your diminished light from the sun. It will really be better that way because when the moon comes out, it will grow darker and My creatures on earth will know it is time to rest."

The Man in the Moon: The moon, after Creation, was as smooth and as blank as a highly polished brass pan. But many, many generations later a face appeared on the moon which has remained there ever since. And this is how it happened:

There was a rich man once who was also very wise, but, alas, neither his riches nor his wisdom made him happy. For he had an only son who refused to study and who could learn little. When this man grew very old, he called his son and said to him: "When I die all my wealth shall be yours, provided you can prove that you are able to take care of it. To prove it you must first find the greatest fool in the world and give him this golden apple." He gave his son a box containing an apple made of pure gold, and then he died.

After the customary days of mourning the son started out to fulfill his father's will: to find the greatest fool in the world. But he soon discovered it was not as simple as he had imagined, for each time he met a man who seemed to be very foolish, upon inquiring he found that the man either had a system to his folly, and his stupidity was rewarding; or he was not as foolish as he at first seemed. The young man traveled from village to village, from town to town, and from city to city, year after year, still trying to prove himself worthy of his inheritance. After many years, when his hair turned gray and his breath grew short, he returned home.

There he found his home in ruins, his father's wealth dissipated by faithless servants, and all that was left of any value was the golden apple he had carried about with him as a prize.

He went to his father's grave and confessed: "Father," said he, "I realize too late that the golden apple was meant for me. Any man who would squander his life in search of a fool, is indeed the greatest fool."

God put the face of that man on the moon as a lesson to the arrogant who think they can judge other people's folly but need not judge their own. And that is also why the moon sometimes looks like a golden apple.

There are many other legends about the Man in the Moon. According to one, God placed the face of Moses on the sun, and the face of Joshua on the moon.

The Sun Sets Sadly: The sun was made to shine at all times with the same light. Yet it appears rosy when rising and scarlet when setting. That is because in the morning it passes over and reflects the roses in the Garden of Eden; and in the evening it passes over the entrance to the *Gehinnom* in the wilderness, reflecting the red of the fire and brimstone below.

How Many Stars Are There?: After the sun and the moon were in their orbits in the second heaven, God created the stars. The number of stars created was recorded by God himself as follows:

"Twelve constellations have I created in the firmament, and for each constellation I have created thirty hosts, and for each host I have created thirty legions, and for each legion I have created thirty files, and for each file I have created thirty cohorts, and for each cohort I have created thirty camps, and for each camp I have suspended three hundred and sixty-five thousand myriads of stars, one myriad for each day in the year."

That is exactly how many stars there are.

5. *The Fifth Day of Creation*

On the First Thursday God returned to the earth and stocked all the waters with every conceivable kind of fish — flying fish, climbing fish, rainbow fish, flatfish, fish so small that they cannot be seen with the naked eye, and fish so big that out of one of its eyes three hundred barrels of oil can be extracted, and out of its bones great balconies can be built. He made the good eating fish in a great variety of size, of color and of taste. He made thousands of varieties, each different in appearance, in nature and in purpose.

God then blessed the fish to be fruitful above all other creatures, for He knew that many generations of men would depend on fish for food. And He made the fish so as to offer man good health and virility. That is why he who eats small fish often keeps in good health and remains virile.

After the Fish the Birds: As soon as all the waters were fully stocked, God made the birds on wing: The bittern and the giereagle, the hawk and the cormorant, the cuckoo and the dove, the falcon and the stork, the sparrow and the raven, the glede and the owl, the quail and the ostrich, the swallow and the peacock, the swan and the partridge, the heron and the ossifrage, as well as the hummingbird and the nightingale, the ptarmigan and the pipit, the bird of paradise and the whippoorwill, the meadowlark and the robin, the crane and the flamingo, the drongo and the hammerhead. And he blessed them, too, with great fruitfulness. The goose and the duck are not mentioned anywhere in the Bible. But we know they exist; and that is how we know they were created on that First Thursday.

Then Came the Angels: After the fish and the fowl, God created the angels.

We know that the angels were created on Thursday because it is written that on that day God created all the winged things "flying above the earth," and the ministering angels fly with two wings like birds.

Some sages claim that the angels were created on Monday. But that is not very likely since it is the one day on which the Creator did not say *"and it was good."* Certainly on the day the angels were created, God *"saw that it was good."*

But whether created on Monday or Thursday, the number of angels is infinite. No wonder the number is so great, for the Ruler of so vast a kingdom as the Universe must have a host of ministers to carry out His commands.

The angels, of course, are immortal and do not propagate their species. Yet angels can be destroyed and new ones are constantly created. When strife breaks out amongst the angels and the peace of the world is in danger, so greatly does God love peace, that He may destroy one or a host of angels to preserve peace. New angels are created from every utterance made by God.

Sandalphon, like the angel Metatron, occupies a special place in God's family, because he helps God teach wisdom to the young.

The chief archangels are: Michael, Gabriel, Uriel and Raphael. Michael, guardian angel of Israel, acts as the defender when Satan brings charges against men before God. Gabriel is God's special messenger. Uriel is Prince of Knowledge. Raphael is Prince of Healing. But Michael is the superior of them all and is the only angel called the Great Prince.

Most angels are very good and the friends of man. But there are also many wicked angels whose wickedness is their angelic mission. Each wicked angel is called Satan; and Samael, Angel of Death, is chief of all the Satans.

Since man can freely choose between good and evil, it is the duty of every man to be constantly alert against the power of Satan. The sly Satan first seduces man to choose evil over good; then he accuses him before God for having chosen evil; and then he argues that the punishment should be death; and, if he wins, he metes out the punishment.

Every man is sternly warned never to get in Satan's way. For instance, one must never walk in front of a bull coming up from the river, for Satan then dances between its horns and urges the bull to gore anyone in his way. Nor should one walk in the middle of the street during an epidemic, for at such times Satan struts through the middle of every road and thoroughfare. Also, if one must make a journey and the wicked are taking the same road, the trip should be delayed three days to avoid the evil spirits who surround wicked men.

There are some angels in heaven who exist only to demonstrate moral principles. Most of them exist to prove that if people desire peace, they can always find it. Some say that these angels reside in

the fifth firmament; but some sages insist that they reside in the
seventh heaven, near the Throne of Glory.

6. The Last Day of Creation

Very early on the First Friday God created all the animals on dry
land, the beasts of prey and the beasts of burden, the tame creatures and the wild creatures, the animals that live in the woods,
the animals that live in the desert, and the mountain dwellers. He
released the satyr, the unicorn, the jackal, the dragon, the wild
ass, the covey, the ferret and the behemoth.

Then He created the six-legged creatures, the insects. For every
one of the other species He created a thousand kinds of insects,
some the friends of man and some his enemies. The insects were
ordered to make silk and honey, and wax, and help fertilize the
crops.

The Creation of Man: When all the animals on dry land were
created, God turned to the Holy Law, inscribed with black fire on
the Mountains of the Moon, and said: "Now I want to create Man!"

And the Law said: "The world is Yours, and all that is in it
listens to Your Voice and remains Your witness forever. However,
You propose now to create Man. His days will be few, his transgressions will be many, and Your patience will be strained."

And God said to the Holy Law: "I have been called: 'The
Patient, the Merciful, and the Forgiving' — all in anticipation of
Man."

Truth came and pleaded: "O Lord, do not create Man, for he will
oppress me with his lies and deception."

Whereupon God sent Truth down to earth and said: "Now Man
can be better than the angels. For the angels are all wisdom and
virtue. But Man will have to struggle with temptation. If he con-
quers his desires and walks in the ways of truth, he will be better
than the angels who know no temptation. Man will sin and steep
himself in falsehood. But for his sin he will die. Each man will die
for a sin of his own, and the fear of death will keep him from
wickedness."

Then Peace came and pleaded against the creation of Man, saying that when men grew strong and rich they would war against their neighbors.

And God said: "I shall make Man love righteousness and he will be full of compassion for the poor and the needy."

Then God turned to the angels. The angels were immediately divided, some arguing in favor of Man's creation; and others, against it.

God said to them: "If a great ruler existed on earth who had many treasures and many feasting tables, but not a single guest of honor, of what good would all his possessions be to him?"

But the angels were still divided in their opinion.

The romantic angels argued, "Create Man, for he will bring love to the world."

The realistic angels argued, "Do not create Man, for he will bring envy to the world."

Then God said: "Since the seas were created the mighty breakers come singing to the shores unceasingly. And they proclaim: 'The Lord on High is mighty! The Lord on High is mighty!' If the breakers of the sea, which have neither mouth nor tongue, can offer such praise, how much more will I be extolled when I create Man!"

And God created Man.

In four ways God made Man like the animals, and in four ways like the angels. Like the animals, Man eats and drinks, propagates his species, relieves himself, and dies; like the angels, Man stands erect, uses language of many words, possesses an intellect, and can see with the inner eye of vision.

Some sages claim that all the creatures of the earth, the seas and the sky were created before the First Man, so that he should never, in his pride, claim that he was God's favorite and was created before the others, even though he was given dominion over all the other creatures right from the beginning. Others claim that the world was created to the last blade of grass in preparation for Man, as one prepares for a distinguished and beloved guest.

The Ten Wonders of the World: As twilight approached on the First Friday, just before the Sabbath arrived, God created the Ten

Wonders of the World: the mouth of the earth that swallowed Korah who rebelled against Moses; the mouth of the well that gave water to the Children of Israel in the desert; the mouth of Balaam's ass that spoke wisdom; the rainbow as the covenant with Noah that there shall never be another deluge; the manna, bread from heaven; the rod of Moses; the *shomeer* that Solomon used in building the Temple; the shape of written letters; writing to convey meaning; and, most important of them all, the Tablets of Stone on which the Ten Commandments were inscribed.

7. *The Perfect Creation*

Now the Six Days of Creation were ended.

Among all the things that God had created there was nothing useless. Everything served a purpose. He created the snail as a cure for scab; the fly as a cure for the sting of the wasp; the gnat as a cure for the bite of the serpent; the serpent as a cure for a sore; and the spider as a cure for the sting of a scorpion. Even such things as might at first seem unnecessary were created as parts of a Universe in which each thing has its purpose.

God created the world with an infinite variety of qualities. But in all of them He included the attribute of justice and the attribute of mercy. If the world were created with only the attribute of mercy, sins would multiply beyond all bounds, and if it were created with only the attribute of justice, the world could not last. By creating it with both attributes, God showed that He wanted the world to endure.

At the end of Six Days of Creation the Universe was complete and perfect in every way.

When a king builds a palace, people will enter and say, "If the pillars were a little taller they would be more graceful." Or, "If the halls were a little wider the proportions would be better." But has any man ever said, "If I had three hands or three eyes it would be better?" Or, "If I walked on my head it would be pleasant?" Or, "If my head were turned backward, I should have preferred it?" Has anyone ever said, "I wish the sun were blue and the moon square?" Or, "I wish water flowed uphill and that birds flew back-

wards?" Has anyone ever said, "I wish our days would flow back-
wards so that each day we forgot part of our lives, rather than remembered the new day lived?" None has ever heard that said. For
all that God made in the Six Days of Creation, He made with per-
fection.

8. *The Sabbath*

On the Seventh Day God rested from all His work and He blessed
the Seventh Day and sanctified it.

So honored is the Sabbath in the eyes of God that He created
an extra soul for every human being, which enters the body as
soon as the first star appears on Friday night (when the Sabbath
begins) and departs the moment the first star appears on Saturday
night (when the Sabbath ends). On the Sabbath one must rest
from all labor, avoid idle talk, and make every meal into a feast.

CHAPTER TWO

The Garden of Eden

1. *God's Dilemma*

On the Sixth Day of Creation God was confronted with a dilemma. Up to that day He had worked one day in heaven and the next day on earth, to avoid any jealousy between them. If on the last day of Creation He worked entirely in heaven, earth would be grieved. God therefore devoted most of the First Friday to the creation of Man, whose body is of the earth and his soul of heaven.

2. *The First Hour of Man's Creation*

On the first hour of the Sixth Day, God took some dust from the very center of the earth, where the Holy of Holies was later to be built. Then he took dust from the four corners of the earth in equal measure. Some of the dust was red, and some black, some white and some as yellow as sand. These he mixed with water from all the oceans and the seas, to indicate that all the races of mankind shall be included in the First Man and none be accounted the superior of the others.

(Arabic lore makes the claim that the First Man was created from part of the Holy Stone, called the *Kaaba*.)

3. *The Second Hour of Man's Creation*

During the second hour of the Sixth Day God molded the clay, and in making the human body, He created a work that, by its very form, was to excite the boundless wonder of the world and to declare the wisdom of the Creator, forever.

Two hundred and forty eight limbs and parts of limbs were placed in the body for perfect balance, one limb for each of the two hundred and forty-eight positive Articles of Faith in the Mosaic Law beginning with: *Thou shalt* —

In each part the human body is a marvelous construction; but the greatest achievements are to be found in the human head. The face was made to measure no more than the distance between the outstretched fingers of one hand, yet it contains four varieties of water which do not intermingle: the water of the eye is salty, so that tears smart the eyes to keep one from grieving overlong; the water of the ears is oily, so that bad news and idle gossip can enter one ear and go out through the other; the water of the nose is fetid, so that when an unpleasant odor is inhaled it is tempered by the nose and does the lungs no harm; and the water of the mouth is sweet, so that if a man takes into his mouth food that is spoiled he can spit it out and the sweet water of his mouth washes away the bad taste and he is happy again.

The eyes, the ears and the nose are not under Man's control, for he often must look on things he would rather not see, listen to words and sounds he would rather not hear, and inhale smells that he would rather not smell. But the mouth is under his control. He can speak and he can be silent. He may use blasphemous language or he may speak the language of the Holy Book. The tongue in Man's mouth, therefore is capable of great good and great evil.

To keep the tongue from evil talk, two rows of teeth were placed around it, like locking doors; and like walls around them both were placed the closing lips.

Inside Man's head God placed a brain. Every man has desires as restless as the sea, which would surely overwhelm him if the Creator had not given him a brain as strong as the mountains that keep the seas from flooding the earth.

The Importance of the Tongue: Life and death, it is written, are in the power of the tongue.

And the story is told of a king whose only son became ill with a strange illness. The royal doctors said the prince would surely die unless he were given the milk of a lioness. The king proclaimed a great reward for anyone who could obtain the milk.

One day a man appeared at the palace and promised the milk within ten days, provided he were given ten goats. The goats were brought to him and the man left for the desert, where he found a den of lions.

On the first day he fed a goat to the lioness and kept out of sight as she devoured it. The second day he brought another goat and came closer to watch the lioness eat. He repeated this day after day for nine days, each time coming nearer and letting the lioness know who fed her. On the tenth day, while the lioness ate the last goat, the man milked her without difficulty.

Then he started out for the palace with the milk.

On the way he fell asleep, and the parts of his body began to quarrel.

Said the feet: "The reward for getting the milk belongs to us, for we carried you to the desert."

Said the hands: "The reward belongs to us for we milked the lioness."

Said the eyes: "The reward belongs to us, for we discovered the lion's den."

Said the ears: "The credit belongs to us, for we heard of the reward."

Said the heart: "The credit belongs to me, for I advised the use of the goats to tame the lioness."

Said the tongue: "The credit belongs to none of you for it belongs to me."

All the parts of the body laughed at the tongue, which lies hidden from view, and asked: "What have you done to deserve the credit?"

Just then the man awoke and went on to the palace.

"Here," said the tongue to the king, "is the milk of a bitch, which I promised to bring you."

On hearing that the man had brought the milk of a dog, the king condemned the impudent man to be hanged the next morning.

That night, when the man fell asleep, the tongue said to the other parts of the body: "Because of me all of you will die. And only I can save you!"

"Please save us," all the other parts of the body pleaded, "and we will forever recognize you as our superior."

The next morning, as the man was taken to be hanged, he said to the king: "I brought you the milk of a lioness as I had promised. But you see, I am from Israel, and in Israel a lion is sometimes called a dog, and a lioness, in Hebrew, is a bitch. Give the milk to your son and you will see that I am telling the truth."

The milk was given to the prince and he immediately recovered.

The Image of the Universe: God created Man's body so as to reflect the entire Universe. Whatever may be found in the Universe outside, Man's body has its counterpart.

But the eye, above all members of the body, was chosen for special meaning: the eye as a whole was made to resemble the earth floating in space, the white of the eye was made to represent the oceans surrounding the earth; the iris represents the dry land; the pupil represents the City of Jerusalem; and the image mirrored in the pupil is the Holy of Holies.

The body was made so that in each man part resembles part, excepting the face as a whole. Though every living person is cast in the die of Adam, no two human faces are alike. This was done to protect Man from committing adultery through mistaking other women for his own wife.

4. *The Third and Fourth Hours of Man's Creation*

During the third hour on the First Friday, God covered the clay image with skin. And during the fourth hour He blew the living soul into its nostrils. When God said: *"Let Us make Man in Our Image,"* he referred only to the soul and not to the body. That is why when a man dies, his body, which comes from the earth, is returned to the earth, and his soul, which is from God, returns to Him in Whose image it was made.

Man's divine semblance was given him so that no man should ever despise another, remembering that hatred of any man is hatred of God, in whose image Man's soul was created.

Where Man's soul resides is as great a mystery as the residence

of God. But we know that Man's soul is to be found in his name
and in his words: for Man alone of all the creatures on earth
has a separate name for each individual member of the race, and
his name exists as long as the man lives; and only Man of all the
creatures on earth can speak in many words and in seventy languages. In this respect Man is the superior of even the angels, who
speak only Hebrew, excepting, of course, the Angel Gabriel, who
knows all the languages of Man and beast.

Man's body is the scabbard of his soul. Therefore the soul is to
the body what God is to the Universe; with it, it is everything;
without it, it is nothing.

5. *The Fifth Hour of Man's Creation*

In the fifth hour of the day, God commanded Man to rise, saying: "I name you Adam." Adam arose and stood on his feet. He was
like an angel, and his body reached from earth to heaven. His skin
was as bright as daylight and covered his body like a luminous
garment. The first words he uttered were a psalm unto the Lord,
as he looked about him on the Garden of Eden.

He saw that the Garden was at the entrance of the Celestial
Paradise. Sixty myriads of ministering angels, the face of each
bright as the splendor of the firmament, stood guard at the ruby
gates. But the gates of the Garden of Eden toward the world outside, in Beth-Shean, were unguarded.

Adam saw that the Garden of Eden was sixty times as large as
the earth outside it; eighty myriads of species of trees grew in the
garden; and in the center of them all arose the Tree of Life, on
which grew five thousand varieties of fruit, each different in appearance, in aroma, and in taste. The branches of the Tree of Life
extended over all the other trees and reached from one end of the
Garden of Eden to the other. And over the Tree of Life bright
clouds floated like bridal canopies, driven by the four winds of
heaven, and they filled the world with the fragrance of the Garden
of Eden.

And from every corner of the Garden, above the sound of the
nightingales, were heard the soft sweet voices of angels singing.

Adam lifted his eyes and said: "How wonderful are Thy Works, O Lord!"

Then he walked all over the Garden to see what he could see. And when he tired, he sat down in the shade of a tree.

6. *The Sixth Hour of Man's Creation*

In the sixth hour of the Sixth Day of Creation Adam arose, and God brought all the animals before him to be named.

Satan came up before God and pleaded: "You created me before Adam and I should like the privilege of naming all the living things."

Satan had hated Adam from the start. He had been against the creation of Man to the last. When Adam first arose and sang a psalm unto the Lord, the Archangel Michael commanded the angels to pay homage to the Image of God. And all the angels obeyed, excepting Satan. Whereupon Satan was banished from heaven to the nethermost part of the abyss.

Now Satan came to claim a prior right to name the living things on earth.

"Name them," said God to Satan, "and name all the fruits and all the berries and all the herbs and all the things that I have created, including the insects."

Satan tried. But he no sooner named one animal than he changed his mind and gave that name to another. When he came to the insects he grew so confused that he did not know how to go on and hung his head in silence. Then God told Adam to go on with the naming.

Adam named each creature according to its nature: the ass he called *ass*, because it was clearly the most foolish creature, and "ass" means "fool"; the horse he named *horse*, because he liked its joyful nature, and "horse" means "joyful"; the eagle he named *eagle*, because he knew that every ten years this bird would shed its feathers, and, at the age of a hundred years, would fly straight up toward the sun until the heat scorched him, and he would fall down into the great ocean and die, and "eagle" means "falling down."

One creature in the sea he named *Leviathan,* because he was as large as a continent. And Adam said to God:

"That pair of Leviathans, O Lord, are so big, that if they are fruitful as You commanded them to be, they will soon fill the sea and even destroy the whole world."

God then emasculated the male Leviathan, and killed the female and preserved its flesh in the briny deep for the great feast to celebrate the coming of the Messiah.

Adam then went on and named all the other creatures and all the growing things. And whatever name Adam gave each creature, that was forever its name.

When all the living things had been named, God asked: "What will you call me?"

Adam answered at once: "Your Name shall forever be *Adonoi,* for You are the Lord of All."

And God said: "I am Adonoi and that *is* My Name!"

7. *The Seventh Hour of Man's Creation*

As Adam named all the creatures, he noticed that each creature had a mate. Though there were many beautiful females in the Garden of Eden, Adam saw none that he wanted for a wife. Yet he felt lonely.

When he finished naming all the animals, they prostrated themselves before Adam, and tried to worship him. Adam pointed toward heaven and said: "The same hand that shaped you, shaped me. He alone is our King! He alone is clothed in majesty!"

The angels, too, when they saw Adam in God's image naming all the creatures, wanted to worship him. Whereupon God brought a deep sleep over Adam and called the angels to gaze upon him.

"Look," said God to the angels, "Adam is not even your equal. For you never sleep."

(And since then the angels are known as "The Wakeful.")

The Creation of Woman: As Adam slept, God looked at him and thought: From what part of Man shall I make his mate?
If she is made of his brain, she will be too proud —
If she is made of his eye, she will be too envious —

If she is made of his ear, she will be too curious —
If she is made of his mouth, she will be too talkative —
If she is made of his heart, she will be too possessive —
If she is made of his hands, she will be too acquisitive —
If she is made of his feet, she will be too adventurous —
Therefore He made her from the thirteenth rib of Man's right side, which is covered with flesh and cannot be seen.

But, alas, all this caution was of no avail. For though Woman was not created from the brain, women are proud and walk with outstretched necks; though not made of the eye, women want to see everything and are envious; though not made of the ear, women are eavesdroppers and curious; though not made of the mouth, women delight in gossip; though not made of the heart or the hands, women are possessive and acquisitive; though not made of the feet, women can't stay still and must gad about.

8. *The Eighth Hour of Man's Creation*

In the eighth hour of the Sixth Day of Creation, Adam awoke and beheld Woman beside him. And he saw that she was more beautiful than any of the angels. God had adorned her with the splendor of a bride, with wimples and bracelets and earrings and a caul shining with rubies, and rings on her hands and tinkling ornaments on her feet. Adam looked at her, and he embraced and kissed her.

God led Adam and his bride under a series of ten canopies studded with gems and pearls and ornamented with gold. The archangels Michael and Gabriel acted as grooms, and God pronounced the blessing.

After the ceremony, a watch was set over the bridal chamber and the angels danced in the Garden, beating their timbrels and singing songs.

The Story of Quarina: In Arabic lore, the creation of Adam and his marriage to Eve is told with refreshing difference:

Adam was fashioned out of clay in two halves, one male and the other female, joined at the hips like Siamese twins. After some time the two bodies miraculously separated and they lived happily as man and wife. But their joy did not last. For the woman, called Quarina, refused to allow Adam to rule over her, since she was made of the same dust and by the same Master as he. When Allah heard of Quarina's rebelliousness, he drove her from the Garden of Eden, and she became the mate of Satan, called Iblis.

Since that day Quarina hates all the children of Adam, particularly all males, and she tries to snare them into evil ways from the day they are born to the day they die.

When Quarina was banished, Adam longed for his mate. And when his loneliness became very great, the Angel Gabriel took him to the top of Mount Ararat in the land of Aral where Adam met Eve. He took her as his wife in place of Quarina. And they lived happily in the Garden of Eden.

The story of Quarina is obviously based on the story of Lilith, described in Talmudic lore as the principal female demon, who tries to harm women in childbirth, snatches children from their parents and, more particularly, snares husbands away from their wives.

9. *The Ninth Hour of Man's Creation*

Adam's happiness made Satan sad. And Adam's wedding made Satan miserable.

Satan plotted Adam's downfall. But he did not know just how to accomplish it until the ninth hour of the Sixth Day of Creation.

For in that hour God called Adam and his wife before him and said:

"The Garden east of Eden is yours to inhabit, and you shall have dominion over all the fish in the seas and the birds on wing and the living creatures that move over the earth. You may eat the Bread of Angels, and your meat may be all the sweet-smelling herbs and the fruit of every tree. But in the center of the Garden, next to the Tree of Life, there is the Tree of Knowledge. He who eats of the fruit of this tree becomes wise in the ways of good and evil. But also he who eats thereof becomes the pawn of Satan and the creatures of evil desire. You must promise not to eat the fruit of the Tree of Knowledge. For if you do, on that day you will surely die!"

Adam and his wife promised.

Why Cherries Are Red: As God was about to leave them, Adam said: "O, Lord, you have made the cherries and the good fruits of the earth for the birds. But You have made none for us."

"I have made the cherries and all the other fruits sweet and good to eat especially for you," said God.

"But how can we tell when we may eat them?" asked Adam. "If we eat them before they are ripe, they will hurt us. And if we wait too long, the birds will eat them before we do."

"I will give you a sign when cherries are ripe and good to eat," said God. "Do not touch them as long as they are green. But when they turn red, you may pick them and eat them."

Then God left Adam and his bride.

They were happy with each other in the Garden of Eden, but, alas, not for long.

CHAPTER THREE

The Fall of Man

1. *The Plot of the Serpent*

When God forebade Adam and his wife to eat from the Tree of Knowledge, Satan gloated, and he plotted to kill Adam by inducing him to eat the forbidden fruit. Since Satan could not enter Eden, he planned to use his friend, the serpent, as an accomplice.

At that time the serpent looked like a man, talked like a man, and could love like a man. But his heart was the heart of a snake. The serpent saw Adam's wife and he fell in love with her. He was willing to help Satan kill Adam, but he schemed to spare Woman so that she could become his own wife.

The serpent gave Woman a love potion and then sought every opportunity to be alone with her. The more he saw of her, the more determined he was to kill her husband. Finally he worked out the plan to destroy Adam: He would convince Woman that the forbidden fruit could be eaten without hurt; if she could be induced to agree, he was certain she would first take it to her husband to pronounce the proper blessing before tasting it; as soon as Adam tasted the fruit, the serpent planned to snatch it from his hand to prevent Woman from eating it. Then Adam would die, and he, the serpent, would marry Woman.

When the evil plan had been worked out the serpent found Woman alone in the center of the Garden of Eden. He came near and began to flatter her, telling her many things sweeter to her ears than the music of angels. Then he asked slyly why it was that God had forbidden her and Adam to eat *any* fruit. Woman protested and said that she and her husband were the keepers of the Garden and permitted to eat all and every kind of fruit.

"All?" asked the serpent.

"All but the fruit of the Tree of Knowledge," said Woman. "That one we may not eat nor may we even touch the tree."

(The wise men say that was the first sin Woman committed. She told a lie. Touching the Tree of Knowledge had never been forbidden them. That lie, which seemed so innocent, gave the serpent the opening he needed.)

As they walked along, the serpent took Woman's hand and pushed it against the trunk of the Tree of Knowledge.

"You see," said the serpent, "nothing happened. You touched the tree but you did not die." And he added quickly, "Nor will you and Adam die if you eat of its fruit."

Woman would not listen to his beguiling words.

Then the serpent said: "It was forbidden to you to eat the fruit of this wonderful tree, for if you do, you will become like the angels. The angels are jealous of you and Adam. They did not want you and Adam to be created in the first place."

Now Woman listened.

And the serpent added quickly: "You and Adam were the last to be created and that is why you have dominion over all the other creatures which came before you. If you do not eat of this fruit and become wise, the jealous angels will convince God to create a new being wiser than you and who will rule over you."

Woman listened and thought: "The angels did object to the creation of Adam. They might be jealous. They might induce God to create a being who would become our master —"

The serpent could see that Woman was wavering. He plucked some fruit from the Tree of Knowledge and held it out to her. Before the serpent could stop her, Woman had taken the fruit from his hand and bit into it.

At that moment all the adornments God had given Adam's bride fell away from her. And she saw that she was naked. She hid from the serpent, but as she looked up, she saw the Angel of Death approaching her.

"I shall die," she thought in panic, "and my husband will live after me. God will create another woman to take my place. If I make Adam eat of this fruit he, too, shall die and know no other beside me."

She ran to her husband and told him what had happened.

"If you must die," said Adam sadly, "then I, too, will die with you." He pronounced the proper blessing, and ate of the fruit.

In that very instant Adam, who had been a giant, diminished in stature to the size of an ordinary man. The brightness of his skin, which had covered him like a garment, disappeared. And Adam, too, saw that he was naked.

Some say the forbidden fruit was the fig, for as soon as Adam and his wife had eaten it, they sewed fig leaves together to hide their nakedness, and those leaves, it is believed, came from the Tree of Knowledge. Some say that it was a grapevine, from which Adam and his wife made wine, and it was after they drank the wine that they felt ashamed. And some claim that it was the Apple of Paradise, a fruit the like of which is found only in the Garden of Eden.

2. The Deathless Hoyl

Adam took of the fruit of the Tree of Knowledge and gave it to all the creatures on earth so that they, also, should know death. All the living things ate of the fruit but one strange bird, named Hoyl, who refused to eat what God had forbidden. He spread his golden wings and flew away.

And to this day the Hoyl does not know death. It lives a thousand years. At the end of that time the giant bird goes to sleep. A divine fire consumes the nest and all that remains is an egg. Out of the egg comes a little bird that slowly grows in size and splendor until it is a full-grown Hoyl, which again lives a thousand years.

This goes on forever.

3. The Judgment

In the tenth hour of the Sixth Day of Creation Adam and his wife sinned; and in the eleventh hour they were judged.

The sun was beginning to go down. God came into the Garden and called out: "Adam, where are you?"

And Adam answered: "We heard You moving in the garden, Adonoi, and we hid ourselves because we are naked."

"How did you learn that you are naked? Have you broken My commandment and eaten of the fruit of the Tree of Knowledge?"

"My wife, whom You created out of my bone, and whom, as You commanded, I regard as my own flesh, ate the forbidden fruit. I ate of it, too, because if she must die, I also want to die. I shall cleave to her in gladness and in sorrow. But I repent what we have done, Adonoi!"

Then God asked Woman: "Why have you done this?"

"My Lord, the serpent beguiled me. He plucked the fruit, not I. We were forbidden, I thought, to pluck the fruit off the Tree of Knowledge and eat it; but since it had already been plucked by another, I thought there could be no harm in eating it."

The serpent stood nearby in silence.

God did not ask the serpent why he misled Woman, but meted out His harsh judgment at once, so that forever it would be known that he who causes others to sin is punished more severely than the sinner. God took the power of speech away from the serpent, changed his face, and cursed him to crawl on his belly and live in the dust all the days of his life.

Then God cursed Woman with nine curses, in addition to death, because of her disobedience.

And to Adam he said: "You were warned that on the day you ate of the fruit of the Tree of Knowledge you would surely die. But you have repented. So great is the power of repentance that you may live one of My days — which is one thousand years."

Adam, who was endowed with the power of prophecy, foresaw in that moment that King David was doomed to die three weeks after birth. Adam thanked the All-Merciful for permitting him to live one thousand years, but asked that seventy years of his life be given to King David, and his request was granted.

Then God said: "Because you disobeyed My commandment you shall no longer live on the Bread of Angels. Instead, you shall eat herbs of the earth."

"Adonoi, must I and my donkey eat out of the same manger?" asked Adam.

Whereupon angels came down and taught Adam all of the husbandman's arts, all the crafts, and how to work in iron, so that he would never be kin to the donkey.

Adam then turned to his wife and said: "Woman, I will rename you *Eve*, which means 'She Who Speaks,' for you have been hasty in speaking to the serpent; and your name shall be Eve also because it also means 'Mother of All Mankind.'"

4. *The Expulsion*

God commanded Adam and Eve to leave the Garden of Eden, to till the soil from which they came, and with hard labor to produce their bread.

"If we leave the Garden of Eden," Adam pleaded, "all the wild beasts will attack and kill us."

God then gave Adam and Eve two coats made of snakeskin, and on them were painted all the beasts and birds on earth. When they wore the coats, Adam and Eve were told, all creatures on earth would fear them.

Adam knew that they were to leave the Garden of Eden to till the ground for their bread. He did not know that they would never again be allowed to return. Had he known that, he would have preferred instant death. But God did not want him to return lest he and Eve be tempted to eat of the fruit of the Tree of Life, and live forever.

As Adam and Eve left the Garden, its great gates were shut, and the Terrible Angels with flaming swords took their place to guard the entrance.

It is recorded that God banished Adam and Eve from the Garden of Eden in the twelfth hour of the Sixth Day of Creation, just as the first Sabbath arrived.

5. *The First Tears*

When Adam and Eve were driven from the Garden of Eden, their sorrow was greater than they could bear. And God saw how heavy were their hearts and He came to them and said:

"My poor children! You have sinned and your sin was punished as you deserved. But My love for you is unending, and I have brought you from My treasury a gift — these tears. From this time forth when you are in sorrow, the tears will rise in your eyes and stream down your faces, and your hearts will be comforted."

And Adam and Eve sat down near a brook outside the Gates of Eden and wept.

An angel came to them and asked:

"Why are you so sad? Your fate is still in your own hands. If you fully repent, your deeds will bring you joy."

"I don't know my way," said Adam, "and that is why we are so sad. I don't know whether to turn right or to turn left."

The angel gave Adam a book called *God's Secret,* and said: "Whenever you or your descendants are in trouble or in doubt, consult this Book and it will show you the way to follow."

Adam and Eve walked slowly toward the Cave of Treasures, which was to be their new home. As they neared the cave Adam said to Eve: "Look at this cave that is to be our prison in this world, and the place of our punishment!"

Eve took his words as a reproof, and she prayed: "O God, forgive my great sin which caused our downfall, and remember it not against me!" She leaned her head on her husband's shoulder and wept bitterly.

Adam and Eve entered the Cave of Treasures and for seven days neither ate of the fruit of the earth, nor drank of its waters in all that time.

6. *The Light of Fire*

Two hours before sunset on the First Friday, Adam and Eve ate of the forbidden fruit. One hour later they were driven from the Garden. God wanted to extinguish the lights of the world, for Man was no longer worthy of them. But the Sabbath was near, and for the sake of the Sabbath the lights were left on until the Sabbath day was over.

Then darkness came upon the world.

Adam and Eve, out in the wilderness east of Eden, began to tremble in fear that the snake would come in the darkness and bruise their heels. To reassure them, God sent down the Stone of

Darkness and the Stone of the Shadow of Death. When struck against each other, they produced bright flames to light the darkness of the night.

Adam raised his eyes and said: "Blessed art Thou, Lord our God, Creator of the World, Creator of the Light of Fire."

7. The First Family

When Adam realized that he and his offspring would never again enter the Garden of Eden, he refused to live with his wife, and they had no children. Then Adam was shown, through his great powers of prophecy, that twenty-six generations later the Ten Commandments would be given to Israel; and he reunited with his wife. They went to bed two, and they arose seven: Adam and Eve, Cain and his wife sister; Abel and his wife sister; and another daughter.

8. The Child in the Mother's Womb

Before the first child was conceived, it was determined that the infant in the mother's womb should lie like a closed book, its hands upon the temples, its arms upon the knees, the heels upon the buttocks, and the head set between the knees. The mouth is closed and the navel is open. When the child is born, the mouth that was closed, opens; and the navel that was open, closes. Otherwise the infant could not survive even an hour.

Just before birth a light is kindled upon the infant's head so bright that it can see the world from one end to the other. Then an angel comes and teaches the infant the whole of knowledge and wisdom. That is the happiest time in the life of a human being.

But just as the infant leaves its mother's womb, another angel flicks its mouth on the center of its upper lip and causes it to forget all it had learned. (And that is why the upper lip is indented in the center, and that is also why men must learn all over again what they knew before birth and had been made to forget).

At birth each infant promises, on oath, to do good and not evil;

and he is told that the soul given him is pure and it is his duty to keep it pure. If he fails to do so, he is warned that it will be taken from him.

And that is how it has been since the first childbirth.

9. *The First Winter*

As Adam and his wife started their family in their great adversity, they noticed that the days were growing shorter and the dark nights longer.

"I must have sinned again," thought Adam, "and soon we will be punished with eternal darkness."

Adam fasted and prayed and bathed himself in the River Gihon. Seven times seven days Adam prayed and purified himself and, on the fiftieth day, he noticed that the day had grown longer again. Then Adam knew that God had accepted his prayer and decided upon the Seasons of the Year.

10. *Why the Swallow Has a Forked Tail*

One year after Creation, God called together all the living things and all the growing things on earth, and asked them whether they were pleased with their lot. All bowed to God and said they were satisfied — all but Adam.

Adam complained that the snake was forever near, making all his days full of fear and misery. He asked that the snake be taken from the face of the earth.

"The snake was created before you, Adam," God said. "I shall not kill it; but I shall banish it from your door so that it will not molest you."

"You might as well kill me," said the snake. "For if I am banished from Adam's door, I shall surely starve."

"You will not starve," said God. "You shall live and feed on the best food in the world."

"What is the best food in the world?" All the living and growing things wanted to know, including the snake, and each hoped that he was not the best food.

"I will make a creature who will be a taster of food. For one full year he will taste all the foods on earth. Exactly one year from now all of you shall return and hear his report. That report will be my Law."

Then God created the gnat and sent it out on its mission.

A year later, on his way to report to God, the gnat met the swallow.

"Well," said the swallow to the gnat, "did you find out what is the best food in the world?"

"I did," said the gnat proudly.

"What is it?" asked the swallow, flying closer to the gnat.

"Man's blood is the best food in the world."

"What did you say? I can't hear you." And the swallow flew very close to the gnat.

"Man — man —" the gnat called, its mouth wide open.

In a flash the swallow's beak entered the gnat's open mouth and tore out its tongue.

When all the living things appeared before God, the gnat was asked to report. But the only sound the gnat could make without a tongue was "Tzzzz — tzzzz." It flew about in circles and repeated again and again, "Tzzzz — tzzzz."

"If I were given permission," said the swallow, "I could tell you what the gnat found out. For as we were coming here, just before he lost his tongue, he told me what he learned."

"What did he tell you?" All the animals wanted to know.

"He said it was the frog," said the swallow.

"Then the snake shall live on the frog," said God, pleased that Adam had been spared. And He sent all of them home.

On the way home the swallow met the snake and said, "You thought you were going to live on man, but instead you'll have to be satisfied with frogs ... "

The snake leaped up in anger and caught the swallow by his tail. The swallow tore out of the snake's grip, leaving some tail feathers behind.

Ever since then the swallow has a forked tail. And ever since then, too, it is the duty of man to put out some food every Sabbath morning, when the snow is on the ground, so that the good swallows may not know hunger.

11. *The Quarrel of the Brothers*

Abel was a shepherd and Cain worked in the fields. But every time the brothers met, they quarreled. Whatever one of them did was sure to anger the other. And no matter what one of them said, the other was certain to take offense. When shepherd Abel brought his flock to pasture, farmer Cain would come running and order him off. He would say that was just the field he had planned to plow, or the place he had selected in which to plant trees.

"Then let us divide the ground between us," said Abel, "so I will know which is mine, and you will know which is yours."

"Wherever you stand," said Cain, "that is the ground I want."

That is how it went.

Whatever Abel wanted, Cain wanted; and whatever Abel rejected, Cain rejected. For though they talked about the land, it was really their sister Luluwa that they meant. She was the cause of all their anger.

"I am the first-born," thought Cain, "and I am entitled to have my pretty sister as my extra wife."

And Abel thought, "My youngest sister was born after my wife, and that is a sign she was meant for me."

Cain and Abel continued to quarrel about many things, but they never said a word about their love for their sister Luluwa.

One day Abel's sheep strayed into the field where Cain was tilling. Cain said in anger: "Why do you bring your sheep to my field?"

"And why," said Abel, "do you drink the milk of my sheep, and take their wool to spin your clothes? If you will take off your clothes and stop drinking the milk, I will keep the sheep out of your fields."

"You make my anger rise," said Cain. "If I were to kill you now, who would ask an accounting for your blood?"

"He Who created us all will ask for an accounting," said Abel. "For He is judge and He is just."

Cain turned away from his brother. But there was murder in his heart.

That night Satan came to Cain and said: "Your parents love

your brother Abel more than they love you. That is why they want him to marry your beautiful sister Luluwa, and expect you to be satisfied with the ill-favored Akleima. Therefore, kill your brother and avenge the injustice."

A few days later Abel selected his best sheep and brought them as a sacrifice to God; but Cain ate the best fruit of his trees and brought only the culls as a burnt offering. God accepted Abel's sacrifice and rejected Cain's. And Cain blamed his brother.

"Why do you blame your brother for your own faults?" God asked. "If you will repent, I will forgive you and accept your sacrifice as I have accepted your brother's. But if you do not repent, I will bring you to the brink of *Gehinnom* and Satan will destroy you."

Cain would not listen to the voice of God. He ran to his brother in the field and began to abuse him. In great anger Abel threw his brother down on the ground, jumped on him and pinned his arms down.

Cain pleaded for mercy: "We are the children of the same father, yet you are hurting me."

"It is not I who began this quarrel," said Abel, and released his brother.

As they arose from the ground, Cain suddenly turned on his younger brother and killed him.

12. *Cain's Punishment*

When Abel fell dead at the hands of his brother, all the animals and wild beasts and birds of prey and, particularly, the serpent, rushed toward Cain to destroy him. But God warned them that whoever touched Cain with evil intent would be punished seven-fold. Then God said to Cain:

"Where is your brother, Abel?"

"I do not know," Cain lied, for he knew that the birds and the beasts of the field had buried Abel.

"You are trying to cover murder with falsehood," said God. "Your brother's blood cries out to Me from the ground."

Then He marked Cain's forehead with the letter "C" so that all the living creatures would recognize Cain and shun him.

Only then did Cain sob in repentance. Though his remorse came late, God pitied Cain, and commanded him to go off with his wife to the Land of the Wanderer — the Land of Nod.

After Cain received his judgment from God, he found his father waiting anxiously.

"How great is your punishment, my son?" asked Adam.

"Because I have repented, my punishment has been lessened," answered Cain.

Adam lifted his eyes to heaven. "I know that the power of repentance is great, but I did not know that it could even lessen the punishment of one who committed murder."

Abel was dead, and Cain banished to be a wanderer. Yet Adam was glad that God had spared his wicked son.

Cain and his wife gathered their possessions and wandered off. Wherever Cain went the earth shook under his feet, and all creatures ran from him in fear. Not until Cain reached the Land of Nod, far to the east of Eden, did the earth grow quiet under his feet, and then he knew that he could settle there.

After some time Cain's wife gave birth to their first born son, Enoch; and he was followed by other sons and daughters. They, in turn, had children. And before very long the Land of Nod was full of people.

13. *The Heart of a Fox*

In the days when Cain and his family multiplied, Samael, the Angel of Death, came before God, his seven thousand eyes full of tears.

"I am full of fears," said he, "and shame," said he, "because I am called the Angel of Death, yet the power over the death of every living creature has not yet been granted me. Adam is still alive. Eve is still alive. Their children live. And even some of the lower beings that came out of the Garden of Eden are still living. At this rate, it would seem, they will live forever."

"They will die," Samael was assured. "And if you promise never to kill any living thing before its time, the power you ask will be granted you."

"I promise," said Samael. "And as a covenant that this power was granted to me," said he, "let me drown a pair of every living creature in the ocean Okeanus, and their kind shall forever be in my power, when their time comes."

And this request also was granted.

Samael rushed down to earth and enticed a pair of cats to the seashore. They were suspicious but curious. And Samael drowned them. Then he drowned a pair of donkeys. After the donkeys came the lions. And after the lions came the monkeys.

Soon Samael had drowned a pair, male and female, of every specie of living creature on earth, excepting the foxes.

When Samael finally called on the foxes, he found them weeping.

"Why do you weep?" asked Samael.

"We weep," they answered amid sobs, "for our father and our mother, whom you drowned yesterday."

"But I have drowned no foxes as yet," Samael protested.

"Yes, you did," said the foxes. "Come to the seashore and we will show you their bodies floating in the water."

They ran out on a rock at the edge of the water and pointed to their own reflections below, shouting: "There are our parents! And don't you dare drown us, too, for you have promised not to kill anyone before his time!"

And Samael let them go home.

One year later, the Leviathan, king of the oceans, gave a great feast to all the creatures that were drowned in his waters. When the guests arrived, the Leviathan saw that the foxes were not amongst them. Upon inquiry he learned that the fox had outsmarted the Angel of Death.

"I want to become as cunning as the fox," said the Leviathan to his councilors. "And it is up to you to tell me how."

"It is really very easy," said the councilors. "Catch a fox and eat his heart, and you will be as cunning and as wise as he."

"Then go and bring me a fox," the king commanded. "If you fail," he added, "I shall have you all beheaded."

The councilors swam to the shore where a fox was sunning himself in the sand and said to him: "Come and be our king, and the king of all the creatures in the ocean."

"What is wrong with your King Leviathan?" asked the fox.

"He is sick and dying," said the councilors. "And we have decided that our next king should be the wisest of all the creatures. That is why we came to you."

"You have chosen well," said the fox. "Take me to your palace that I may rule over you, and everyone shall bow down to me and call me King Fox!"

He jumped onto the backs of the councilors and they started swimming toward the home of the Leviathan.

When they were quite far from shore, one councilor said to the fox: "The Leviathan will certainly be happy to see you. He had heard of your cunning, and decided to become as wise as you."

"How can he do that?" asked the fox, as he nearly fell into the sea.

"Don't you know? He will eat your heart and then he will be as wise as you."

The fox began to laugh. "Why didn't you tell me in the first place it is my heart that you are after? Had I known it, I would have brought my heart with me."

"Don't you have it now?" asked the fish.

"Of course not! We foxes always leave our hearts at home, unless we go courting."

"If we bring you to our king without your heart," said the councilors, "he will have us beheaded."

"Then take me back to shore," said the fox. "I will run home and fetch my heart. Then you can take me to your king."

The fish swam back and the fox jumped ashore, never to return.

"I have fooled the Angel of Death," said the fox to his wife. "But I was nearly drowned and eaten by a fish because I listened to flattery."

14. *Lemech's Family*

One of Cain's great-great-great-great-grandchildren was Lemech, son of Methuselah. When Lemech reached one hundred and eighty years of age he decided that it was time for him to marry. He took two wives, as was the custom in those days. One wife was for child-bearing; and the other he fed herbs to keep her barren, so that she would remain beautiful for a long time. And Lemech treated her forever as a bride. The names of Lemech's wives were Adah (meaning "getting things done"), and Zillah (meaning "shadow," for Lemech always liked to sit in her shadow).

Adah had two sons and Lemech named them Jabal and Jubal. Jabal was the first man to domesticate cattle. Jubal was the first musician and spent all the days of his life making harps, organs, tabrets, cymbals and pipes. But he liked best of all the instruments that made a joyful sound when he plucked their strings.

Zillah envied Adah her two gifted sons. Not even Lemech's love could make up for her yearning for children. Zillah prayed for children and God listened to her prayers. She gave birth to a son, who was named Tubal Cain, who worked in brass and iron and invented many metal tools.

During the days of Methuselah and Enoch, Adam, having reached the age of nine hundred and thirty years, died. Adam was created on a Friday, and he died on a Friday. And he was buried by Enoch and his father in a cave near Mount Moriah.

CHAPTER FOUR

The Great Deluge

1. The Fallen Angels

Noah was Adam's son, ten generations removed. And in the ten generations much had happened since Adam and Eve were expelled from the Garden of Eden.

In Noah's time people lived much longer than in all succeeding generations.

Men lived longer, and women were more beautiful.

So beautiful were the women of Noah's day that when the angels in heaven looked down and saw them their thoughts wandered. Many stricken angels quietly left heaven. They made love like angels, and the women could not resist them. The children, offspring of fallen angels and human wives, were tall as the mountains and swift as the eagles. A man could uproot a cedar of Lebanon in passing as easily as we uproot a blade of grass. And the bites of the leopard and the lion were to them as bites of fleas.

The children of the fallen angels were beautiful, both men and women, and as wicked as they were comely. The angels knew they could never return to heaven and knowing this they became wicked. And none are more wicked than the righteous gone astray.

2. From Wickedness to Idolatry

The first great sin of the generation of fallen angels was incontinence.

The husbands had lust for their own wives; and then for the wives of their brothers, or of others, or for widows, or girls yet unmarried. The women indulged in adultery, and the men in rape and incest. And all the days of their lives were steeped in debauchery.

For the sake of the women, men thieved; and for the sake of men, women lied. Their sins multiplied. Every variety of vice and knavery became known to them. They lived long and transgressed often.

And then they began to deny God and turn to idolatry.

They worshiped the sun, and the moon and the stars. They worshiped the night and the wind and the rain. They made images to represent their nature gods. And they went on to make all kinds of images. They made images of clay and of wood and of bone and of stone. They made small images to wear as amulets and ornaments; and they made huge images that towered above them.

These images they worshiped. They liked the idols because they had eyes, yet could not see; they had ears, yet could not hear; they had noses, yet could not smell; they had feet, yet could not move; they had mouths, yet could not forbid anything to the people. The idols were powerless to punish, and the people were free to follow in their evil ways.

From lust and idolatry, the road led to murder and cannibalism.

Even the animals became corrupted and fed upon each other. Up to that time all men and beasts ate only herbs and fruit. But in the days of Noah they began to eat meat.

3. *The Man Who Walked with God*

Noah's great-grandfather, Enoch ben Jared, saw the evils of mankind and turned away from them to devote himself to prayer. He was not in seclusion long when an angel of the Lord came and commanded him to go out and teach the people how to be pure of heart, to shun evil, and to love what is good in the eyes of God.

Enoch did as he was told and he soon found many followers. His fame began to spread throughout the land. Kings from distant parts came to hear his words of wisdom, and they returned to instruct their subjects to follow in the ways of Enoch, the man who walked with God.

One day the one hundred and thirty kings of the earth came to

Enoch to persuade him to rule over all of them and to teach them the ways of peace and justice. For two hundred and forty-three years Enoch ruled the people of the world and led them in the path of righteousness and mercy.

At the end of that time all the people had learned to live in peace and to honor God, and Enoch said: "Now I wish to withdraw and devote myself day and night to the worship of the Lord." The people were grieved and begged Enoch to come out of seclusion from time to time to teach them. This he did, but the periods between his appearances grew longer and longer.

Then one day Enoch appeared before all the kings, the judges, the high officers and the people, and said:

"The time has come for me to leave you."

At that instant fiery steeds drawing a chariot of flame, and surrounded by angels, came down from heaven and stopped in front of Enoch.

"Promise me," said Enoch to the people, "that you will live peacefully and deal kindly one with another."

The people promised. Enoch entered the fiery chariot and ascended to heaven.

When the distance between Enoch and the Throne of Glory was six hundred and fifty thousand miles, the angels cried out:

"Lord of the Universe! How can a man born of woman mingle with us and live in Your Presence?"

And God said:

"Mankind forsook Me for idols of wood and stone and followed in the ways of corruption and evil. But Enoch brought mankind back to My ways. Therefore I shall exalt him and sanctify him."

God opened a thousand gates of knowledge and of wisdom for Enoch. He blessed him with five hundred thousand three hundred and twenty blessings; and He gave him seventy-two wings, each extending to the end of the earth. Then He gave Enoch five hundred thousand three hundred and sixty eyes with which to see all things in the entire Universe; and Enoch became an angel who could dwell with God.

When the people saw that Enoch had gone and did not return, they went to his son, Methuselah, and crowned him king.

But although Methuselah tried to follow in his father's footsteps, the people did not heed his words and slowly turned from good to evil, from peace to war, and from virtue to sin.

4. Enoch the Writer

(In *The Book of Jubilees,* also known as *The Little Genesis,* Enoch is credited with being the first among men who learned to write; and that he recorded his knowledge, his visions and his wisdom in a book. Arabic lore claims that Enoch was the author of thirty books. These contained his divine prophecies, the noble visions in which he saw all that would happen to the children of men to the end of time, his dissertations on wisdom and magic, and tractates on all the sciences. According to this legend, these thirty books are kept in the Treasuries of Allah.)

5. The Little Deluge

At first God thought the wickedness of man was due to his long life, and He decreed that in succeeding generations men should not live beyond one hundred and twenty years. But this decree did not diminish the iniquity. If anything, it increased the evil-doing. Men and women tried to commit as many pleasurable sins in one hundred and twenty years as had been committed before in seven or eight hundred years.

It was then that God began to plan the deluge. At first He opened the springs of the River Nihon, that flooded three parts of the earth; and wherever the flood rose, there neither man nor beast survived.

God thought that those saved from the flood would mend their ways and repent. But they did not. The wicked multiplied and the good men died off, until all the good men were dead, excepting Methuselah and his grandson, Noah.

God's patience was at an end. But for the sake of two good men, He would not destroy the world.

6. *The Good Noah*

A stranger once asked: "Why did God create Man in the first place, since He must have known that the children of Adam would become wicked and that He would then want to destroy them?"

And he was answered: "You have a son, and when he was born you were very happy. Did you not know that some day your son would have to die? Why then were you happy at his birth?"

And the stranger answered: "One should be happy when it is the time to be happy: and when the time comes for grieving, then one must grieve."

And the stranger was told: "That is the answer to your question. God created Man knowing that the righteous and good would come into the world. And the wicked live by virtue of the righteous. As long as there were any good men, as long as Methuselah and Noah lived, God refrained from completely destroying the world."

Noah was a good man, threefold: He was a just man in the midst of injustice; he was a humble man in the midst of pride and arrogance; and he would not turn away from the path of God no matter what the people about him said or did. For this threefold goodness, Noah was rewarded threefold: it was given him to see the world built up in the days of Adam; to survive the destruction of the world by the deluge; and to rebuild the world again through his own offspring.

7. *Noah Preaches Repentance*

When Noah was four hundred and eighty-two years old, God came to him and said:

"Noah, go out every day with your grandfather Methuselah and warn the people that My patience is at an end. Let them repent and I will forgive them. But if they do not turn away from their wickedness, I shall destroy them!"

Early every morning and late every day Noah and his grandfather went from street to street and from house to house repeating God's warning. But the people were stiff-necked and would not listen.

Then God said to Noah: "Methusaleh is growing old and soon will die. I want you to get yourself a wife and raise a family so that the righteous shall not disappear from the earth."

Noah began to look about him for a wife. After seven years, at the age of four hundred and eighty-nine, he married his great-aunt Naomi, daughter of the good Enoch, who was five hundred and eighty years old on her wedding day. She gave birth to three sons, Shem, Ham, and Jepheth, and they were brought up by their father and grandfather in the ways of the just.

In a now lost Apocrypha, called the Book of Noria, *the story of Noah's wife, named Noria, is told in full. She is presented as a very wicked woman, often the tool of Satan.*

8. *Noah Builds an Ark*

Noah started to build an ark on dry land, according to fixed specifications, as he had been told to do by God. The ark was to be made of gopherwood, three stories high and large enough to house Noah and his entire family, one pair of all the living creatures on dry land, and food enough for all of them to last throughout a long, long journey.

When the people saw Noah and his sons putting down the keel of a ship as large as the Leviathan, they looked on with wonder and asked in derision: "What are you building, Father Noah?"

"I'm building an ark that can float and withstand a great deluge. If you continue in your wickedness, the Great God will surely destroy you in floods worse than the floods we have had. In the coming flood, none will be spared. But I and my family will be saved in this ark."

"If God wants to spare you," the people mocked, "why can't He do it by a miracle?"

"He can if He wants to," said Noah, and went on with his work.

"Why doesn't He?" they insisted.

"Because the Great God wants me to build this ark for one hundred and twenty years. He knew you would come and be curious, and it is my duty to preach repentance and prophesy your doom if you do not listen to God's warning. He is merciful and He gives you time to repent."

"One hundred and twenty years, you say?" the people laughed. "We'll wait and see."

As the years went by, the ark began to take shape. It was three hundred cubits long, fifty cubits wide and thirty cubits high. There were three decks, with doors and windows, and it was waterproofed from the inside with pitch.

9. *How Big Is God?*

During the years, Noah's ark became an attraction for the people, who came to marvel at this seaworthy vessel on dry land, and to mock its builder.

"You mock me now," said Noah, "but the Great God will mock you later."

"Why do you always say 'the Great God'?" asked the people. "How big is your God, anyway?"

When Noah heard them say "your God" and not "our God" he knew they were beyond salvation. Yet he answered them:

"Do you really want to know how big our God is? My great-grandfather Enoch was once taken up to the top of a high mountain by the Angel Gabriel. There Enoch saw a bird so large that its head reached the clouds and its feet rested on the bottom of the sea. And do you know how deep the sea is?" asked Noah.

"As deep as a deep well," said the people.

"Once," said Noah, "a carpenter crossed the sea in a boat and when he was over the deepest part he accidentally dropped his axe, and it took seven years before it reached the bottom of the ocean. Yet the bird Enoch saw rested its feet on the very bottom of the sea."

"What else did Enoch see?"

"He saw a frog larger than a city. Then he saw a snake that swallowed that frog, as a chicken swallows a grain of wheat. Then the bird came along and swallowed the snake. The bird flew away over the mountains and the seas until it came to a forest. And there it lighted on a branch of a giant tree."

"Then what happened?" the people asked.

"Nothing happened. But that bird, and that frog, and that snake and those trees were only a few of the things God created by uttering a single word. Now can you imagine how great God is?"

"We can," said the people.

"Then repent," said Noah.

But the stiff-necked people would not repent.

10. *Invitation to the Ark*

Finally the ark was complete in every detail. The period of one hundred and twenty years of grace was over and the people had not repented. The deluge was about to begin. But just then Methuselah died at the age of nine hundred and sixty years. He was buried with great honor, and God allowed Noah and his children to complete the seven days of mourning before the deluge began.

Messengers had gone out to invite one pair of all the living creatures on dry land to board the ark. Soon great swarms of insects, flocks of birds, herds of beasts of the field, reptiles, wild boars, buffalo, yak and zebu, and every other kind of living creature came streaming toward the ark, trying to get in.

Noah, who feared they might destroy the ark in their stampede, placed two lions, two elephants and two tigers at the gates. These animals kept all the passengers in order as they boarded, the males going one way, and the females going another way, so that the sexes were separated for the duration of the journey in the ark. The first to enter the ark was the ant; and the last was the stubborn ass, who had to be prodded before he would cross the gangplank and pass into the lower story of Noah's ark.

11. *Falsehood and Misfortune*

Among those who came to the ark was Falsehood. But Noah would not admit him, saying: "God commanded me to gather into the ark only pairs, male and female of each kind. Since you are alone, I cannot let you enter."

Falsehood left Noah to look for a mate before it was too late. On the way he met Misfortune.

"Why do you look so downcast?" asked she.

"Noah will not let me enter his ark because I have no mate," he answered. "If you would come as my mate, both of us would be saved."

"What will you give me if I become your mate and save your life?" asked Misfortune.

"After we leave the ark I will give you all that I earn," Falsehood promised.

They returned to the ark as a pair and Noah admitted them.

(Later, when they left the ark, Misfortune took away all that Falsehood earned. When Falsehood complained, Misfortune reminded him of their pact before they entered Noah's ark.)

12. *The Decree of Continence*

When all the animals were in the ark, the food for the journey was loaded, and God blessed the food, so that it should not spoil.

Then Noah and his family entered the ark. The men and the women separated, for although the deluge was about to punish men for their wickedness, it was nevertheless to be considered a great disaster, and in times of disaster a good man does not indulge in pleasure. Noah decreed that neither man nor beast should be with their mates from the time they entered the ark until the day they left it. And this Decree of Continence was made known to all within the ark.

Noah was exactly six hundred years old when he entered the ark and locked its doors. And a gentle rain began to fall. It was a pleasant rain, and men strolled near the ark, laughing and saying: "This is a nice, warm rain. What is there so strange about a rain like this?"

Noah called to them through a window that God was All-Merciful and would give them one last chance to repent. But the people only laughed, and said: "For a hundred and twenty years we have heard nothing from you but 'repent,' 'repent.' Haven't you learned any other words in all your six hundred years?"

13. *The Deluge Begins*

God opened the springs of the deep and pulled the stoppers out of the heavens, and the waters that came up from the deep and down from heaven were boiling hot. The people realized in sudden horror that the long-threatened deluge was upon them. Seven hundred thousand men, women and children rushed toward the ark, wailing and shrieking, and blaming Noah for this misfortune.

"Why should we die?" they shouted. "Are we worse than the animals you have in the ark?"

"The animals," Noah shouted back, "have no free will to do good or evil. But you were warned with great patience. You were given one hundred and twenty years to turn away from wickedness. Now it is too late."

"If we must die," the people threatened, "you and all those that are with you in the ark shall die with us!"

They ran toward the ark to overturn it. But the wild beasts from all over the earth reached and surrounded the ark first, and they killed the people who intended to harm Noah.

Man, last to be created, was first to be destroyed in the deluge.

Fear magnified the pain of the scalding waters tenfold. The people cried out in torment and in terror. The scalded animals roared and screeched and bellowed and howled and whined and whimpered, and their anguished voices commingled, until Noah could bear it no longer, and prayed for peace.

Then the skies darkened and the torrents increased. After a time all the noise subsided. Soon all that could be heard was the sound of the downpour against the wood of the ark.

Neither sun nor moon nor stars were out and the darkness was complete. God gave Noah a bright stone that shone in the dark like a bright lamp to guide him in his work throughout the days of the deluge.

14. *Tragedy in the Ark*

For forty days and forty nights the rains came down, and the waters of the deep continued to rise. The ark was lifted on the rising waters ever higher and higher until, at the end of forty days, it floated fifteen cubits above the highest peaks of the highest mountains on earth.

At the end of forty days, God sent out a great wind to close the springs of the deep and to shut the windows of heaven. And the rains from above and the floods from below ceased.

For one hundred and fifty days after that the ark drifted, with nothing in sight but water. One hot summer morning Noah looked out of a window and saw in the distance the tops of mountains sticking out of the water like low islands.

During this time a tragedy had taken place in the ark: three transgressed against the Decree of Continence. The first was Noah's second son, Ham, and his punishment was that his children should be black and known as Moors; the second was the hound, and he was punished to lead a wretched life; and the third was the raven, and his punishment was that he would be neither good for the table nor acceptable as a sacrifice.

Thirty days later the ark settled on Mount Ararat. Noah wanted to send out the raven to find out how far the waters had subsided, but the raven refused to go for fear that he might not be allowed to enter the ark again.

"Because of your sin," Noah said, "you have been punished. But if you refuse to obey me, I will cast you out of the ark so that your kind may disappear from the face of the earth."

But God intervened and said: "Let the raven be. In the days of Elijah the Prophet, I will send the raven to save My prophet from starvation."

Noah then sent out the dove. And after some time the dove returned with an olive leaf in its beak.

Many have wondered where that leaf came from, since all the trees in the world had been destroyed by the deluge. That leaf, the wise men say, came from the Garden of Eden. And when the flood subsided, the dove was allowed to enter the Garden to obtain a sign for Noah. The dove could have plucked a leaf from the fig tree or the myrtle, the tamarisk or the cedar of Lebanon, the citron or the pomegranate, but it brought the bitter leaf of the olive so that Noah would know that it is better to take the bitter from the Lord than the sweet from man.

And when the dove was sent out again the following week, it did not return.

15. *The Covenant of the Rainbow*

Though Noah and his family could now see that the land was dry, they did not stir. God had commanded them to enter the ark and they waited for Him to tell them when to leave. One year after Noah had entered the ark, he was told to leave it.

When the ark was emptied of all the people and living things in it, God told Noah to be fruitful. But Noah was apprehensive. He built an altar and offered burnt offerings on the altar, and said:

"O, Lord! Why do You command me and my sons to multiply? If my offspring do not follow in Your way, another deluge would destroy them. Why bring them into the world?"

And God said: "I shall establish a covenant with you and your offspring and all the living things that, as long as the earth abides, never again shall a deluge destroy the flesh. And every time the clouds gather for rain, and the day draws to an end, I shall plant the rainbow in the east for all to see and remember the everlasting covenant."

"O, Lord!" said Noah. "Even if a deluge does not destroy me and my seed, the wild beasts, who know that they are no worse than the wicked, will destroy us. Should we multiply just to feed the wild beasts?"

And God said: "Fear not, for the fear of you and your seed shall be upon all the creatures of the earth. Their meat shall be your meat to eat, and they shall all be accountable to you."

"O, Lord!" said Noah, "But what about man? What if in their anger and in their envy they war with each other and destroy one another?"

And God answered: "Fear not, for I shall keep every man accountable for his brother, and he who sheds blood, his blood shall be shed. If a man kills a man, he shall be punished. And if a man train an animal to kill a man, his crime shall be accounted even greater. And he who sends a messenger to kill a man, his crime shall be double, for he is guilty both of murder and of causing his messenger to commit murder. I shall keep each one accountable for the shedding of blood. Fear not, and remember the covenant."

16. *Noah's Vineyard*

When Noah had entered the ark he took along a vine. He had been a gardener before he built the ark, and when he settled again on the land after the deluge, he planted the vine once more and returned to his old occupation.

As he worked in the garden, Satan came to him and said:

"If you will let me help you, I can show you how to make grapes grow on that vine by tomorrow."

"That," said Noah, "is something worth seeing."

Satan helped Noah plant the vine. Then Satan took a lamb, a lion, a monkey and a pig and watered the plant with their blood.

(That is why, after the first glass of wine, one becomes gentle as a lamb; after the second glass of wine, as daring as a lion; after the third glass one is apt to make a monkey of himself; and after the fourth glass of wine, a man becomes drunk and behaves like a pig.)

17. *Noah's Story*

Noah lived three hundred and fifty years after the deluge and he saw his family grow into a multitude. When Noah was very old, he told a young man, named Abraham, about his father Lemech, who saw Adam the First, and he also told him about the deluge and how it all happened. Abraham told the story to his son, Isaac. And Isaac, in turn, told it to Jacob. And Jacob told it to his children. And that is how the story from Adam to Noah was preserved.

At the age of nine hundred and fifty years Noah died. By that time his children, grandchildren and great-grandchildren had dispersed over the earth and the nations of the earth were again established.

CHAPTER FIVE

The Age of Confusion

1. *Nimrod the Hunter*

Cush, the son of Ham, had many children, and all of them have long since been forgotten, all but his oldest son, Nimrod. Not that there was any greatness in Nimrod. He was neither wise nor strong, neither pure in heart nor a great magician, neither splendid in appearance nor dazzling in wit. The word "ordinary" describes Nimrod up to the age of twenty.

But on his twentieth birthday Nimrod received from his father a snakeskin coat that Cush had obtained from his grandfather, Noah, and which had belonged to Adam. Grandfather Noah claimed that there were two of these coats which were given to Adam and Eve when they were expelled from the Garden of Eden. Eve's coat had been lost. But Adam gave his coat to Cain. Cain gave it to Tubal Cain. And so it was handed down until it was given to Nimrod as a birthday gift.

When Nimrod received the coat, he put it on, took his bow and arrows and went out hunting. All Nimrod ever did was hunt. He was not a brave hunter. The sound of a wolf struck fear in his heart; and the thought of a tiger weakened his knees. Nimrod hunted rabbits.

On this day, as he reached the hunting grounds, Nimrod was petrified at the sight of a vast number of small game and big game coming toward him. And the sky was suddenly darkened by flocks o: every conceivable and coveted bird. Nimrod was so frightened that he just stood still, wondering where he could hide. Then he saw that all the birds had settled in the trees and all the animals had come to rest and were bowing to him, as meek as the rabbits he usually hunted. Though he shot at them with arrows they did not run away.

That day he returned home with more game than any hunter of his generation. People came to admire his catch and wondered how he did it. Nimrod related many wild exploits and claimed the game as only the just reward of his courage and prowess.

The next day Nimrod went out again (wearing his snakeskin coat), and returned with an even greater catch. Little by little it dawned upon him that when he wore Adam's coat, he had dominion over all the wild animals.

After that, when he planned to go hunting he would say to people: "I am going hunting tomorrow. What do you want me to catch?"

"Bring us a hundred golden ptarmigan," they would say jokingly. Or they would say: "Bring us a koodoo, a nilgai and a springbuck."

Nimrod would put on his hunter's coat and go out. And soon he would return with whatever animal or bird his friends had mentioned, and in any number that he could carry. But he never revealed how he got them, always claiming he was braver and nimbler than any man on earth.

Nimrod's fame traveled fast, and it traveled far and wide. His prowess was even exaggerated. People admired him and began to fear him. And their fear became Nimrod's strength, as it is believed that the fear in the heart of the people becomes the weapon of the wicked.

2. Nimrod the King

At that time King Japhath and his army of giants terrorized the nations. The people came to Nimrod and said: "You are such a great hunter and such a brave man. You are the man to go out and fight King Japhath and his men!"

Nimrod went out all alone (with his snakeskin coat on) and a vast horde of wild beasts followed him. When they neared Japhath and his men, the animals fell upon them, and the vipers bit them, and the scavengers of the air fed upon them. King Japhath and his men were utterly destroyed.

When Nimrod returned victorious, there was jubilation in the land of Shinar and dancing in the streets of Accad, Babel, and

Calneh. In gratitude, Nimrod was proclaimed king by the people of his own land. Yet he was not content. King Nimrod waged war after war with all his neighbors until, in the end, he became King of All the Nations on Earth.

Nimrod was not a saint to begin with. And the more powerful he grew, the more wicked he became. When his only son, Mardon, grew up, Nimrod taught him in all the ways of wickedness. Though the King of All the Nations on Earth was still afraid to go out at night alone (without his snakeskin coat on), he told his people not to depend on God but on their own strength. Power, he said, was justice; and whatever one man could wrench from another, that was rightfully his. So wicked were Nimrod and his son Mardon, that they gave rise to the proverb: "Out of the wicked can come only wickedness."

3. Nimrod Wants to Be God

Now that he was king of the entire earth, Nimrod wanted to be remembered forever.

"I shall build cities, so many and so great," said he, "that as long as a single man remains on earth, he will see them and remember their builder."

Then Nimrod built Babylon, Erech, Caleh, Ressed, and many more equally great.

Still he was not satisfied. Now that the cities were completed, he began to be jealous of God in heaven.

Nimrod then built a stone tower higher than any mountain. On top of the tower he placed a throne of cedar. Upon the throne of cedar he placed a throne of iron. Upon the throne of iron he placed a throne of copper. Upon the copper throne he placed a throne of silver. Upon the silver throne he placed a throne of gold. Upon the golden throne Nimrod placed a diamond so large that he could sit on it with comfort. Over the diamond he hung lamps which, when lighted, were reflected by the diamond in rays that could be seen all over the world.

Nimrod seated himself on the golden throne, lit the lights, and the people came to pay homage as if he were a god.

And still Nimrod was not satisfied.

4. *The Tower of Babel*

Then the idea arose of building a tower that would reach to the seventh heaven.

Some say that the wise men in Nimrod's court believed that the skies were weakening and foretold that exactly within 1656 years from the date of their prediction, the skies would cave in. They advised their king to build four brick towers to support the four corners of the skies.

Others say that the wise men of that day advised the king that another deluge was in store, unless they could build a tower that would reach to heaven, open the great windows in the skies and let the waters out. Still others believe that the idea was entirely King Nimrod's, who said: "God took heaven for himself and gave only the earth to man. I will build a tower so high that all men can enter heaven at will and enjoy that, too."

Nimrod gathered six hundred thousand men and began to build what he called the Pillar to Heaven. All the people in Nimrod's day were rich but, strangely enough, they loved each other, and they enjoyed working together on a tower that would take them to heaven. They built a large round foundation, and upon it began to rise above the desert plains of Shinar a great brick tower, the walls of the tower rising cubit by cubit. On the east side of the tower and on the west side were stairways, and the workers who carried mortar and bricks up the east stairway descended on the west stairway so that no worker was ever in the way of another.

As the tower rose, the builders became divided in their hearts. One group thought: "When this tower is completed, we will move into heaven and live there!"

Another group thought: "When we get to heaven, we will establish our gods there and worship them!"

And still others thought: "As soon as we reach heaven, we will declare war on God!"

Whatever the different groups thought, they said nothing to each other, and continued their work in peace and with unflagging enthusiasm.

Forty-two years after the tower was started, it reached to a height of twenty-seven miles. It took a hod carrier a full year to get up from the ground to the top; and a brick was more precious than a man. For if a man fell down, there were others to take his place; but if a brick fell down, it took a year to replace it.

5. *The Confusion of Tongues*

King Nimrod looked at the tower that reached far beyond the clouds and was certain that the top was already quite near to heaven. He ordered the men on top of the tower to shoot arrows into heaven. All the arrows returned to the ground covered with blood, each arrow a warning to Nimrod and his men. But they were so blinded by power that they believed their arrows had killed the angels in the first heaven.

For a long time God did not punish the builders of the tower because they were at peace and loved each other. And so great is the power of love and peace that, even when people band together to defy God, He will not destroy them. But when the sign of the arrows was not heeded God said to the seventy angels surrounding Him: "Go down and confuse their tongues that they may not understand each other."

Up to that time all the people of the earth had spoken the same language, the Holy Language of Creation. Now each angel brought down a new language, and the builders of the tower talked in seventy different tongues, and not one of them, not even King Nimrod, knew more than one language. The hod carriers could not understand the bitumen mixers; the bitumen mixers could not understand the brick makers; the brick makers could not understand the bricklayers; the bricklayers could not understand the carpenters. And so it went.

There were seventy names for each object and seventy words for each action, and the loud talk sounded like the babbling of madmen.

Soon the confusion turned the Pillar to Heaven into the Tower of Babel. Each worker blamed the others for the lack of understanding and for doing the wrong thing. Up to that time they had worked in peace; now the workers began to quarrel, though, of course, neither quarreler understood the other. Accidents began to happen. One worker asked for mortar and he was given a brick. He threw the brick back in anger, and it toppled the first worker off the twenty-seven-mile-high tower.

Soon the tower had to be abandoned.

6. *The Fate of the Tower and Its Builders*

One third of the Tower of Babel sank into the ground of its own great weight; one third was destroyed by fire, due to the confusion of tongues, before the task was abandoned; and one third remained standing as an omen and a warning to succeeding generations who lived in the Land of Shinar.

The ruins of the Tower of Babel can be seen to this day. But he who sees them is cursed with the loss of memory. All the people on earth who go around saying: "Who am I?" "Who am I?" are the ones who have seen the ruins of the Tower of Babel through which men aspired to reach heaven and war against God.

As for the builders of the tower: those who aspired to move into heaven and live there, God dispersed to the four corners of the earth; those who aspired to establish their idols in heaven, God confused in thought as well as tongue; and those who planned to declare war on God when they completed the tower and reached heaven, God turned into monkeys, sea cats and demons. That is why monkeys, sea cats and demons look a little like human beings to this day.

And that is how it came to pass that the generation of wickedness in the days of Noah was followed by the age of confusion in the days of Nimrod.

PART II

The Patriarchs

The great saga of the Patriarchs, covering a period of
three hundred and sixty-one Biblical years (1996–
1635 B.C.), is fully recorded in Genesis XII–L. Within
the space of about fifty printed pages the Old Testament
details, with seeming leisureliness, the adventures of Abraham in many lands; his trials and triumphs; the story of
Sodom and Gomorrah; the feud between Isaac and
Ishmael and between Jacob and Esau; Jacob's memorable
vision of angels, and his troubles in Laban's house; and
the wickedness of Dinah's avenging brothers; and ends
with the stirring and magnificent story of Joseph and his
brothers.

These adventures of the human spirit attributed to the
Patriarchs, far away and long ago in the early nomadic
days of the race, particularly intrigued the folk imagination. And we note a marked tenderness in the legends
about the characters and events as given in Genesis, beginning with God's order to Abraham to depart from his
country and his kindred and ending with, "So Joseph died,
being an hundred and ten years old; and they embalmed
him, and he was put in a coffin in Egypt."

CHAPTER SIX

Father Abraham

1. Miracles at Birth

In the days of King Nimrod there lived a man named Terah who made clay idols and sold them. There were many dealers in idols in those days but Terah is remembered because he was the father of three sons: Abraham, Nahor and Haran.

When Abraham was born, a star appeared in the east so bright that all the stars around it paled in the sky. The royal stargazers came running to King Nimrod and said: "Your Majesty, a son has been born to Terah who will destroy our gods and convert all the inhabitants of the earth to his beliefs. There is but one thing to do, and that is to destroy him before he grows up. Terah is a faithful subject. Therefore offer him gold and silver to turn over his son to you. If Terah refuses, behead him as well as his child."

Nimrod sent for Terah and said: "I am told that a son has just been born to you, and the seers predict evil things for him. Therefore I will give you as much gold and silver as your son weighs if you will turn him over to me that I may destroy him."

Terah replied: "Your Majesty, you remind me of the man who said to the horse, 'I will give you much rye and wheat to eat, but first I must cut off your head.' And the horse said, 'Who will eat the rye and wheat if my head is cut off?' "

"Meaning what?" asked the king.

"Meaning that if you kill my first-born son, who will inherit the gold and silver you wish to give me?"

"If you do not bring your son Abraham to me within three days, I shall have your head cut off, too," said Nimrod in anger.

Terah went home and took the stillborn child delivered by one of his handmaidens and brought it to the king, and said:

"When I came home I found that my first-born son had died. Here he is, for you to do with as you please."

2. *Abraham in the Cave*

Then Terah hid his son Abraham in a cave. And within the cave two stones began to pour out oil and honey mixed with flour, on which the child fed.

Abraham did not leave the cave until he was thirteen years old. On the day he came out for the first time and saw the world about him he wondered: "Who created heaven and earth and Who created me?" He observed the brightness of the sun and assumed that the sun was the Creator. All day long he prayed to the sun, and he prayed in the Holy Language, which he knew through the power of prophecy.

Then evening came and the sun went down and the moon and stars appeared. Abraham now thought the moon was God and the stars his servants, and he prayed all night to the moon. But when the moon and stars faded at dawn, Abraham knew that there must be a Creator who had created sun, moon and stars, and everything else in the world, and that He was God in heaven.

Thus Abraham was the first man to perceive the existence of God without having been taught this knowledge.

Abraham prayed and then returned to his father's house.

3. *Abraham the Idol Breaker*

Terah was still making idols and selling them for a living. One day Terah left his oldest son alone in the shop where his idols were sold. Soon a woman came in and wanted to buy an idol to protect her family from thieves.

"Don't you have one?" asked Abraham in surprise.

"We had one, but it was stolen," she replied.

"How can you expect an idol to protect your family against thieves when it can't protect itself against them?"

"But I must worship something!" the woman insisted.

"How old are you?" Abraham asked.

"Who, me? I'm sixty years old."

"There's not an idol in my father's shop that is more than a week old. And if you want to see how powerful these idols are, just watch me —"

Abraham took an axe and started to smash the clay idols. The woman ran from the store in horror, but Abraham just went on smashing the idols until all but the largest one were destroyed. Then he put the axe in the hands of the large idol and waited for his father.

When Terah returned, he demanded: "Abraham, what have you done?"

"I have done nothing," said Abraham calmly. "A woman came in and offered some flour as a sacrifice to one of the idols. Whereupon that big one took the axe and destroyed all the others, as you can see."

"Abraham, you know these idols have no spirit in them. They cannot move nor can they fight."

"If they have no spirit, Father, what good are they?" asked Abraham.

"If I fail to report this to the king and he finds out about it from someone else he will surely kill us all," said Terah. And he went off to the palace of the king.

4. Trial by Fire

When King Nimrod heard what had happened, he called Abraham before him and said:

"Since you will not worship idols because there is no spirit in them, then worship fire."

"I would rather worship water, because it can extinguish fire," said Abraham.

"Then worship water," said Nimrod.

"I would rather worship the cloud, because it carries off water," said Abraham.

"Then worship the clouds," commanded the king.

"I would rather worship the wind which disperses the clouds," said Abraham.

"Then worship the wind."

"I would rather worship God in heaven, who created everything, including the wind," said Abraham.

"Bow down to the idols!" commanded the king. "If you refuse I will throw you into the fire so that you will be destroyed by the fire we worship."

Abraham refused to bow to the idols, and he was thrown into the fiery heart of a furnace.

Gabriel called three angels to go down with him to rescue Abraham. But God said: "I am One in the Universe, and there is none like Abraham on earth. I will rescue him Myself."

At these words, the flames in the furnace turned into trees bearing flowers and fruit, and the fruit trees arrayed themselves in rows, as in a watered garden. Abraham walked between the rows of trees for three days and three nights, singing songs in praise of God.

At the end of the third day King Nimrod and his princes and their attendants assembled to watch the opening of the furnace. The gates were opened and, to their amazement and bewilderment, Abraham walked out of the furnace unscathed.

King Nimrod and all his princes bowed low before Abraham and offered him gifts of gold and silver. And when Abraham left, three hundred men followed him, saying:

"We are your servants. Wherever you go, we will go; and whatever you command us to do, we will do with joy."

5. Haran's Error

After Abraham came out of the fire unharmed, Nimrod asked Abraham's youngest brother:

"And you, Haran, what do you believe in?"

"I believe in the same God Abraham believes in," said Haran, thinking that if his brother had been saved by a miracle, he, too, would be saved by a miracle.

The king's henchmen threw Haran into the furnace. And the fire consumed him.

Haran's death was a lesson to future generations that a man

should always follow the honest dictates of his conscience and not count on miracles.

6. *Abraham Leaves Home*

After Abraham's trial by fire, God commanded him to leave his father's house, his kinsmen and his country, and travel to far-off lands to denounce the idol worshipers and convert them to the ways of God.

A man who travels far from home is diminished in three ways: it is harder for him to raise a family; it is harder for him to accumulate possessions; and it is harder for him to establish a good reputation. God therefore told Abraham that He would bless him with offspring as numerous as the stars in the skies; with great possessions; and that the fame of his name would precede him everywhere.

Abraham declared that he wanted to serve God and obey His commands without any compensations. For, if one does good only for compensation, Abraham reasoned, to that degree his goodness is diminished. But God convinced Abraham that whereas a poor and obscure man gains few converts, wealth and a great name would make it easier for him to win followers.

Abraham took his wife, Sarah, and his nephew, Lot, and his wife, and all their menservants and maidservants, and all their possessions, and they traveled to the Land of Haran.

Wherever they went, Abraham preached against idolatry. But he gained fame more for his kindness and his love of all people. His fame as a peacemaker preceded him wherever he went. Soon all those who had differences came to Abraham instead of to their own judges, and he made peace between them with justice and loving-kindness. His fame grew and his wealth grew. But Abraham left his wordly affairs in the hands of his chief steward, Eliezer, and dedicated his life to doing what is good in the sight of God.

7. *Abraham in Egypt*

All went well, until a great famine threatened Canaan. Abraham decided to move to Egypt, for he feared that the Canaanites might say: "Abraham came to us and turned us to his religion; and now we are afflicted with famine as a punishment for abandoning our gods."

One day, on their way to Egypt, Abraham sat down near a lake to rest. In the waters of the lake he saw the reflection of his wife, Sarah, standing near its edge, and he suddenly realized how beautiful she was. He said to her:

"Sarah, we are coming to a land where the men are full of lust and there is not one woman to compare with you in comeliness. When the men see you, they will surely kill me and take you away. Therefore, if they ask you who I am, tell them I am your brother."

(Then and there it was decreed that because Abraham showed lack of faith and fled from Canaan, and because he tried to save his life by a lie, his offspring would have to serve as slaves for four hundred years in the very land in which he and his family hoped to save themselves from hunger.)

Abraham hid his wife in a chest so that she would not be seen when they entered Egypt. But as they crossed the border, the king's men stopped Abraham to collect a tithe on his possessions. When they came to the chest, they asked:

"What have you there? Is it barley?"

"If you think it is barley," said Abraham, "I will give you the tithe on barley."

"Is it wheat?" asked the king's men.

"If you think it is wheat, I will give you a tithe on wheat."

"Perhaps it is pepper," said the Egyptians.

"Then I will give you the tithe on pepper."

"Perhaps you have gold in that chest," said the guards.

And Abraham said: "Ask whatever you want of me to the extent of all my possessions and I will give it to you, but do not ask me to open the chest."

"That chest must be full of precious stones," thought the king's men.

They opened the chest by force, and Sarah's radiant face almost blinded the guards. They took her at once to Pharaoh, and when the king saw her, he fell in love with her and wanted to make Sarah Queen of Egypt. But as he came near, an angel with a drawn sword held him back. In terror, Pharaoh demanded to know what this meant. Then Sarah told him that she was married, and that Abraham was actually her husband.

In the morning the king called Abraham and told him to leave Egypt at once. None of Abraham's possessions were taken away; instead, the king gave him many gifts, realizing that only the wife of a very holy man would be protected by an angel. And among the gifts the king gave to Sarah was his own beautiful daughter, Hagar.

"It is better that you become the handmaiden of this holy man," said Pharaoh to his daughter, "than remain a princess in my house."

8. *The Wickedness of Sodom*

When they left Egypt, the shepherds of Abraham and Lot began to quarrel among themselves. Abraham called in Lot, his nephew, and said to him:

"You are my brother's son. I have no sons of my own, so that you will be my heir. Why then should we quarrel? Let us separate. You may have your choice between the land over the Jordan, where the pastures are green and the water abundant, and I shall stay here. Or I'll move across the Jordan and you can stay here."

Lot chose to move across the Jordan, partly because he thought that was a better choice, and partly because, as he grew rich, he wished to be far away from Abraham and close to the people who lived in Sodom and Gomorrah, about whom he had heard so much.

The citizens of Sodom and Gomorrah were wealthy cattle dealers who despised the poor. They suspected any stranger in their midst who was not as rich as they were. And their courts had become known for their infamy and corruption. Their chief judges were four in number: Liar, Falsifier, Bribe-Taker and Soul-Stealer.

If a man was attacked without cause and beaten until the blood covered him, the judge ordered the victim to pay the attacker a doctor's fee "for bloodletting."

If a man struck a pregnant woman and she miscarried, the man was fined to sleep with the woman until she conceived another child.

If a poor man asked for bread and water, he was given gold and silver. But the coins were marked "beggar" on one side and the name of the giver on the other. The merchant who would accept those coins for food was beheaded.

For strangers who sought a night's lodging, there were beds of a fixed length. If the stranger was too tall, his legs were chopped off; if he was too short, he was stretched to the length of the bed.

9. *The Voice That Reached to Heaven*

One day a young girl of Sodom, who was at a well drawing water, was asked by a stranger for a drink and she gave it to him. When this became known, she was taken to an apiary, stripped of her clothes, and covered with honey, so that the stinging of the bees would kill her. In her death agony she cried so loud that her voice reached to heaven.

"Because the cry of Sodom and Gomorrah is great and their sin grievous," God said to Abraham, "I shall destroy them and all their inhabitants."

"Surely You will not destroy the righteous with the wicked?" said Abraham.

God promised that even if there were only ten righteous men in Sodom and Gomorrah, he would not destroy the cities.

Abraham did not plead any longer. For he knew that ten is the smallest number of a community. God will save the world for the sake of the smallest community, but He will not save it for the sake of individuals, no matter how good and just they may be.

10. *The Destruction of Sodom and Gomorrah*

Two angels, disguised as travelers, arrived in Sodom as the sun was setting. On that day, Lot had been elected judge and he sat at the gates of the city. He rose to welcome the strangers, as his uncle Abraham had taught him, and invited them to be his guests for the night. At first the angels demurred. But finally they accepted the invitation. They washed their feet of the dust of the road, and seated themselves at the table to eat the food which Lot had set before them.

Idith, Lot's wife, objected to her husband's hospitality. When Lot prepared the food for his guests his wife said: "We are out of salt. I shall have to borrow some from our neighbor." She then went to their neighbor and confided that Lot was entertaining strangers counter to her wish and the customs of Sodom.

The news traveled from one end of Sodom to the other that Lot was entertaining strangers. That night a mob of old and young surrounded Lot's house, banged on the door and demanded that the strangers be turned over to them for the treatment always given unwelcome guests.

Lot came out and locked the door behind him. He pleaded with the mob to go away. The more he talked the angrier grew the Sodomites. In desperation, Lot offered his two young daughters to them if they would leave his guests unharmed. But it was of no avail.

The crowd threatened: "If you do not stand aside and let us lay hands on your guests, we will deal more harshly with you than with them. Open the door, or we will break it down!"

The door opened suddenly and the angels snatched Lot in, and locked the door again. They smote the crowd with blindness so that they could not find the door and began to fight among themselves.

The angels then revealed themselves to Lot, and said: "We have come to destroy Sodom and Gomorrah. For the sake of Abraham, you and your family will be saved. Therefore tell your sons-in-law to get ready to leave the city. And you and your two virgin daughters and your wife must also prepare to leave at once."

Lot went to his sons-in-law and urged them to come with him and steal away from the city before it was destroyed. But they only laughed at Lot and refused to come with him.

It was growing late, and the angels urged Lot to hurry. Lot wanted to take his gold and silver and other possessions, but the angels told him they had come to save lives, not wealth. And they warned Lot, his wife, and their two daughters not to look behind them as they escaped from the city.

Under cover of darkness they fled. And as they escaped through the gates, a heavy downpour of brimstone and fire fell upon Sodom and Gomorrah. Lot's wife could hear the roaring of the fire behind them, and she thought of her daughters who had remained with their husbands in the burning cities. She turned to look behind her. Instantly she turned into a pillar of salt, which can be seen to this day near the River Kidron. Every day the cattle come and lick it until only a small lump is left by nightfall. But in the morning the pillar of salt rises as high as on the day Idith, Lot's wife, turned to look behind her.

And when the rains come the salt of the pillar washes down into the Salt Sea and covers it with the salt, pitch and sulphur that rained down on Sodom and Gomorrah.

Lot and his daughters escaped to a cave in the Mountains of Zoar, believing that not only Sodom and Gomorrah, but all the cities on earth had been destroyed.

Said Lot's older daughter to the younger: "There are no men left on earth, and our father is growing old and will soon die, and mankind will disappear from the face of the earth. Therefore, let us give our father wine and lie with him so that we may have children."

In those days it was permitted for the sons of Noah to take their daughters to wife. But Lot's daughters were shy and carried out their plan so that their father in his cups did not know what had happened.

Both conceived and had children. The offspring of one daughter were the Moabites, and the offspring of the other were the Ammonites.

11. *Isaac Means "Joy"*

Abraham was seventy-five years old when he left Haran for Canaan. He was already rich then, and his wealth multiplied so that within ten years his possessions and cattle were beyond count in one day and his gold and silver too heavy for one camel to carry. Yet he and his wife were not happy. For they had no children.

Sarah began to despair about her barrenness and she took her pretty Egyptian maid, Hagar, to her husband, as was the custom in those days. Hagar bore Abraham a son, and he was named Ishmael.

One day, when Ishmael was thirteen years old, God came to Abraham and said: "Sarah, your wife, shall have a son."

Abraham laughed and said: "My Lord, I am ninety-nine years old and Sarah is but ten years younger than I, and we are both stricken with age. Only through a miracle can Sarah now conceive."

"Long before the world was created, miracles were created," he was told. "A man cannot say two things at the same time, but God can utter Ten Words and the Universe is created; a man cannot listen to several people at the same time, but God can hear the pleas of all the people in the world at the same time."

Within a year Sarah gave birth to a son, and they named him Isaac, which means "joy," for Abraham and Sarah were filled with joy when he was born.

A rumor began to spread that Sarah had adopted the son of a servant and called him her own. Whereupon Abraham and Sarah arranged a great feast, and when all the guests had assembled, Abraham asked the women who had infants to give them to Sarah, that she might feed them. Sarah's breasts flowed with milk in two white streams and all the infants at the feast were fed by her. Then all knew that Abraham and his wife had been found worthy in the eyes of God, and that Isaac was Sarah's son.

At this feast, Satan, disguised as a poor man, came to the door begging for food. Sarah, who was occupied in breast-feeding the infants, and Abraham, who was busy tending to the needs of the guests, paid no attention to Satan.

Satan then went before God and said: "You have praised Abraham, and yet today when a poor man begged for food at his door, there was no one to hear him. He cannot be a man of great faith."

(God decided to test Abraham's faith and to ask him to offer his son Isaac as a sacrifice.)

12. Abraham's First-born Leaves Home

When the feast was over and all the guests had gone, Sarah said to her husband: "At the feast I saw Ishmael going from guest to guest and mocking: 'What is all this festivity about? I am Abraham's oldest son and I shall inherit his wealth and his name!' You must do something about him and his mother, my servant Hagar!"

(For Sarah's jealousy and the mistreatment of her servant and the child, it was decreed that Sarah should die before her time, forty-eight years before her husband, and that he should remarry Hagar after Sarah's death.)

Abraham said nothing and did nothing at the time. But when Sarah reported later that Ishmael, instigated by his mother, had tried to kill Isaac with his bow and arrow, Abraham sent Hagar and Ishmael back to Egypt.

On the way, as they wandered about in the desert, Hagar was visited by an angel who told her that her son would thrive and establish a great nation.

In Egypt, when Ishmael was old enough to marry, his mother found a wife for him, named Meribah, and Ishmael moved with his mother and his family into the desert to establish his own flocks of sheep and cattle.

13. *Abraham's Visit to Ishmael*

News of his son Ishmael reached Abraham's ears from time to time. He was happy that his son prospered, and he yearned to see his first-born. When his yearning became great, Abraham said to Sarah:

"It is long since I have seen my son, Ishmael, and I have decided to pay him a visit."

"His mother, Hagar, lives with him," said Sarah, dryly.

"She lives with him, and with his wife and children," said Abraham.

And Sarah said: "You must promise me not to descend from your camel."

Abraham promised, knowing what she meant.

A camel was saddled for him, and Abraham rode into the desert. At midday he arrived before the tent in which his son lived. Ishmael and his mother were not home but Meribah, Ishmael's wife, and her children came out to see the stranger.

"Where is Ishmael?" asked Abraham.

"He is away hunting," Meribah replied. But she did not ask the visitor who he was nor what he wanted of her husband.

"I am thirsty," said Abraham.

"I have neither water nor bread in my tent for strangers," she replied.

The children, full of curiosity, hung onto their mother's skirts. Meribah cursed them and ordered them into the tent. Abraham's heart ached for his son and his grandchildren. He said to Meribah:

"When Ishmael comes home, tell him that an old man came to visit him. Describe me to him. Then give him this message: 'Your tent needs a new lining and your threshold is faulty.'"

That afternoon when Ishmael and Hagar returned home, Meribah told them of the old man and the message he had left. Ishmael's face became wreathed in smiles.

"Why are you so happy?" asked Meribah. "That message makes no sense to me."

"No, indeed!" said Ishmael. "But it makes a great deal of sense to me."

For Ishmael understood that his father had come to see him and had left a message that Meribah was not a good wife.

14. Abraham's Tenth Trial

Ten times Abraham's faith was tried to test whether he was worthy that his offspring should receive the Ten Commandments. And the tenth trial was the hardest of them all. For God said to him:

"Abraham, take your son to the top of Mount Moriah and place him upon the altar as a sacrifice and as a burnt offering."

"I have two sons," said Abraham. "Which shall it be?"

"The one you love," said God.

"I love them both," said Abraham.

"Take Isaac and place him upon the altar."

Early the next morning Abraham arose and gathered sacrificial wood lest there be none on Mount Moriah. He packed on the back of an ass the wood, food for the long journey, and the sacrificial knife. Then he told Sarah that he was making the annual journey to the top of Mount Moriah to offer a sacrifice. He said nothing to her about God's command to sacrifice their son. And before she could ask any questions, he left with Isaac.

15. *The Meeting with Satan*

On their way to Mount Moriah, Abraham and Isaac met Satan disguised as an old man.

"Where are you going, Abraham?" asked Satan.

"I'm on my way to pray," answered Abraham.

"Why then the wood and the fire and the sacrificial knife?"

"We shall be on top of Mount Moriah several days and will use them to prepare our food."

"You are an old man and you have only one son with your wife Sarah, yet you are willing to sacrifice him," mocked Satan.

"As God told me to do, so shall it be," answered Abraham.

Satan then addressed Isaac: "Where are you going, Isaac?"

"To study God's wisdom," said Isaac.

"Do you intend to study after you are dead? For your father intends to sacrifice you."

"If God wishes to accept me as a sacrifice, I am glad to do His will."

Satan ran ahead to the foot of Mount Moriah and caused the stream to rise and overflow. Abraham and Isaac tried to wade across but the water reached over their heads.

"You have asked me to sacrifice my son," Abraham prayed, "but I shall not be able to fulfill Your will if I drown."

The waters at once receded and father and son proceeded to the top of the mountain.

16. *The Promise*

Now Isaac knew what was to happen. But together father and son built the altar on the very spot where Adam had offered up his first sacrifice. And when all was ready, Isaac said to his father:

"Father, promise me that you will not tell what has happened here to Mother while she may be standing on a roof, or near a well, or on the edge of a ravine. For the shock might cause her to fall and die."

Abraham promised.

Then Isaac said: "Tie me, Father, and make haste. For I am young and you are old, and when I see the sacrificial knife above my neck I may push you against my will and do you injury."

Abraham placed his son upon the altar, tied his hands and feet, then raised the sacrificial knife.

At that moment a voice called out commanding Abraham to stay his hand.

"Who are you?" Abraham asked.

"I am Michael, an angel of the Lord," came the answer.

"The command to sacrifice my son came from God," said Abraham, "and the command not to sacrifice him comes through His messenger. Whom shall I obey, the Teacher or His disciple?"

"I am not rescinding My command," said God. "You were told to place your son Isaac as a sacrifice upon the altar to test your faith. You have done that, and I command you now to take him off the altar."

Abraham closed his eyes and prayed: "O God, in the days to come should my offspring sin against you, remember my willingness to sacrifice my beloved son as a vicarious sacrifice for their sins, and deal mercifully with them."

And God spoke to Abraham a second time and said: "Because you have done this thing, and have not withheld your son, your beloved son, from Me, that in blessing I will bless you, and in multiplying I will multiply your seed as the stars of heaven, and as the sand which is on the seashore. And in your seed shall all the nations of the earth be blessed!"

Then Abraham untied his son and whispered: "Blessed art Thou, O Lord, Who resurrects the dead!"

For to Abraham it was as if Isaac had been resurrected.

As Abraham looked about him, he saw a sacrificial ram, whose horns were entangled in the thicket. That ram had been there since the Sixth Day of Creation, waiting to take the place of Isaac. Abraham placed the ram upon the altar and mixed his burnt offering with the seven fragrant substances: frankincense, galbonum, stacte, nard, myrrh, costum and spice. And the air from the top of Mount Moriah to the first heaven became filled with sweet smells.

(Out of the bones of that ram, it is recorded, the foundations of the Sanctuary in the Holy of Holies was built; its veins became the strings of King David's harp; its skin was made into a girt and belt for the Prophet Elijah; of the left horn was made the *shofar* used by Moses on Mount Sinai; and the right horn was made into the *shofar* which the Prophet Elijah will blow on Mount Moriah to announce the coming of the Messiah.)

17. *Sarah's Death*

When Abraham returned from Mount Moriah to Beersheba he found the door of Sarah's tent shut and the light within extinguished. And Sarah was not there.

Abraham went to the neighbors and asked: "Have you seen my wife Sarah, and do you know where she is?"

And the neighbors replied: "While you were gone an old man came to Sarah's door and told her that you had taken your son Isaac to Hebron to be sacrificed on the altar as you would sacrifice a lamb. And Mother Sarah remembered that you had left with wood for a fire and the sacrificial knife, but without a ram for the altar. Then she left for Hebron to seek her son — her only son Isaac."

Abraham rushed to Hebron and there he learned that when Sarah came and could not find her son, her soul fled. When Abraham saw her dead, he wept long and bitterly, and he lamented:

"O, orphans and widows, weep for Sarah, who fed you when you were hungry, and gave you drink when you were thirsty, and clothed you when you were naked.

"How has the tongue that always spoke words of comfort become silent!

"How have the hands that wiped the tears from the eyes of those in sorrow grown helpless!

"How have the eyes that always looked on all with compassion closed forever!"

And Abraham wept until he could weep no more; and he sat on the ground as silent as a stone.

Sarah was one hundred and twenty-seven years old when she died. And the city in which she died was called Four Corners, because of the four giants there who guarded the entrance of the Cave of Machpelah, where Adam and Eve were buried.

Abraham bought the cave and there he buried his wife Sarah.

18. *Abraham Prays for Death*

After Isaac married, Abraham was left alone. He was gray and old and lonely. It is said that four things cause a man to turn gray: disobedient children; a shrewish wife; taking part in war; and fear of old age. Abraham feared loneliness in his old age. He knew that Hagar had never remarried and that she had changed her name to Keturah, meaning "separation," for she had known no other man and considered herself only separated from her husband. Abraham went to her and married her again and they had many children.

Although Abraham was old, he was still filled with the strength of youth, and he prayed to be allowed to live forever. God listened to his prayer and said:

"You have walked before Me in truth, therefore your soul will not be taken from you unless you pray for it. But the laws of nature shall not be changed for you."

Years passed and Abraham still wished to live forever. Until one day a very old man came to ask for food and drink at Abraham's door. Abraham took him in and saw that the old man's knees trembled and that he faltered as he walked, both because his muscles were weak and his eyes were dim. When Abraham gave him food to eat, the spoon fell from his trembling hands and the food spilled over his garments. Abraham watched him with pity and a troubled heart.

"How old are you?" Abraham asked his guest.

"Just a few years older than you," the old man answered. "But such are the laws of nature that when age sets in, the senses wither like flowers in autumn."

When the old man left, Abraham prayed and said: "O Lord! Let me die with the strength of my senses undiminished rather than live to be a burden to myself and my kin."

God heard Abraham's prayer and fulfilled his wish.

Abraham died at the age of one hundred and seventy-five years. And he was buried in the Cave of Machpelah.

CHAPTER SEVEN

Isaac and Jacob

1. *Rebekah of Nahor*

After Sarah's death Abraham called in his old and trusted steward, Eliezer, and said to him:

"I want my son Isaac to marry a member of my father's family in Haran. For I do not want it to be said in Canaan that God could not keep His promise to give this land to my children unless Isaac marries one of their daughters. Go without delay and bring a wife for Isaac, and the God who has guided me since childhood will send you guidance."

"What if your family will not allow their daughter to leave her native land?"

"Then your obligation shall have been fulfilled," said Abraham.

Eliezer took ten of Abraham's servants and ten of his finest camels and they loaded the camels with ten measures of gold and ten times ten measures of silver and precious cloth and rare stones and herbs of many kinds, and started out for the city of Nahor.

Although Nahor was a distance of seventy days by camel, an angel guided them, and they made the journey in three hours. Eliezer left his master's house at noon, and before sunset he and his men and their camels were already resting near the wells at the outskirts of Nahor.

They had hardly settled when a young girl with a pitcher on her shoulder approached the well. She was more beautiful than any woman Eliezer had seen since his mistress Sarah was young. He noticed that the girl was very shy, but when he asked her for a drink of water, she surprised him by saying:

"You may have all the water you want for yourself and your men and your camels."

She had noticed the camels and knew they belonged to Abraham because Abraham's camels were different from the camels of all the desert people in that they were never allowed on the road without muzzles, so that they could not graze on the fields of strangers.

"What is your name?" asked Eliezer, convinced that she had been brought to the well by an angel.

"I am Rebekah, daughter of Bethuel, granddaughter of Nahor, who was Abraham's brother."

Eliezer then took out a golden noseband and two bracelets of great beauty, and earrings set with precious stones, and gave them to Rebekah as gifts from her great-uncle Abraham.

2. Marriages Are Made in Heaven

Rebekah hurried home to tell her father and her mother and her brother Laban what had happened. The wicked Laban envied her the gifts and hastened out to meet Eliezer, hoping that there would be presents for him also, and invited Eliezer and his men to the house.

While the camels were fed and bedded and the men washed their feet from the dust of the journey, Bethuel and his son conspired to poison Eliezer at the meal, so that all the wealth in his possession would fall into their hands.

But an angel exchanged the dishes of Bethuel and Eliezer. At the end of the meal Bethuel cried out:

"I am in pain! I am in bitter pain!"

And he fell upon his face and died.

The next morning Eliezer told Laban and Rebekah's mother about Abraham and his great wealth, and asked them to let Rebekah accompany him to become Isaac's wife.

"Since it is God's will," answered Laban, "there is nothing we can say." (Laban and his mother knew that forty days before a man is born the angels in heaven call out the name of the girl to be his bride.) "Here, then, is Rebekah. Take her to Isaac that she may be his wife, as decreed in heaven."

Eliezer unpacked the many gold and silver goblets, the fine

cloth, the rare fruits and the fragrant herbs which he had brought as presents, and that evening they celebrated the engagement of Rebekah and Isaac.

Early next morning Eliezer was ready to depart. But Laban, the sly one, asked that Rebekah remain home for a year to have her wedding clothes prepared. He knew that Eliezer would not want to wait and he hoped Eliezer would offer money and precious stones to receive permission for Rebekah to leave without delay.

Eliezer was not deceived. "Rebekah is now an orphan and we must ask her what is her wish in this matter," said he.

Rebekah had long deplored the wickedness of Laban and wished to leave her home as soon as possible.

"If you go today," said Laban, "we can give you nothing but our blessings."

"I will take your blessings," replied Rebekah, and she took leave of her mother, her brother and all her friends and left with Eliezer on the seventy-day journey.

Once more at sunset of the first day the long journey was over, and when Rebekah looked up, they were already near Hebron and a man was coming across the field to meet them.

"Who is that?" she asked.

"My young master, Isaac, who comes here each day to pray in solitude."

Rebekah slid down from her camel, covered her face with a veil, and waited for her betrothed to draw near.

Eliezer presented Isaac's bride to him, saying:

"Her name is Rebekah, but all who know her call her Rose, for she grew up as a rose among thorns."

3. *The Twins*

Isaac was forty years old on his wedding day, and when he was forty-nine years old, Rebekah came to him in tears, and said:

"When a woman is barren for ten years it is the right and duty of her husband to divorce her. We have been married nearly that long, and I am still childless."

"What can we do?" asked Isaac. For he loved Rebekah and

wanted neither to divorce her nor to take any other woman.

"Your mother was barren, and your father prayed for her until she had a child," said Rebekah. "Pray for me!"

"I will pray," said Isaac. He prayed, and he was told that his prayer would not be heeded, because it had been decreed that his wife, the daughter of an idolater, would have two sons, one resembling Abraham and the other resembling Bethuel. And the good would be withheld because of the evil.

Isaac did not tell his wife. But when another ten years passed and she pleaded again with him, he took her up to Mount Moriah, to the place where his father had been ready to offer him up as a sacrifice. They prayed there together and Isaac admitted to God that for Rebekah's sake he was willing to father even a reprobate if she would have also a good son.

In due time Rebekah knew that she was pregnant, and bearing twins, and that the twins would be unlike each other. For each time Rebekah passed a place where there were idols, one of the twins wanted her to enter and pushed the other; and each time Rebekah passed a House of God the other twin wanted her to enter. And the twins constantly struggled.

When they were born, the first child was red and covered all over with hair, and they named him Esau, the Hairy One; the second child was born holding onto the foot of the first-born, for he should have really been first, since his soul was created first. And the second child was named Jacob.

4. *Esau and King Nimrod*

When Isaac's twin sons were fifteen years old, bold Esau spent his days hunting, and quiet Jacob remained at home with his aging grandfather, Abraham, from whom he learned about God and all that had happened since Creation.

Isaac was proud of his carefree and nimble Esau; Rebekah took greater pride in Jacob.

One day Esau went into the woods to hunt and met King Nimrod.

"I hear that you are quite a hunter!" said the king.

"As good as any in the land," Esau replied without shame.

The king then made a wager: "Let us go hunting until the sun passes the zenith and we shall see whose catch is greater and worthier. If I win, you shall be my servant; and if you win you can have anything you want, up to half of my kingdom."

They separated for the hunt and at the end of the day met at the appointed place. King Nimrod returned with his attendants carrying a lion, two leopards, and a number of rare birds. Esau appeared empty-handed.

"Have you caught nothing at all, great hunter?" King Nimrod mocked.

"I am a great hunter, but I am not a giant. And not even a giant could carry all the lions, yak, gazelles, capuchins, ibex, and the many birds and beasts I cannot name, yet killed this morning. You shall have to send a hundred men to bring them all in."

He led King Nimrod and his ten servants to the place where his morning's catch lay, and they saw that Esau had told the truth. King Nimrod kissed the victor's hand, and asked him what he wanted as his reward.

"All I want is your snakeskin coat, Your Majesty!" For Esau knew that was the coat which had belonged to Adam the First.

5. *Because of a Pot of Lentils*

Esau returned home that day very happy, but so famished that he thought he would die of hunger. As he entered his father's house, he found Jacob in tears.

"Why do you weep?" he asked his brother.

"Grandfather Abraham died this morning."

"If Grandfather Abraham died like any ordinary man," said Esau, "then I know that there is no God and no reward for virtue." Then he said: "I am weary and hungry. Let me have some of the lentils you have cooked."

"You may have it," said Jacob, "if you will give me your birthright."

Esau gladly gave him the birthright for he knew that after Isaac's death the son with the birthright would have to perform the sacrifices and serve God faithfully. And Esau was interested only in hunting and in making hunting weapons.

Jacob served the lentils to his brother Esau and nothing more was said about the birthright. Excepting that when Isaac heard about it, he was very upset; and when Rebekah heard about it, she was very glad.

6. *Esau and Satan*

When he was a hundred years old, Isaac's eyes grew dim, and his feet feeble. He called in his favorite son one day and told him to prepare a feast and bring it to his father and receive his blessing.

"But do not," added Isaac, "prepare for me any food you have not rightfully obtained." For although he loved his son Esau he knew all his faults.

Rebekah overheard Isaac and decided that the benediction for the first-born rightfully belonged to Jacob.

While Esau was out hunting food for his father, Rebekah prepared a feast, then sent for Jacob, who was in the Shem and Eber house of study. She dressed Jacob in hunter's clothes, covered his hands with skins, had him put on Adam's snakeskin coat, then urged him to go to his father and pretend that he was Esau.

When Jacob understood what his mother wished him to do, he began to tremble and to weep, and refused to deceive his father. But the angels Michael and Gabriel came down, took him by his arms, and led him into his father's chamber. Jacob then knew that it was God's will that he should obey his mother.

"Who is there?" asked Isaac.

"Father, arise and eat the food I have prepared for you," Jacob replied, and fainted.

"How did you get back from the hunt so soon?" Isaac asked suspiciously, for the voice he heard was the voice of Jacob. "Come near, and let me kiss you."

The angels revived Jacob and brought him nigh. Isaac touched the skins upon Jacob's hands, smelled the fragrance of the Garden of Eden which Adam's coat carried with it, and said:

"May God bless you with the dew of heaven (meaning the City

of Jerusalem), and the fat of the land (meaning the Temple sacrifices), and may you forever walk in the ways of righteousness."

Meanwhile Esau was out hunting. He caught a gazelle, bound it, laid it down under a tree and went to catch another. When he returned with the second gazelle, the first one was gone. "I must have been careless in binding it," thought Esau, and bound the second one more carefully before continuing the hunt. But when he returned with the third gazelle, the second was gone. This went on for some time, until Esau realized that he had been hunting Satan, disguised as a gazelle. Esau began to fear that he might have to return empty-handed to his father, when he caught a bird. He hastened home to prepare it. And when the food was ready, he went to his father and called:

"I have brought your food, Father, and I have come for your blessing."

"Who are you?" asked Isaac.

"I am your first-born son," Esau answered.

"Then who was he I have just blessed?"

Old Isaac trembled when he realized what had happened and Esau cried out in a loud and bitter voice.

7. *Jacob's Dream*

Esau threatened that, as soon as his father died, he would kill his brother Jacob.

Rebekah went to Isaac and said: "Esau has threatened to kill Jacob on the day you die, and surely God will kill Esau as a punishment. Thus I shall be widowed and bereft of my two sons in one day. Therefore I ask you to send Jacob away to my brother Laban in Padanaran and let him stay there until Esau's anger dies down."

Jacob left for Haran, and on the way he ascended Mount Moriah. The sun went down, though it was still early in the afternoon, so that Jacob would be obliged to remain there overnight.

Jacob prepared for the night and gathered some stones to protect him from the wild beasts. The stones began to quarrel among themselves. "I want to be the one," said each stone, "upon which this holy man will rest his head." For the stones knew what was to happen. God made peace between them and all of them turned into one great stone which surrounded Jacob like a fortress.

Jacob fell asleep and dreamt that he saw a ladder rising from the earth into heaven, and a myriad of angels going up and coming down. First the angels went *up* to look at Jacob's face engraved on the Throne of Glory, and then they came *down* to do honor to the sleeping Jacob. Then God came to Jacob in his dream and told him that the land upon which he rested would belong to his offspring, and that his offspring would be numerous as the stars, when they were good, and as the dust on the road, when they were wicked.

Jacob awoke and realized through his power of prophecy that he was on the very spot where all the world's prayers go up through a gate in heaven and that the stone he had slept upon was where the Holy of Holies in the Temple would be built. He anointed the stone with oil and vowed that if he prospered he would bring tithes unto the Lord.

The stone upon which Jacob slept, known as Jacob's Pillow, according to legend, exists to this day. It is a slab of yellow sandstone, nearly a cubit and two hands in length, over a span and a half in width, and fully a span in thickness. It is called the Stone *of Destiny; and it is called the* Stone of Scone. *Until the end of 1950 the coronation chair of England, in Westminster Abbey, rested upon it. Then it was dramatically stolen, and much later returned unharmed. How Jacob's Pillow came from Bethel, in the Holy Land, to the Monastery of Scone, in Scotland, is a wonderful legend that unfortunately does not belong in this book. But that the Stone of Scone is Jacob's Pillow, the Irish Kings of the Hills of Tara and John de Baliol, King of Scotland, never doubted.*

8. *Jacob Falls in Love*

Jacob started out from Mount Moriah in the morning and early that afternoon he reached the outskirts of Haran. Soon a number of shepherds came down to the wells with their flocks.

"Tell me, my brothers, do you know Laban, the grandson of Nahor?"

(He called them "brothers" to show that all men are brothers in the eyes of God and should be treated with respect and love, unless they prove themselves unworthy.)

"We know him," they replied.

"Is there peace between you and Laban?"

"There is peace between us," said they.

"Then God is with you," said Jacob. "Now tell me, how is Laban's household? Is all well with them?"

"There was a plague among Laban's sheep and only a few survived," said the shepherds. "Those he gave to his daughter Rachel to tend, and she should be here soon to water them."

While they were speaking there came to the wells a young shepherdess, straight as an arrow, proud as a cedar, supple as a willow, her eyes shining like jewels, and her lips the color of ripe cherries. Jacob fell in love with her as soon as he saw her.

"This is Rachel," said the shepherds, "the daughter of Laban, about whom you asked."

"I am Jacob, son of Rebekah, your father's sister," Jacob told Rachel; and he embraced his cousin and kissed her.

Then tears came to Jacob's eyes, for through the power of prophecy he could foresee that Rachel would not be buried with him in Machpelah, and though he had just met her, it pained him to think of parting with her even after death.

When Rachel returned home and told her father of the meeting with Jacob, Laban hurried out to greet him. He remembered how Eliezer had come laden with presents, and expected Jacob to be surrounded by an even greater number of camels, more servants, and bearing more precious gifts.

Laban was disappointed when he saw Jacob standing alone near the wells. Then Laban embraced his nephew, hoping to discover whether Jacob had gold and precious stones hidden upon his person.

When Laban could feel no hidden treasure he was greatly grieved, and said:

"You are as welcome as a bone from which the meat has been removed. But you are a kinsman. Abide with me for a few days."

9. *She-Leilah*

The moment Rachel's older sister, Leah, set eyes on Jacob, she fell in love with him. But Jacob hardly noticed her, for he loved Rachel. And after a short while in his uncle's house, he asked for Rachel's hand. Laban told the poor young relative that he would have to work for seven years to earn the right to marry Rachel.

Seven years is a long time. And seven years' work was a great price to pay for a wife. But Jacob agreed, so great was his love for Rachel.

Leah wept when she heard of Jacob's pact with her father. For seven years she wept, and her eyes grew weak.

"Why are Leah's eyes so red and weak?" asked Jacob of his cousins, Laban's sons.

"She was told that she is to be the wife of Esau," they replied. "Ever since then she has been praying to God not to let her fall into the hands of the wicked and she has been weeping all this time. That is why her eyes are weak and red."

"God is near the broken-hearted," said Jacob. "He will surely listen to her prayers and grant her what she wishes."

At the end of seven years Jacob demanded Rachel, his bride, for whom he had labored so long.

Laban arranged a wedding feast to which he invited all the townspeople and revealed to them that he planned to give Jacob, not his bride Rachel, but Leah.

The guests drank their wine, and when they were in their cups they began to sing a song consisting of only two words: *She-Leilah* — *She-Leilah*. They hoped that Jacob would catch the clue in their song which told him of Laban's scheme. But Jacob was so happy that he heard nothing, and thought only of the hour when he would be at last alone with his beloved.

Late that night Laban brought to Leah all the gifts Jacob had given to Rachel during the seven years of his courtship. Then Laban took Leah to Jacob's chamber. In the antechamber he placed Zilpah, Rachel's young maid, and then he blew out all the lights.

Jacob saw Zilpah in the antechamber and assumed her mistress

Rachel was within. But when Laban began to blow out the lights, he asked:

"Why do you do that?"

"It is the custom of our land," said Laban. And he left Jacob in the darkness.

In the morning Jacob saw that Leah was beside him. He went to Laban in anger.

"Why did you deceive me? It is for Rachel that I worked seven years."

Laban answered with indignation: "We do not permit a younger sister to marry before her older sister. If you still want Rachel, you shall have to work another seven years. But you may marry her now, and work for her after the wedding."

And Jacob so longed for Rachel that he was willing to work for her for another seven years.

10. *Jacob Marries Rachel*

Jacob blamed Leah for what had happened to him and he disliked her. Leah had wept before she was married because Jacob did not love her; and she cried after their wedding because he still loved only Rachel. To comfort Leah's troubled heart, God blessed her with children.

Now it was Rachel's turn to be jealous, for she was childless like Rebekah and Sarah before her. Rachel could bear it no longer, and she said to Jacob:

"Give me children, or I shall die."

Jacob became angry and said: "The fault is not mine."

But the fault was his. For he foresaw that Rachel would die in childbirth, and he could not bear the thought of her death.

Rachel then brought her maid, Bilhah, to her husband, as was the custom, and Bilhah bore two sons. And then Leah gave birth to a daughter, and they named her Dinah. But Rachel was still without a child of her own.

Just when Rachel began to despair, she gave birth to a son. She thanked the Lord for taking the shame of barrenness from her and she named her son Joseph.

11. *Jacob Goes Home*

When Joseph was born, Deborah, Rebekah's maid, arrived in Haran with the message that Jacob's father and mother were growing old and wanted their son to return to Canaan to look after their welfare. But Laban would not let his son-in-law go, for he knew that God had made him and his sons rich for the sake of Jacob. He offered Jacob all the spotted and the speckled among the goats and the dark among the sheep to induce him to remain in Haran. But in his heart Laban plotted to trick his son-in-law. And God ordered the angels to punish Laban and to reward Jacob. And Jacob's flocks multiplied a hundredfold faster than the flocks of his father-in-law.

Before very long Jacob's flocks grew so great that six hundred thousand dogs were required to keep them from straying.

Naturally, the sons of Laban were jealous, and they plotted secretly to kill their brother-in-law. The plot became known to Jacob. Quietly and secretly, on the night Laban's sons planned to kill him, Jacob left Haran with his wives and children, his shepherds and servants, and all his possessions on camels.

When Laban awoke in the morning he found them gone. He followed after his son-in-law and caught up with him seven days later.

"If you had told me you were determined to leave," Laban shouted, "I would have sent you away with joy and song. But instead you have taken away my daughters and their children as if they were captives of the sword. You did not let me kiss them farewell. And besides, you have stolen my gods."

Jacob's children, who had crowded around, turned red with shame.

"Why do you blush, my grandchildren?" Laban asked them. "Why did your faces turn red when I said your father had stolen my gods?"

"Because you have shamed us today," said the children.

"How did I shame you, my grandchildren?"

"You are old and gray," they answered, "yet you speak as one who does not know his right hand from his left. If the idols you worship were really gods, could they be stolen? And if they were stolen, could they be gods? Yet you said to our father, 'You have stolen my gods.'"

And Jacob said in anger to Laban: "Search me and my household and all my men, and on him that you find your idols, he shall be put to death!"

Laban went through from tent to tent, his search in vain. At last he came into Rachel's tent. Rachel had taken the idols to teach her father and brothers that the idols they worshiped were useless and could be stolen. But when she heard Jacob's vow of death for the person who had taken the idols, she hid them in the saddle of her camel and sat down upon it.

"Forgive me, Father, for not rising," said Rachel to her father when he came into the tent. "I am in the period of women."

Laban left his daughter without saying a word because it is forbidden to disturb a woman at such a time, and it is a bad omen even to talk to her, or to look at her, or to remain in her presence.

Laban took leave of Jacob and his daughters and their children and returned home.

12. *Jacob and the Angel*

On the way to his father, Jacob had to pass through Edom, where his brother Esau lived. Though twenty years had passed since Esau threatened to kill him, Jacob was still afraid. He sent messengers ahead to tell Esau of his coming, and to tell him also that it was not the father's blessing that had made Jacob rich, but that all he had he had paid for with twenty years of labor; yet, should Esau want any of his possessions, he could have them.

Along the way they forded the Jabbok River. The day after they crossed, Jacob went back alone for some precious vessels that had been left behind.

As he was collecting them, an old man approached him and said: "Do me a favor and take my lambs across the river and I will carry your vessels. For I am old and tired and night will soon be upon us."

Jacob lifted up as many lambs as he could carry and took them across the river. Then he returned for more. He made many trips, but the number of lambs which remained seemed to increase rather than to decrease. And when the sun began to set, Jacob looked up and saw that the stranger's flock was now so great that it filled the valley and the meadows and the mountains beyond.

"Are you a magician?" asked Jacob.

The old man bent down and touched the ground with his finger in answer. And the earth shook and a great flame went up to the heavens.

"You cannot frighten me with your magic, nor shake my faith in God," said Jacob.

Then the old man caught Jacob and began to wrestle with him. All night they wrestled in silence. Toward morning the old man said:

"Let me go, for you have wrestled with an angel of the Lord and he could not destroy you."

"I shall not let you go until you bless me," said Jacob.

The angel touched the hollow of Jacob's thigh and dislocated it. But though Jacob was in great pain he would not let go. "When the angels came to my grandfather, Abraham, they did not leave until they had blessed him."

"They were sent to bless Abraham, but I was sent to try your faith," said the angel. "Now let me go for it is already dawn."

"Are you a thief that you are afraid of the light?" asked Jacob.

"At dawn the angels sing before the Lord. Let me go that I may return to heaven."

"Today the angels will have to sing without you," said Jacob.

"If I do not sing today," said the angel, "then tomorrow my company of angels will say: 'You did not sing yesterday; you cannot sing today.' And I shall never be allowed to sing again."

"Then bless me, and I will let you go."

"I bless you," said the angel. "And from this time forth your name shall be Israel, which means that you will be a ruler 'with the aid of God.'"

"What is your name?" asked Jacob.

"An angel's name changes with each mission he performs. Therefore do not ask my name. One thing I can tell you: You need not fear your brother Esau, for God has softened his heart toward you."

Then the angel disappeared.

13. *The Wages of Curiosity*

When Jacob and his great household reached the outskirts of Shechem in Canaan, the Patriarch bought a large field and consecrated with it an altar to God; and there he and his family lived in peace with the Hivites and their king, Hamor.

Until one day Dinah, Jacob's daughter, wandered out alone into the Canaanite city, full of curiosity. On the way she met King Hamor's son, Prince Shechem, whose honeyed words exceeded his discretion as much as his passion exceeded his restraint. He spoke flatteringly to the beautiful Dinah and induced her to come to his chambers in the palace.

King Hamor heard of it and called his son to him and said: "The sons of Jacob will not allow their sister to be treated as a harlot. To avoid strife, you must marry her."

"My soul cleaves to hers," said Shechem. "Go to her father and get me Dinah to wife."

The king went to Jacob and said: "Your grandfather was a chieftain and I am a chieftain, therefore give your daughter Dinah to my son as his wife."

"My grandfather Abraham was likened to an ox," said Jacob, "and you have been likened to a mule, and our Law forbids harnessing an ox and a mule for the plowing."

"The plowing and the seeding has been done," said Hamor. "I am talking of the reaping."

When the sons of Jacob heard what had happened to their sister, they went to the king and said:

"We will let you marry our daughters, and we will marry yours. But first, all your men must be circumcised, for the uncircumcised are an abomination in the eyes of our God."

The king agreed and issued a decree that all the men in Shechem were to be circumcised. On the third day, when the men of Shechem were weak from pain, Simeon and Levi bared their swords and descended upon the city. They killed all the men, plundered their possessions and took their women captive.

Then they took their sister Dinah and cast her out because her indiscretion had caused so much bloodshed.

Jacob grieved when he heard of the evil his sons had committed:

"You have made me as a stink in the nostrils of the nations," he lamented.

And in fear of their lives, they left their fields in Shechem and went toward Bethel.

14. *Rachel's Death*

Between Bethel and Ephrath, in Canaan, Rachel was taken in labor. And that which Jacob had so long feared now happened. Rachel died in childbirth. The son that was born to her he named Ben Oni, meaning "Son of My Sorrow." Then he renamed him Benjamin, meaning "Son of My Right Hand."

Where Rachel died, there she was buried, which is in a place called Bethlehem. Upon her grave Jacob erected a monument, which is there to this day.

By the time Jacob and his family reached Four Corners, Rebekah had been dead for many years, and Isaac died soon after Jacob's return. The two brothers, Esau and Jacob, buried their father in the Cave of Machpelah.

(When Jacob had left home he promised to return soon, but he stayed twenty-two years. It was therefore decreed that he should be punished by having his son Joseph remain in Egypt for twenty-two years without getting in touch with his father.)

15. *Pearls in the Sand*

The stories of Abraham, Isaac and Jacob are many, whereas the stories of Esau and Nahor and Laban and Lot and all the others of their day are few. That is because, when one loses pearls in the sand, one sifts the sand until the pearls are found; then the sand is thrown away.

They who follow the dictates of their desires are as common as the sand, but the men of God are rare as precious pearls.

CHAPTER EIGHT

The Great Famine

1. *Joseph the Dreamer*

There were twelve sons in Jacob's house and many daughters. Yet none compared with Joseph in beauty of countenance and in grace of movement. As he grew, so increased his comeliness. It is said that ten measures of beauty were given to the world, and nine of them went to Joseph. People from afar came to look upon him, and the sight of his face, it was believed, could cure afflictions of the eye. By the time Joseph was fifteen years old, the people from Padanaran to Goshen, when they wanted to flatter anyone, would say: "You resemble Joseph ben Jacob!"

Jacob loved Rachel's first-born above all his other children and adorned him with garments finer than any given the others. Naturally Joseph's brothers and sisters resented him.

When Joseph was sixteen years old he began to dream dreams, which he would relate at the family gatherings, and the resentment of his brothers and sisters turned into hatred. For these dreams did not please them, and sometimes angered even his doting father.

"I dreamt last night that we were all picking fruit in a garden," Joseph related one day. "Your fruit spoiled before it was brought home, but my fruit did not spoil."

"What does that mean?" asked Judah.

"I don't know. Ask Father," said Joseph.

The next day he told of another dream. "We were all out in the fields binding sheaves of rye. My sheaf remained standing upright, but your sheaves surrounded mine and bowed to it."

"Does that mean that you expect to be our ruler?" asked Levi.

"I don't know what it means. It is only what I dreamt," said Joseph.

Soon he related still another dream. "I dreamt that the sun and the moon and the twelve stars appeared in the firmament, and the sun and the moon and eleven stars bowed to my star."

"Do you mean, son," said Jacob angrily, "that you expect me and Bilhah, who brought you up, and your eleven brothers, to bow down to you?"

"I don't know what the dream means," said Joseph.

"Your dreams are mere fancy and lies," said Jacob before all his children. For Jacob understood what the dreams meant and he knew that they foretold the future. But he dealt harshly with his son to lessen the hatred Joseph aroused in his brothers.

When left alone with his son, Jacob warned: "O my child! Tell not your dreams and visions to your brothers, lest they devise some evil plot against you. For Satan seeks out the envious to inspire them with mischief."

But Joseph continued to dream dreams and he continued to tell them. And the enmity of his brothers increased.

When Joseph was seventeen, Jacob started to send him out to his brothers in the fields on various missions. Joseph would return with reports that made his father's heart heavy with sorrow. Joseph reported that the sons of Leah called the children of the servants "slaves"; and that was forbidden. He reported that the sons of Zilpah ate the meat of a lamb which had been torn to pieces while still alive; and that was forbidden. Then he reported that his brothers took liberties with the daughters of their overseers and the wives of strangers; and that, too, was forbidden.

(What Joseph did not know was that slander was as great a sin as any he reported; and that he slandered even though such was not his intention. Therefore he was punished. For accusing his brothers of eating the flesh of living things, his shirt was dipped in the blood of a kid; for accusing his brothers of calling their servants "slaves," he was sold into slavery; and for accusing his brothers of lusting after married women, he was accused by Potiphar's wife and sent to prison.)

2. *Joseph Is Sold as a Slave*

One day Jacob received no word from his sons, who were feeding their flocks in distant fields of Hebron infested with robbers, and he sent Joseph to find out whether all was well with them.

Joseph went toward the Valley of Hebron and looked for his brothers but could not find them. As he wandered about, the Angel Gabriel came to him, disguised as an old man, and directed him to his brothers in Dothan.

When the brothers saw him coming, they said to each other: "Now, now is the time to rid ourselves of this slanderer."

Only Reuben, the oldest brother, rebuked them, saying: "Shed no blood!"

"We shall not shed his blood," said Levi. "We will release our dogs and they will tear him to pieces as they do the wild beasts."

The brothers released the dogs, but they joyfully ran up to Joseph and licked his hands.

Still the brothers were intent on destroying Joseph. When he came near, they laid hands upon him, stripped off his clothes and then Simeon threw him into a dry well full of snakes.

"If the snakes do not kill him," said Simeon, "he will die of hunger and thirst. Yet we shall not have shed his blood."

Late that same day a group of Midianites stopped at the well for water. Instead of water they found a youth at the bottom unhurt among the snakes. They lowered a rope and drew the boy out. But when they saw that he was circumcised they threw him back into the pit, thinking that he had been mutilated.

Just then a caravan of Ishmaelites, bearing a cargo of wax, pepper, wine and spices to Egypt, also approached the well in search of water. The Midianites drew Joseph out again and offered to sell him to the Ishmaelites for twenty pieces of silver. The Ishmaelites were ready to buy him, for they themselves practiced circumcision and knew that there was nothing wrong with Joseph.

Joseph's brothers, who had watched from a distance, came up to the pit to find out what the strangers wanted.

"Who is this boy whom we have just drawn out of the pit?" asked the Midianites.

"He is one of our slaves, whom we cast into the pit because he refused to obey our orders," the brothers replied.

"If he is your slave, sell him to us," said the Ishmaelites. And they offered twenty pieces of silver, the price set by the Midianites.

The brothers accepted the silver, glad to be rid of the dreamer whose dreams angered them.

The Ishmaelites placed Joseph on a camel, naked as he had been thrown into the pit, and the caravan left. Joseph clasped tightly in his hand an amulet his mother had placed about his neck, and prayed. And before the astonished eyes of the Ishmaelites, a silken garment softly covered his naked body.

3. Reuben's Grief

That night Reuben came to the pit to save his young brother. But the pit was empty. Reuben returned to his brothers and demanded they tell him what had happened to Joseph. Judah told him that a group of Ishmaelite merchants in search of water found Joseph in the well and had taken him with them to Egypt.

"What shall we tell our father?" Reuben asked.

Issachar answered: "We have his silk shirt. Let us tear it and dip it in the blood of a kid and send it to Father. He will think that Joseph was killed by wild beasts."

When a messenger brought the bloodstained garment to Jacob, he rent his cloak, put on sackcloth, and sat down in ashes to mourn Joseph's death. His sons and daughters came to console him, but Jacob would not be comforted and said:

"My mourning will never end, for I shall mourn my son Joseph until the day I die."

Later Jacob said to his sons: "Go and find the beast that killed my son; and bring me Joseph's bones that I may bury them."

The sons of Jacob went into the wilderness and caught a wolf. They brought the animal to their father and said:

"Here is the beast that devoured your son Joseph. But of his bones we have found no trace."

Jacob then spoke to the wolf bitterly: "You wretched beast, why have you killed my son, who did you no harm and never carried sword or arrow?"

And the wolf answered in a human voice: "Before the Lord I swear that I did your son no harm. I myself have come from distant places to look for my own son whom I have lost, and I do not know whether he is still alive or dead."

Jacob sent the animal away unharmed, knowing that the Lord

had given the wolf speech. He was no longer certain that Joseph was dead, and his grief lessened.

But Reuben's grief was even greater. For he knew that his brothers had added falsehood to malice against their brother Joseph.

4. *Joseph in Potiphar's House*

Joseph was brought to Egypt and sold to Potiphar, Captain of the King's Guard. Potiphar noticed that whatever Joseph did, he did well; and that whatever he planned, succeeded. Before very long Potiphar appointed Joseph overseer, and entrusted him with the household affairs.

Potiphar admired Joseph because he was skillful and because whatever he did prospered; and his wife, Zuleika, admired Joseph from the day he had entered her home, because there was not another man in Egypt as handsome as he. She consulted him on all matters, and consulted him often. She ordered that Joseph be given clean linen each day, and that his bed be sprayed with perfume. She flattered him whenever she saw him. And she sought every opportunity to see him.

One day Zuleika gave a banquet to her women friends and ordered Joseph to serve her when the guests arrived. The guests began to cut the citrons that had been served and instead cut their fingers for their eyes were fixed on Joseph. Soon their beautiful garments were stained with blood. But they seemed not to care as long as Joseph remained in their presence.

When the guests departed, Zuleika tried to entice Joseph with gold and silver, but he would not listen to her, saying that it was against the dictates of his conscience and the will of God.

"Show me this god you speak of so often," she demanded.

Joseph led her to the window and asked her to look up straight into the sun.

"I cannot," said Zuleika, "for it will surely blind me."

"The sun is only one of God's works," said Joseph. "If you cannot look at one of His works, how do you expect to look at Him and live?"

Joseph left her. But Zuleika could not cast him out of her thoughts.

One holiday, when the Egyptians celebrated the rise of the Nile in their temples, Zuleika pretended illness and remained at home in bed. Joseph did not know she was home when he came into the house to attend to his affairs and was surprised to find her alone. Zuleika called to him:

"Come, lie with me."

Joseph replied: "Your husband trusts me with all that he has and I cannot deceive him."

"But there is no one here to see us," said Zuleika.

"There *is* someone here," said Joseph. "God can see us."

Zuleika threw a mantle over the idol in her room. "Now he cannot see us," she said.

"Your god," said Joseph, "but not mine. My God can see everything." And he lowered his eyes to the ground.

"Am I so unworthy that you will not even look at me?" demanded Zuleika.

"Command me to leave," Joseph pleaded.

Zuleika took a spear and placed the point under Joseph's chin. "You shall not leave. And you shall look at me."

"When a man dies, the first question he is asked is: 'Have you dealt honestly with every man?' What shall my answer be?"

"In your religion, not mine," said Zuleika. "I have consulted the stars which we worship, and I see by the stars that I am to have a son with you. I cannot defy the stars."

She put her hand on his coat and tried to draw him near. Joseph fled, leaving his torn garment in her hand.

Zuleika flung Joseph's garment on her bed and began to scream. And when Potiphar came home, she told him that the Hebrew slave Joseph, knowing she was alone at home, had tried to force his attentions upon her, and when she screamed, he ran away, leaving his torn garment behind.

Potiphar sent for Joseph. "For such a crime there is only one punishment."

"But I am not guilty," said Joseph, "and you cannot condemn me on the word of one person who has no witnesses."

"Neither have you any witnesses to prove your innocence," said Potiphar, and began to beat Joseph to make him confess.

At that moment an infant in the room spoke out in the voice of an adult and said to Potiphar: "Why do you beat Joseph? For I heard my mother say to him, 'Come and lie with me.' He ran out, and it was long afterwards that she screamed."

The infant's words were a sign to Potiphar. But to protect the honor of his family, he sent Joseph to prison.

5. *Dreams of the Butler and the Baker*

Joseph remained in prison for twelve years. Toward the end of that time the king's butler and the royal baker were imprisoned; the first because a fly had been found in the king's cup, and the second, because splinters of wood had been found in the king's bread. Three days before the trial the two prisoners told Joseph of dreams they had dreamt and asked him to interpret them.

Joseph knew that a fly might fall into a goblet even after it has been cleaned; and that the court would find the butler innocent. But splinters of wood in bread, particularly a king's bread, can be accounted for only by neglect or a deliberate attempt on the king's life; therefore the baker would be found guilty. After Joseph heard their dreams, he said to the baker:

"This is the interpretation of your dream: within three days you will be found guilty and condemned to hang." And to the butler he said: "From your dream I gather that within three days you will be found innocent and restored to your place in the palace."

"If the king will deal with me as you interpret and I am restored to the palace, I promise to do all in my power to have you released from prison."

As Joseph foretold, so it happened. But once back in the palace, the butler completely forgot Joseph and his interpretation of the dream.

6. *Two Dreams and One Meaning*

King Pharaoh had two troubling dreams one night. In the morning he called together his wise men and said to them: "I dreamt two dreams last night, and neither gives me peace. I will tell you the dreams, and you shall tell me what they mean."

And these are the dreams Pharaoh dreamt. He was standing at the edge of a river and saw seven fat cows come up and feed in the pasture, then seven lean cows came up and devoured the fat cows. The king awoke, and when he fell asleep again, he dreamt that he saw seven ears of corn heavy with grain swaying in the breeze, when suddenly the east wind brought up seven lean and parched ears of corn and they devoured the good and full ears.

The wise men puzzled over the king's dreams for three days and three nights and then they came to him and some said: "The seven fat cows in your dream represent seven daughters that will be born to you. And the ears of corn represent seven kingdoms that you will conquer. The rest we do not understand." And others said: "The seven cows represent seven wives you will take, who will die young, and their children will war against each other."

The king said: "I have no faith in your interpretations for I think you are all wrong." And he commanded that the wise men should be driven from the palace.

The king's butler remembered Joseph and told the king about him. "Hear what he has to say," pleaded the butler, "for he is neither a fortuneteller nor a dealer in witchcraft. He is a Hebrew and both fortunetelling and witchcraft are against his religion."

The king sent for Joseph. When he arrived at the palace, the king was seated on his throne, girt with an ephod of gold and a crown of emeralds upon his head. Seventy steps led up to Pharaoh's seat. It was customary that a man received by the king ascended as many steps as the languages he could converse in, then the king would come down and sit one step above him.

Though Joseph could speak in seventy languages, he ascended only to the third step, and the king came down to the fourth, and said:

"I have dreamt two dreams, and I know not what they mean. I was told that you could interpret dreams."

"With God's help," said Joseph.

The king told his dreams.

"You have dreamt two dreams, but their meaning is one," said Joseph as the king ended. "You have seen the dream in two forms as a warning that what is foretold will come to pass soon. A seven-year famine threatens the land, to be preceded by seven prosperous years. And the warning has come to you so that you may prepare without delay, or your nation will suffer from starvation. Therefore, gather enough grain during the fat years to last through the lean years. In that way you shall save your people from famine."

"How am I to know whether your interpretation is true or false?" asked Pharaoh.

"Before this day is over," said Joseph, "you will rejoice and you will be grieved. Today your wife, the queen, will give birth to a son and you will rejoice. But your first-born son, who is now two years old and very ill, will die, and you will be grieved. If these come to pass you will know that I speak the truth."

As Joseph left the presence of the king, a messenger arrived to announce that the queen had given birth to a boy. The messenger was still speaking, when another arrived to announce that the two-year-old prince had died.

Pharaoh recalled Joseph to the court, took off his ring and placed it on Joseph's finger, and appointed him as supervisor of Egypt's granaries. He then placed a gold chain about Joseph's neck to signify that he had been made Governor of Egypt. And he decreed that Joseph should be recognized second only to the king.

"From now on," said the king, "Your name shall be Zaphnath Paaneah, which means *'He who uncovers the hidden.'*"

7. *Joseph and Asinath*

As soon as Joseph completed the system of granaries and instituted the plans to brace Egypt against famine, he asked the king for permission to marry.

"It is forbidden to us Hebrews to live with our wives or indulge in any pleasures in time of disaster or famine, and I want to start my family during the fat years," said Joseph.

"And whom do you want as bride?" asked the king.

"With your permission, I wish to marry Asinath, daughter of Potiphar."

There was consternation among the courtiers when they heard

that, for Potiphar had caused Joseph to languish in prison on a false accusation. But the king ordered that Asinath be given to Zaphnath Paaneah in a royal wedding.

Joseph had asked for Asinath because he had discovered that she was the daughter of his half-sister Dinah.

When Asinath was born, Dinah's brothers had wanted to kill the child. But Jacob said: "The shame is not on the innocent child, but on Shechem and on you." He then took a piece of gold shaped like a flower, on which he inscribed: "He who takes Asinath for wife joins the house of Jacob." This he placed as an amulet on a chain about her neck. Then Asinath was left among the thorns of the desert. The Angel Gabriel came down and carried the child to Potiphar's house, for Potiphar had expressed the desire to adopt a daughter.

There Asinath grew up, and there Joseph saw her many times without paying her any attention, thinking that she was Potiphar's daughter. When Joseph was appointed governor, a great celebration was held in his honor. Joseph passed through the streets in the royal chariot. One thousand men, their drawn swords glistening in the sun, marched before Joseph, and twenty thousand guards marched behind him. Trumpeters without number announced his coming, and dancers without number followed him.

The streets were filled with the women of Egypt who had come to admire him and threw their jewels into his chariot. Asinath was among the women and she threw into the chariot the amulet Jacob had placed about her neck. Joseph read the inscription and, realizing who Asinath was, sent a messenger to find the owner. Then he asked the king for permission to marry her.

Joseph was thirty years old on his wedding day, and the wedding celebration lasted three weeks throughout the land of Egypt.

The fat years were counted from the day of Joseph's wedding. And during those years, Asinath gave birth to two sons, who were named Manasseh and Ephraim.

8. *The Famine Begins*

The seven fat years passed quickly. The more prosperous people were during these years, the more they grumbled, for they were taxed according to the amount of grain they possessed, and they could see no sense in gathering together so much surplus grain.

Then came the lean years. Famine spread in all the surrounding lands, where there had been no saving and no planning for time of need. After two years of famine all the neighboring nations began to come to Egypt for the stored-up food, and it required even greater wisdom to disburse it than it had to gather and store it.

The famine reached the land of Canaan and into the house of Jacob. One day, when all the food was gone, Jacob said to his sons:

"I have heard there is grain to be bought in Egypt. Go down there with gold and silver and get us some food that we may live and not die."

At first the sons refused to go, each remembering with sudden fear their brother Joseph, from whom they had not heard for twenty-two years. But as hunger tightened its grip upon them they consented to go down to Egypt, provided they would be permitted to go down together.

"Go, my sons," said Jacob, "but leave Benjamin behind to take care of me and our affairs while you are gone. And when you reach Egypt, disperse; for if you come as ten brothers together you might be suspected of evil intent."

The ten brothers went down to Egypt. They agreed between them not to enter the city through the same gate, but to disperse, each entering through a different gate. And they agreed not to seek for grain for several days until they had looked around for Joseph.

9. Joseph and the "Spies"

Joseph had placed a recorder at each of the city's ten gates, and no man was allowed to enter until he had registered his name and his father's name. One day Joseph looked through the records and found in one the name "Reuben ben Jacob"; in the next one, "Simeon ben Jacob"; in the next one "Levi ben Jacob"; and in each of the ten books he found the name of one of his brothers. He pointed the names out to his guards and said:

"When these men come to buy grain, bring them to me."

Three days passed, and not one of them had appeared at any of the granaries. Joseph sent out scouts to find them, and all ten were brought before Governor Zaphnath Paaneah. Though time had changed the brothers very much, it had not changed them enough for Joseph not to recognize them. But Joseph was clean-shaven; he wore the governor's robes; his name was different; when he spoke his voice was harsh. And the brothers did not recognize Joseph.

The governor struck the golden goblet before him with his ring and listened to its sound. After a long pause he said sternly: "My ring and my goblet tell me that you are spies."

The brothers bowed and protested: "We are not spies."

"Then why did you, who are brothers, enter our city each by a different gate?"

"Our father commanded us to do so," Reuben spoke for them all.

"If you come to buy grain, why did you not report at the granaries?"

"We were tired from the long journey and decided to rest first."

Joseph struck the goblet again. "I can see that two of you destroyed the city of Shechem. You are murderers as well as spies."

"Our father can tell you that we are not spies," pleaded Reuben.

"If you were not spies, your father would have sent only one of you with servants. But servants, when caught, cannot be relied upon and when tortured might betray their master. That is why your father sent all his sons so that they could depend on each other."

"But he did not send all his sons," said Simeon. "Our youngest brother, Benjamin, has remained at home with our father."

"I do not believe you unless you produce your youngest brother. All of you but one can buy the grain you need and take it back to your father and his household, in case you tell the truth. But one shall remain in prison here until you return with Benjamin."

And he selected Simeon to imprison, because it was Simeon who had thrown Joseph into the pit. There was a commotion among the brothers when Reuben suddenly upbraided them, saying that their troubles were a punishment for what they had done to their brother Joseph.

They spoke in Hebrew and did not know that the governor understood them. And the guards were astonished when they saw the governor leave the room suddenly, his eyes filled with tears.

10. *The Brothers Return*

The nine brothers bought the grain and turned toward home. On the way, Levi went to feed the asses and was surprised to find on the top of his sack, the money he had paid for the grain. He came running to his brothers and told them what he had found. They all rushed to their sacks, and they, too, found the money they had paid for the grain. They looked at each other in surprise, and they knew that it boded them no good.

When they reached home and told their father all that had happened, he refused to let them take Benjamin back to Egypt. Nor were any of them eager to return after their experience there.

But when the grain they had brought from Egypt was gone, Jacob urged his sons to return for more food.

"We cannot go without Benjamin," they answered. "That was the governor's command."

"Why did you tell him you had another brother?"

"Because he asked, 'Is your father alive? Have you another brother?' How could we tell that he would ask us to bring Benjamin to him?"

Still Jacob would not listen to them.

Finally Reuben said: "It is for you to choose, Father; either you let Benjamin go with us, or we all perish of hunger."

There was nothing else for Jacob to do. He placed in Benjamin's hands great gifts for the Governor of Egypt and ordered his sons to take with them double the amount of money so as to return the money they had found in their sacks, and to have enough to pay for more grain.

And the brothers returned to Egypt with Benjamin.

11. *The Governor's Banquet*

Upon their arrival in Egypt, the brothers were commanded to appear before the governor. They went in fear, but when they arrived at the palace they found Simeon out of prison and they were told that the governor had invited them to a banquet.

When the governor arrived, the eleven brothers surrounded him and bowed to him, like the eleven sheaves of rye in Joseph's early dream.

Joseph took his goblet and struck it with his ring. As if by divination, he announced how the brothers were to be seated, each by name, and each according to his age. And to the youngest he said:

"You have no mother, and I have no mother. Therefore you will sit beside me."

The brothers looked at each other in wonder but said nothing. Soon the servants arrived with wine and food. Joseph's cup was filled, and the butlers were surprised to see him drink. For Joseph had made a vow not to touch wine until he saw his brothers again and knew that his father was well. His brothers, too, had made a vow not to touch wine until they learned what had become of Joseph. But they drank now for if they refused, the governor might believe they were spies, who feared to drink lest in their cups they might reveal their secret.

As they were eating, the governor asked Benjamin: "Are you married?"

And Benjamin replied: "Yes, I have a wife and ten sons."

"What are their names?" asked the governor.

"Ochi, Becher, Naamen, Mophim, Ord, Rosh, Bela, Ashbel, Gero and Chupim."

"Those are strange names," said the governor. "What do they mean?"

"I had a brother whose name was Joseph. And he was lost. My father went to the mountains and hewed out twelve stones and upon each he engraved the name of one of his sons. Then he said: 'Arise, O stones, and bow down before Reuben your oldest brother.' But the stones did not move. Then my father repeated the command, giving each time the name of the son next in age. The stones did not move. But when he named Joseph, the stones bowed down before the stone on which my brother Joseph's name was inscribed. Then my father knew that Joseph is not dead but alive. And he wept bitter tears, for he did not know how to find him. When I married, I decided to name my sons in memory of my lost brother. And their names mean: My brother, the beautiful, more beautiful than the rose, and by right the head of his brothers, has vanished, or has become captive, a stranger in a foreign land, and I have not been to his wedding, nor he to mine, and neither of us could rejoice on our day of gladness."

12. *Joseph Reveals Himself*

The next day when the brothers were ready to leave, Joseph ordered that their sacks be filled with grain, and the price of the grain again placed at the top of each sack. And in Benjamin's sack he ordered them to place his own golden goblet.

Early the next morning the brothers loaded their asses and their camels and started out for Canaan. They had not gone far when they were overtaken by a troop of Egyptian soldiers, who accused them of stealing the goblet which the governor used for divination.

The brothers protested: "We would not do such a thing. He upon whom you find the goblet you may kill, and you can take the rest of us as slaves."

The search began from the oldest brother downwards. As each sack was opened, there on top was the silver they had paid for the grain. And when Benjamin's sack was opened, there was the goblet.

All the brothers were brought back before Joseph. Again they bowed before him.

"How stupid of you to try and steal my goblet. Have you not seen that I can divine such things?"

"There is nothing we can say," said Judah in anger. "Here we are, and we are your slaves."

"We do not punish the innocent with the guilty," said Joseph. "He on whom the goblet was found we shall keep. The rest of you can return to your father."

"Let me take his place," pleaded Judah. "For I have promised Father to bring his son Benjamin back to him in safety." And when Joseph refused, Judah's anger flared up again. "We were accused falsely the first time," he shouted. "We are not spies. And the money and the goblet were planted on us by your men."

"Hold your peace!" Joseph silenced him. "By Pharaoh, my men are not as the men of Shechem!"

When Judah heard that he began to tremble. He prostrated himself before Joseph and said: "Forgive me, my lord, but I am thinking of my old father. He had two sons by his wife Rachel, and the first one left home twenty-two years ago and never returned. Now, if the second one should also not return, he will surely die."

Joseph ordered the guards and servants to leave the room. And when they were gone he called out in a loud voice:

"Joseph, come and see your brothers!"

The brothers looked in awe to the right and to the left, expecting Joseph to come in through a door.

"Why do you look here and why do you look there? I am Joseph, whom you sold as a slave to Egypt. But regret it not, for it was the will of God."

The brothers stood petrified in their places, excepting Benjamin, who had no part in Joseph's fate. He ran to his older brother and threw his arms around his neck and kissed him. Joseph embraced all his brothers and they wept.

After they had told Joseph about their father and their sisters and their household, the brothers said:

"We must ask you for one great favor: that you never tell Father we sold you as a slave. For he would surely curse us for it and end his days in bitterness."

Joseph promised. Then he dispatched his brothers to bring his father with his entire household to Goshen, that they might be near each other.

13. Jacob's Reception in Egypt

When Pharaoh heard that Joseph had found his father and brothers, he was greatly pleased. He invited them to live in his kingdom and arranged a banquet to honor them. Jacob arrived with seventy members of his household. And they were given a royal welcome.

At the banquet Pharaoh asked Jacob his age. And Jacob told him that he was really not very old, but looked old because he had had many troubles in his days, working for Laban and then missing Joseph for so long.

Jacob lived in Egypt seventeen years, and as long as he lived there no woman ever miscarried, no baby was born prematurely, and no one ever suffered from a toothache. And Jacob was held in great respect by all the Egyptians.

(God later told Jacob: "I saved you from your brother Esau and from Laban and from Shechem. And I returned to you your daughter Dinah and your son Joseph. Still you complained. Therefore I shall diminish your years, one year for each word of complaint — thirty-three years in all.")

When Jacob was one hundred and forty-seven years old, he blessed all his sons, and then he died. And he was buried in the Cave of Machpelah with great honors.

PART III
In the Days of Moses

In the Old Testament the entire of the six days of Creation are given in one chapter of thirty-one sentences; and the events in the days of Abraham within twelve chapters of the Book of Genesis. Even the complex story of Joseph and his brothers (which Thomas Mann in our day retells in four large volumes) takes only fourteen chapters in Genesis. But the story of Moses (1571–1451 B.C.) covers three books (Exodus, Leviticus, and Numbers), and a fourth (Deuteronomy) gives the summation by Moses, consecrating the Children of Israel to the One God through the Commandments and the Law.

The lore about Moses, from miraculous infancy to miraculous death, reflects in volume and in content the reverence of the people for the Prophet of Prophets, the Lawgiver whose face, according to legend, is engraved forever on the face of the sun. From this extra-Biblical treasury the following legends were selected.

PART III

In the Days of Madness

CHAPTER NINE

Egyptian Bondage

1. *The Wicked Pharaoh*

The children of Jacob in Goshen multiplied. It was an age when children were born in fours and in fives, and even in sixes. It was also an age when no woman miscarried and no child died in infancy. And the household of seventy, which Jacob had brought down with him to Goshen, multiplied into thousands.

After two hundred years their number became great. Through all the years in Egypt they continued to practice circumcision, kept the Sabbath holy, refused to worship the stars, and believed God could be seen in no temple but was invisible and indivisible.

Some Egyptians in high places began to resent the Hebrews in their midst and plotted against them. As long as the memory of Joseph was fresh in the minds of the rulers and respected in Pharaoh's courts, nothing was done. Then there arose one Pharaoh who knew not Joseph and who listened to his high priests and jealous overlords. He decided to enslave the Hebrews and reduce their number.

2. *Almaqube the King*

In Mohammedan lore the rise of the wicked Pharaoh is explained in the following way:

In the days of the good Pharaoh Rayan Ibn Alhalid, there lived a childless shepherd one hundred and twenty-seven years old, who one day envied the calving cow her fruitfulness. Allah caused the cow to speak to the shepherd and tell him that children had been withheld from him because he was destined to have a very wicked son, and, for the sake of his ancestors, he was spared the shame. Since he complained so bitterly about his fate, said the cow, Allah would give him a son within one year who would be a curse to his family and a mockery to his house.

Within the year the shepherd's wife gave birth to a son and they named him Almaqube. The boy grew up to cause sorrow to his parents and to do evil in the eyes of Allah. But he had great courage and managed to become very rich. He surrounded himself with evil but powerful men and even declared war against Sinjov, the son of the Good Pharaoh. He killed Sinjov in battle, usurped the throne, and proclaimed himself Pharaoh Almaqube.

This was the Pharaoh who oppressed his subjects, ruled the Children of Israel with a heavy hand, and finally decided to weaken and destroy them.

3. *Pithom and Raamses*

Pharaoh decided to build two new cities the like of which had never been known, and to build them with the labor of the enslaved Children of Israel.

The king assembled all his architects, his stargazers, his high priests and governors of districts, and together they decided to build the two cities in the largest desert in the domain. The two cities were to be called Pithom and Raamses. Pithom was to belong to Pharaoh and Raamses to his queen. In these royal cities there were to be banqueting halls so large that all the inhabitants of Egypt and the neighboring countries could be seated at a single table to celebrate Pharaoh's birthday.

After three years the plans were completed. The sites were selected. The Hebrews were moved from Goshen. And the building of Pithom and Raamses began.

"By the time Pithom and Raamses are finished," said the overlords, "the Hebrews too will be finished. The work will kill them."

But they were mistaken. The Hebrews worked hard, complained to God, and multiplied.

"There is only one way to diminish them," said Balaam to Pharaoh, "and that is to separate the males from the females."

"You are right," said Pharaoh.

He issued a decree that all the Hebrew males should work in the fields and sleep there; and their wives should work and sleep in the cities. "In no time at all," thought Pharaoh, "there will be no Hebrews left."

But the women went out to the fields to bring their husbands water to drink and food to eat, and their fertility did not diminish.

4. *Jethro, Job and Balaam*

Pharaoh called in his three palace advisors and asked them what to do. Jethro, meaning "The Pre-eminent," refused to advise him and ran off to Midian, never to return; Job, meaning "The Afflicted," said nothing, and would have no part in the plot; but Balaam, meaning "The Sordid," advised the king to keep a record of the number of bricks a man made the first day at work when he was fresh and strong, and then punish him severely each day thereafter on which he fell short. The slaves would soon be tired out and would not multiply. "Then," he continued, "issue a decree to the midwives to throw all Hebrew male infants into the Nile the day they are born."

Pharaoh followed Balaam's advice. But angels came and sustained the hands of the laborers, and strengthened those who had faith; and the angels gathered up the children who had been cast into the water and set them down safely in the desert, giving each infant two stones, one flowing milk and the other honey. When the children were grown they returned to their parents, and the number of the Children of Israel was not diminished.

5. *Young Rider on a Lion*

One late afternoon, Pharaoh fell fast asleep and dreamt that a young man came riding toward him on the back of a lion, holding onto the mane with one hand and with the other inflicting powerful strokes on the king's head. Then he caught the king by his leg and threw him into the sea.

Pharaoh awoke, trembling with fear, and demanded that his viziers interpret the dream.

"It bodes no good," said they. "Command the midwives to watch more vigilantly all new births, and double the number of your spies."

A few nights later the palace was shaken as by an earthquake and all the idols trembled, then fell from their places and crumbled into dust.

The frightened king called his advisers together, and the stargazers said: "We see that a male child was born this night, in the house of Amram the Levite, who is destined to bring ruin to Egypt unless he is destroyed."

Pharaoh dispatched his chief officer Haman to Amram's house with orders to find the infant and to destroy him by fire. But when Haman came to Amram's home he found the infant in the oven, where a great fire seemed to be burning. Haman left believing that the parents had burned their child to please Pharaoh. He did not know that there was no fire in the oven and that it was the infant's face that glowed like bright flames.

When Haman left, the mother Jocheved took the child in her arms and fed him joyfully. For three months she hid him from her neighbors. And when they could hide him no longer, Amram made a waterproof basket, lined it with down, placed his child in it, and floated the basket down the Nile.

6. Thermutis, "Daughter of God"

Pharaoh's daughter, Thermutis, came down to bathe in the river one day and saw a floating basket. The Angel Gabriel pinched the child within to make him cry and stood by as Thermutis reached for the basket.

The princess suffered from a strange disease which covered her face with sores. But as she touched the basket, her face cleared, and her maids were astonished at her beauty. Princess Thermutis then and there decided to adopt the foundling. She swore her maids to secrecy, and took the infant home to the palace.

The king ordered a great feast to celebrate his daughter's cure, and in the midst of the festivity the princess was asked to appear. She arrived carrying an infant in her arms, and explained that one of her handmaidens had given birth to a child so beautiful that she wished to adopt him.

The infant's face was uncovered, and the great hall became flooded with light.

Everyone praised the child. But when the magicians saw him they whispered in Pharaoh's ear:

"When that child grows up he will take the crown off your head." The king paid no attention to them.

The next day while the princess was again bathing in the river, her handmaidens whispered about the child that had been found and how he refused to take the milk of any nurse, and how they feared the child might die.

Amram's daughter, Miriam, then came forward from her hiding place and asked the princess to try a Hebrew mother who had just lost her child. The princess agreed and Miriam brought Jocheved, her mother.

"What do you call him?" asked Jocheved as she nursed the infant, her son.

"I call him Moses," said the princess, "because that means 'He who was drawn out'! I drew him out of the river to be my adopted son."

"And I will call you Bath Yoh, because it means 'Daughter of God,'" said Jocheved. Since then Pharaoh's daughter, who rescued Moses, is known as Bath Yoh.

7. When Moses Burned His Tongue

Moses was raised in the palace and Pharaoh came to love him as if he were his own grandson. One day Pharaoh was playing with the child, when Moses climbed up on his knees, took off the king's crown and placed it on his own small head.

The king at once called his wise men, Balaam and Job, and told them what had happened.

"Chop off the child's head," said Balaam, "for he has committed an offense punishable by death."

But Job objected: "The child can be accounted guilty only if he knew what he was doing."

"How can we find out?" asked the king.

"Place before the boy a platter with a golden crown on it, and another with glowing coals. If he takes the crown, he is knowing; if he takes the fire, he is not," said Job.

The two platters were brought before the child and he at once stretched his hand out to grasp the crown. But an angel pushed his hand toward the coals. Moses grasped a hot coal, and then stuck his hand in his mouth in pain. He burned his tongue and had a lisp the rest of his life.

8. *Moses Destroys a Wicked Man*

As Moses grew up he visited Pithom and Raamses and went into the fields where the men worked. They labored in gangs seven days a week, week after week, and were never allowed to sleep in their homes. A great anger grew up within Moses as he saw the treatment of the slaves.

He saw an Egyptian beating a brickmaker mercilessly, and asked:

"Why do you beat this man?"

Though Moses was still very young, he was of the king's household, and the supervisor had to answer him.

"He is neglecting the king's work," replied the man.

Then Moses turned to the Hebrew slave. "Why is he beating you?"

"The truth, Your Highness, the truth by the God of my Forefathers! This man wants to kill me because I have a beautiful wife, and when I am at work he goes to her, and she is now bearing his child. When I threatened to tell, he started to beat me. I swear this is the truth!"

"If this man tells the truth, may God in heaven mete out your punishment," said Moses. And he uttered the Ineffable Name.

The Egyptian withered like a leaf fallen into flames. His breath left him and he fell dead to the ground.

A few days later Moses went out again and saw two Hebrews

fighting, surrounded by a crowd who were watching them. When Moses tried to stop the fight, one of them said:

"Who appointed you judge over us? Do you intend to kill us as you killed the Egyptian?"

The rumor that Moses had killed a man soon reached Pharaoh. And Moses was condemned to die. But when he was placed on the executioner's block and the axe fell, it did not touch Moses's neck. The entire court watched in astonishment.

The judge was about to order the executioner to try again, but his tongue cleaved to his palate.

Moses jumped up and started to run away. The command was given to the guard to catch him, but the guard became deaf and could not hear the command.

And when the executioner himself tried to run after Moses, his sight failed him and he could see nothing before him.

The story of how Moses slew a man is told in folklore with many variations; the circumstances of the quarrel, the persons affected, the manner in which the man died, and the consequences in the trial of Moses varying, but all agreeing that Moses did not commit murder, and that the man who died deserved his fate.

9. *Moses in Midian*

Moses escaped to Midian. Near one of the wells that supplied water for the flocks he saw shepherds driving away a young girl and her sheep from the watering trough. Moses upbraided them, then stepped forward and watered her flock. The grateful shepherdess left, only to return soon with a message from her father, Jethro, inviting the stranger to come and break bread with him.

"What is your name?" Moses asked the girl as she led him to her home.

"Zipporah. And yours?"

"My name is Moses, but those who know me well call me Ahub."

Jethro greeted his guest at the door and thanked him for his kindness to Zipporah. But before Moses would cross the threshold he told Jethro about himself so that his host would know he would be harboring a fugitive.

"You are a good man," said Jethro. "You are welcome in my home."

"If I am truly welcome," said Moses, "you will give me your daughter to be my wife."

"I have seven daughters," said Jethro. "Which daughter do you mean?"

"Zipporah, the Morning Star," said Moses.

"You come from Egypt and we are a desert people. In Egypt you were a prince, and here you will be a lowly shepherd," said old Jethro.

"No work that one man must do should be despised by another," Moses answered.

"I see that you are wise," said Jethro. "But I must make certain you are the one deeded for my daughter."

10. *The Rod in Jethro's Garden*

Jethro led Moses into his garden where, among the shrubs and trees, a rod was planted. It looked like an ordinary slender rod such as shepherds used.

"There is a story to that rod," said Jethro. "Once it belonged to Joseph, son of Jacob. When I was adviser to Pharaoh in Egypt I saw it in the royal treasury and the king gave it to me as a gift. Later, when the king wanted me to advise him how to exterminate the Children of Israel and I ran away to Midian, I brought this rod with me. One day I stuck it into the ground where you see it, but I could not pull it out. All the strong men of Midian have since come and tried to pull it out, but none has succeeded."

Moses looked carefully at the rod and saw the Ineffable Name carved on its head above the three words: *Detzach-Adash-Vehachal.*

"There is still another story to that rod," said Moses. "At the end of the week of Creation, God created the Ten Wonders of the World. This rod was one of them. It was given to Adam, who gave it to Enoch, who gave it to Shem, who gave it to Abraham, who gave it to Isaac, who gave it to Jacob, who gave it to Joseph. The Ineffable Name is upon it. And under it are the first letters of Ten

Terrible Plagues that shall befall the evildoers and the oppressors of the weak. It has been decreed that he who can draw the rod out of the ground shall emancipate the Children of Israel from slavery in Egypt."

"How can I know that your words are true?" asked Jethro.

Moses put his hand upon the rod and lifted it out of the ground as easily as if it had been stuck loosely into sand.

"This rod is my rod and was deeded for me," said Moses, "as was your daughter Zipporah."

How great a traveler the folk tale is can be demonstrated by this legend of The Rod in Jethro's Garden, *which was known about two centuries before Christ. This story, in various garbs, appears in many lands. In Norse folklore the story is told of a mighty sword driven to the hilt into the trunk of an oak, and a great prize is offered to him who can pull it out. Sigmund, son of Volsung, succeeds.*

It appears again in the tales about the magician Merlin and King Arthur, when the famed sword Excalibur *is found embedded in a stone before a church door. It is decreed that he who can draw it out of the stone shall be King of England. Many knights try and fail until Arthur comes along and draws it out as easily as Moses drew out the rod in Jethro's garden.*

11. *The Dream Moses Dreamt*

Moses dwelt in the desert for forty years, taking care of Jethro's flocks. Each day he let the young lambs go first to feed upon the tender grass; then he let out the sheep to feed upon the rest of the grass; and the strongest sheep he let out last to feed on the toughest grass.

And God said: "I shall choose him who knows how to shepherd the flock, each according to its strength, to come and lead My people."

One day a lamb ran away from the flock and Moses pursued it. Though its legs were small and spindly Moses could not catch up with it, until it stopped exhausted near a well.

"I did not know you ran away because you were thirsty," said Moses. He watered the lamb, then carried it back to the flock.

And God said: "I shall choose him, who knows how to be merciful to his flock, to come and lead My people."

Moses sat down to rest after bringing back the stray lamb, and soon fell asleep. As he slept he dreamt that Metatron, Angel of the Face, came to him and said: "Moses, God wants you to leave Midian and return to Egypt to become the Shepherd of Israel. But before you go down to Egypt you shall be shown the glories of heaven and the horrors of *Gehinnom*."

Metatron took Moses upon his wings and carried him to heaven. As they approached the first heaven, Moses heard music lovelier than any he had ever heard in Pharaoh's court. And when he asked where the music came from, Metatron said: "They are singing in heaven to welcome you, for the angels know that you are to be the Prophet of Prophets."

In the first heaven Moses saw streams of water flowing upon streams of water, each in a different direction, yet not commingling. And there he saw the angels that minister to the needs of man. (He heard the angels recite the story of the First Day of Creation, and then they sang in praise of the glory of the Ten Commandments.)

In the second heaven Moses saw the Angel Nuriel and his retinue. Metatron explained that here the weather and the seasons were governed. (Moses heard the angels recite the story of the Second Day of Creation, and then they sang in praise of the glory of Israel.)

In the third heaven Moses saw the angels who govern all the growing things. These angels, he was told, are called *Erelim* and are the tallest of all the angels in heaven. (Moses heard the angels recite the story of the Third Day of Creation, and then they sang in praise of the glory of Jerusalem, the Holy City.)

In the fourth heaven Moses saw the angels who preside over the sun, the moon, the stars and all other heavenly bodies. (Moses heard the angels recite the story of the Fourth Day of Creation, and then they sang in praise of the glory of the Messiah.)

In the fifth heaven the angels were fashioned half of fire and half of ice, yet the fire did not melt the ice, nor the ice extinguish the fire. And Metatron explained that they were the *Ishim*.

"What do they do?" asked Moses.

"They do nothing. They exist to prove forever that in God's world even opposites can live in harmony, if they desire peace." (Moses heard the angels recite the story of the Fifth Day of Creation, and then they sang in praise of the glory of Peace.)

In the sixth heaven Moses stopped to listen to the angels who compose the Heavenly Music. (Moses heard the angels recite the story of the Sixth Day of Creation and they sang in praise of the glory of Loving-kindness.)

When they reached the seventh heaven Moses was escorted by two angels of red and black fire. In the seventh heaven Moses saw the Angel of Death, the Angel of Law and Wisdom and all the souls of the unborn prophets of Israel. (Moses heard the angels sing in praise of the glory of the Sabbath.)

Metatron then asked Gabriel to take Moses down and show him *Gehinnom*. When they came to the gates of *Gehinnom*, the Keeper of the Gates, Nasargiel, would not let Moses enter until a Voice from above said: "Keeper of the Gates, before you stands Moses, for whose sake heaven and earth were created. Let him enter!"

Moses entered and saw the torture and pain of the souls of sinners.

Then Gabriel took Moses up to the Celestial Paradise, to see how fared the souls of the righteous on earth. Moses saw them sitting on thrones: the Just on thrones of rubies; the Pious on thrones of diamonds; the Learned on thrones of gold; the Repentant Sinners on thrones of silver. There were brass thrones for those who, though they themselves had been sinners, had brought up just and pious sons.

Moses was about to ask the Angel Gabriel a question, when he awoke.

12. *The Burning Bush*

Moses thought about his dream and wondered what it meant. One day, as he walked along in the desert, he came upon a thorn-bush on fire. But the fire did not consume it. Moses stood looking at it in wonder, when he heard a Voice, saying:

"Moses, take off your shoes, for the ground upon which you stand is holy ground!"

Moses did as he was told.

Then God said to him: "Go down, Moses, into Egypt and tell Pharaoh that I, the God of Abraham, Isaac and Jacob, have seen the affliction he has visited upon My people and I know their sorrows. Tell Pharaoh to let My people go. And you, Moses, shall lead them from slavery into freedom, and from Egypt to Canaan, the land flowing milk and honey, which My people shall inherit."

"I am unworthy," said Moses. (For Moses was the humblest of men, and humility is the greatest of all virtues.)

"I have chosen you," said God. "And fear not, Moses, no evil will befall you. For the Children of Israel shall be given signs, that they may follow you."

"I am a stammerer, O Lord," said Moses. "How can I appear as advocate for my people?"

"Who blunted the axe? Who muted the judge? Who deafened the guard? Who blinded the executioner when you were about to receive his blow in Egypt? I can likewise make the blind to see, the deaf to hear, and the stammerer eloquent. Go, and I will teach you what to say and what to do!"

Moses went home and told his father-in-law, Jethro, that he had been ordered to return to his brethren in Egypt. Jethro blessed him and Zipporah, and his grandchildren, and accompanied them to the border of Midian.

13. *Moses Before Pharaoh*

Moses and Aaron put on their finest robes in preparing to visit the king. For although Pharaoh was an evil ruler, it was their duty to show respect to the symbol of his office. They went to the palace and, in the name of God, asked to see Pharaoh.

The guards would not admit them. Then Moses showed them his right hand, which the guards could see was like their own. He put his hand into his bosom and brought it out withered as a dead branch. The guards now believed that Moses was a great magician. They knew that Pharaoh liked to see magicians but they feared to admit a man with a leprous hand. Whereupon Moses put his hand into his bosom again, and when he took it out it was as healthy as his left hand.

The two brothers went before the king and demanded in the name of God that he let the Hebrews leave the land for three days.

"What is the name of your god?" asked Pharaoh.

"His name is Jehovah, Lord of Hosts."

Pharaoh looked in the Book of Gods but could not find the name of Jehovah.

"In what land does your god rule and what can he do that I should hearken to his voice?" Pharaoh asked.

"The whole Universe is filled with the might and power of God. He existed before the world was created. It is He Who stretched out the heavens above like a curtain, and laid down the foundations of the earth below. When He speaks the mountains are rent asunder and the rocks are shattered. His Voice is flame, and His Words are flame. His shield is the clouds and His sword the lightning. He causes the rain to fall and all things to grow. If you concede the Universe, you must concede Him. For He created everything out of nothing — even you, the ruler of this kingdom."

"That cannot be," said Pharaoh, "for I am a god, the son of a god, the son of a god, the son of a god, who created himself and created the Nile that gives life to the world."

Moses threw his rod on the floor. Instantly it turned into a hissing snake. Pharaoh laughed. He was an Egyptian. Ten measures of sorcery and magic have been given to the world: Egypt took nine, and the rest of the world, one.

"Just another sorcerer's trick," said Pharaoh, and he commanded his magicians to show what they could do.

They threw down their rods, which instantly turned into snakes. They were all laughing, when Moses bent down and picked up his snake by the tail. It turned into a rod again. But first it swallowed all the other rods.

Pharaoh was still not convinced.

Moses then asked for a pitcher full of water. When it was brought to him, he spilled it before the king, and the water turned into blood.

"Now do you believe me?" asked Moses.

"Another sorcerer's trick," said Pharaoh. He sent Moses and Aaron out of his sight, with orders that they were never to be admitted again.

14. *The Penitence of Jannes and Mambres*

The next day Moses and Aaron appeared before Pharaoh. Though a hundred guards had been placed at each palace gate to keep them out, all the guards temporarily lost their sight as the two brothers passed them and walked up to the foot of the throne. Again Moses demanded of Pharaoh, in the name of God, to let his people go. Pharaoh was enraged and sent for the far-famed magicians, the brothers Jannes and Mambres, to put Moses and his brother to shame.

A multitude of magicians gathered to see the contest between the brothers Moses and Aaron and the brothers Jannes and Mambres. Those who fixed their eyes on Moses believed his words, for his face was like the face of an angel and brighter than lightning; but those who listened to his stuttering speech laughed at him and said in their hearts that if he were truly a man of God he would first heal himself of his stammering.

Then Jannes and Mambres tried all their magic and witchcraft against Moses and his brother. But as light dispels darkness, Moses dispelled their wicked deeds. When everything they tried had failed them, Jannes and Mambres took a goblet full of wine, secretly added the venom of vipers and dragons; and when it was ready they gave it to Moses, asking him to drink to the health of the king.

Moses smiled as he took the goblet and signed it with the name of God, then drained it. He turned to Pharaoh and the magicians, saying:

"This wine was poisoned with the venom of serpents, yet it can do no harm to one in the service of God."

At this, the brothers Jannes and Mambres fled from the court to do penance. But the heart of Pharaoh had not softened and he again drove Moses and Aaron from the palace.

15. *The Plague of Blood*

The next morning Moses and Aaron went down to the Nile. Since Moses had been brought up in the palace, he knew that Pharaoh, who claimed to be a god, with none of the needs of man, ate and drank in secret. And early every morning he went to the Nile alone, to commune with other gods. Anyone who looked at the king at that time, it was believed in Egypt, would die instantly.

Moses and Aaron waited in hiding until the king was ready to go into the water to bathe. Moses then again demanded of Pharaoh to let his people go. Again Pharaoh refused. Aaron struck the Nile with his cane and the water in the river turned into blood.

When the king returned to the palace and tried to wash off the blood, he found that the water in the wells had also turned into blood. And all the wells in the land were filled with blood.

For seven days the plague lasted. Finally Pharaoh said to Moses that if the waters of the land were purified, he would let the Hebrew slaves go.

But when the waters were purified Pharaoh changed his mind.

After a respite of three weeks, Moses inflicted another plague on Egypt, which again lasted seven days. The land became covered with frogs that filled every vessel and hid in every bed. Again the king said he would let the Hebrews go if the plague were removed. And again he changed his mind when the frogs were gone.

This went on for nearly a year. A plague would cover the land for seven days and Pharaoh would promise to obey God's will; the plague would be removed and Pharaoh would change his mind; three weeks of grace would pass and then Moses would bring another plague upon Egypt.

Then came the plague of the first-born. All the first-born were stricken with a strange disease, and Prince Raamses, Pharaoh's first-born, was among the stricken. Pharaoh summoned Moses in haste, implored him and his people to leave without delay, and begged that the prince be spared.

And so it came to pass that four hundred and thirty years after Jacob had come to Goshen, his descendants left Egypt for the Promised Land.

CHAPTER TEN

The Long Migration

1. *The Parable of Father and Son*

When Moses led Israel out of Egypt to Canaan, he took them first in a roundabout way through the Desert Shur; to test their faith, to accustom them to war, and to have them witness miracles which would strengthen their loyalty to God.

Only one fifth of the Hebrews left Egypt; the others, who lacked in faith and feared to leave, perished in darkness. But six hundred thousand men with their wives and children left Egypt and wandered into the wilderness toward the Red Sea. And God protected His people with a pillar of cloud by day and a pillar of fire by night. Where there was danger ahead, both pillars went before them; where there was danger behind, the pillars followed after them. And when danger both confronted and followed them, the pillars divided, and stood before them and after them.

There is a parable of a man who went on a dangerous journey with his only son, and he allowed his child to walk beside him. When brigands came to kidnap the child, the father placed his son behind him. When a wild beast came up from behind, he placed his son in front of him. Later, when brigands approached from the front, and wild beasts from behind, he took the child in his arms. When the glare of the sun troubled the boy, the father took off his outer garment and covered the child's head. When the boy was hungry, the father fed him; when he was thirsty, the father gave him water.

Even so did God care for Israel when He delivered His people from Egypt.

2. *The Crossing of the Red Sea*

Moses had asked Pharaoh to let the Hebrews go for three days into the desert. When the three days were over, Pharaoh gathered an army of six hundred generals with six hundred chariots, each leading an army of two thousand foot soldiers, and they pursued Moses and his people to the shores of the Red Sea.

When the Israelites saw Pharaoh and his army approaching, they divided into four camps; one camp complained to God, saying He had brought them out into the desert to destroy them; another wanted to go to war against Pharaoh; another argued in favor of returning to Egypt; and the last group prayed.

Moses ordered his people to be calm. Then he turned to the sea and commanded the waters to separate and let Israel pass in safety. But the sea refused to obey and said: "You are not my master, but the master of the Nile. Go and split the Nile."

Moses struck the sea with his rod. Still the sea refused to obey. Then God commanded the sea: "Obey Moses as you would obey Me!"

Instantly ten miracles took place:

The waters formed a tunnel so that the Israelites were protected from all sides;

The floor underneath them was hard and dry;

When the Egyptians entered, the same floor was muddy and they sank into it;

The waters all around them were frozen;

The frozen walls were not as one stone but as the stones in a wall;

There were twelve separate ice tunnels, one for each tribe;

The ice was so clear that the tribes could see each other and see that all passed in safety;

The ice was sweet and melted easily when they needed water to drink;

Fruit grew in the icy pillars so that when a child became hungry, the mother had only to pluck a pomegranate or an orange and feed her child;

And the tenth miracle happened to a fish.

3. *The Miracle that Happened to a Fish*

As Moses struck the waters with his rod, the Red Sea divided with such startling suddenness that a fish, caught in the very middle, was split in two.

The fish complained to God and said: "You created us, Lord, before Adam, and now You are going to kill us for his children's sake."

Moses agreed that it was unfair, and for his sake both sides of the fish remained alive. That is why in many parts of the world the flounder, the halibut and the sole are to this day called Moses-fish.

4. *Pharaoh and His Hosts*

The last of the Israelites was leaving the Red Sea, when Pharaoh and his mighty army rushed into the icy tunnels after them. All went well with them until they reached the center of the sea, when the towers of ice turned into torrents of water. The sea covered the army and they sank like lead in the mighty waters. Some tried to escape by flying up in the air, through magic, but the angels Michael and Gabriel dropped them back, like stones, to join their wicked brothers.

Moses gathered all the men to celebrate and to sing a song in praise of God. Miriam, sister of Aaron and Moses, gathered all the women to dance and to sing God's praise.

The ministering angels in heaven too wanted to sing a song of triumph over the Egyptians in the Red Sea. But God rebuked them, saying: "Though the men were wicked, they were made in Our Image. The gates of prayer are sometimes open and sometimes closed, but the gates of repentance are ever open. Though nine hundred and ninety-nine angels should testify against a man and only one attest in his favor, I incline the scales in his favor. And evildoers that must be punished are punished in sorrow." And the angels were silent.

Pharaoh's bitter end in the Red Sea not only saved the Israelites from destruction, but the news traveled and soon reached the ears of rulers throughout the earth, and they were thereby warned against any evil designs they might have against Moses and his people.

5. *Bread from Heaven*

The Israelites in the desert were hungry and began to grumble.

For miles and miles around them there was nothing but desolate land inhabited by scorpions and vipers so deadly that when the shadow of a bird on wing passed over them, the bird dropped dead. Some of the people began to abuse their leader and said that Moses had taken them away from a land flowing milk and honey to a desert filled with danger and devoid of food and water.

"You are a stiff-necked people of little faith," said Moses. "The Lord, who freed you from slavery with a strong arm and who drowned your enemies in the sea, will not let you starve. Tomorrow, and unto the day you enter the land you are to inherit, you shall be fed on manna."

"What is this manna?" they all wanted to know.

"Bread from heaven," said Moses. "You shall be fed on the food of the angels."

Early next morning, when they awoke, the people found the ground covered sixty cubits high with a grain that looked like hoarfrost. It was white as sugar and sweet as honey. The Israelites thought that manna was just another kind of food. But they soon discovered its many differences from any food that had ever been known.

Though it tasted like sugar at first, they found that it had all the tastes and flavors in the world. To the man who liked meat, manna tasted like meat. If he liked cheese, it tasted like cheese. Whatever he liked best — that was what manna tasted like to him.

They noticed another strange thing: no matter how much manna was gathered, when they returned home there was always exactly one *omer* for each member of the family. If a man was a big eater, the *omer* contained more food; and less, if he naturally ate little. The manna lasted for twenty-four hours, and when it was kept more than twenty-four hours it turned bitter.

Every morning the manna fell, excepting on the Sabbath. The manna gathered on Friday lasted through Saturday without spoiling. On all the other days it spoiled if hoarded. The people had to depend on the Bread from Heaven, and they had to have faith every day.

The food not gathered by the people melted and flowed down into the streams. The fish in those streams and the cattle and birds that drank of their waters tasted a little like manna, so that the desert nations gained a faint idea of what manna was like. Just as a man entering the room of a beautiful woman who is absent may imagine her beauty from the fragrance of her perfume, so those desert nations could imagine the manna, yet did not really experience the infinite goodness of the heavenly food.

If the people had been worthy, they would live on manna to this day. But the record shows that they were not worthy. A measure of manna, along with the Rod of Moses, has been preserved in a cave under the Holy Temple. And when the Messiah comes the people will again taste of the Bread of Heaven.

6. *The War with Amalek*

When the Israelites reached a place called Rephidin, they were told that Amalek and his armies were coming against them. Amalek was a stargazer and magician. He knew when a man's days were numbered, and when his end was still far off; and he selected a small but powerful army of soldiers whose days were many by the stars, and therefore could not be destroyed. Amalek also knew by the stars the lucky hours for his army.

Moses turned to the chief of the Hebrew armies, Joshua ben Nun, and said to him:

"We cannot kill Amalek's men because their days are many, but we can weaken them and make them run away. They count on given hours in which they will be fortunate in battle. We must therefore confuse them and shuffle the hours of the day."

"How will you do that?" asked Joshua.

"I will pray and ask God to make the sun stand still as long as the battle goes in our favor."

Joshua led his men into battle, and Moses prayed. He raised his hands, and the sun stood still. As long as the sun remained in its place, Joshua's men were victorious. But when Moses tired and lowered his hands, the sun moved again and Amalek's men gained favor. Moses then called his brother Aaron and a leader named Hur who supported his hands until Amalek and his men fled from the field of battle.

(God told Moses to write down the record of that battle in a book, and he did. But, alas, to this day that book has not been found.)

7. *The Ten Commandments*

Three days after the battle with Amalek, Moses brought his people to the foot of Mount Sinai, and there they encamped. God then called Moses to come to the top of Mount Sinai to receive the Ten Commandments. At that moment all the people in Israel that were blind opened their eyes and could see; the deaf could hear; and the mute could speak. And the people said in one voice:

"We shall obey the Lord and we shall listen to His Commandments!"

Sixty myriads of angels came down from heaven and they placed two crowns on each of the people: one because they had said they would obey; and the other because they had said that they would listen.

Moses told the people that he was going up to the top of Mount Sinai and would be gone forty days, but on the sixth hour of the fortieth day he would return. And he bade them to sanctify themselves for the Holy Commandments. God forbade the people to ascend or even to touch Mount Sinai. But they were promised that they would hear God's voice as he spoke to Moses.

As Moses started to ascend a bright, shimmering cloud covered Mount Sinai. Twenty-two thousand Levites stood as a guard of honor at the foot of the mountain, and twenty-two thousand angels came down in lightning and fire in front of the guard of honor.

The angels blew the Great *Shofar*, made from the left horn of the ram sacrificed by Abraham on Mount Moriah, and as long as Moses remained on Mount Sinai its sound filled the air, yet the people three miles distant could hear each word Moses spoke, and each word spoken to Moses.

As he entered the cloud, Moses composed a psalm.

"I will say of the Lord, He is my refuge and my fortress; His Truth shall be my shield and my buckler."

And all of Israel at the foot of Mount Sinai heard him and said: "Amen!"

When Moses reached the top of the mountain, the earth quaked, lightning rent the skies asunder, and thunder shook every corner of the earth.

And as God uttered the Ten Commandments they were heard in seventy different languages throughout the world.

8. *The Meaning of the Ordinal*

The Ten Commandments, it is believed, are the core of all truth and the hub of all justice. They cannot be increased by as much as one letter without profanation; and they cannot be diminished by as much as one dot without transgression. Nor can the order of the commandments be changed without injury to their meaning.

"Honor your father and your mother," for instance, is the *fifth* commandment because man has five foundations: His parents, the earth, fire, water, and air.

A man has five colors: the white of bone and ligament received from the father; the red of the blood, from the mother; the color of his skin, from the race; the color of his hair, from the maternal grandparents; and the color of his eyes, from the paternal grandparents.

There are also five kinds of living things: human beings, cattle and wild beasts, birds, fish, and insects.

Five is also the number of vegetation: grain, fruits, herbs, vegetables, and woods.

There are five kinds of metal: iron, lead, copper, silver, and gold.

And just as all the things a man's life depends on come in fives, so man's soul depends on the Five Books of Moses. Therefore one must honor his father and his mother as one honors God.

"You shall not steal" appears as the *eighth* commandment because there are eight kinds of theft in the eyes of the Lord: theft by the manipulation of numbers; theft by false measures; theft by fixing the scales; theft of finders becoming keepers; theft of a person sold into slavery; theft of money or property; theft of good will (as in the case of one who invites a man to dinner knowing that he cannot accept, yet thereby obtains his good will); and finally, the theft of a guardian who marries a widow or an orphan, not for love but to appropriate an inheritance.

The most important ordinal of the commandments is the *tenth*, *"You shall not covet."* For covetousness leads to war, and it is written: "God created heaven and earth and all the living things with *ten* words and He created everything out of nothing, with *Peace*."

9. *Not for Israel Alone*

When Moses received the Ten Commandments he asked if they were meant exclusively for Israel. He was told that this was the Law of Mankind and any man who obeyed the Ten Commandments would be the equal of the High Priest.

Israel received the Holy Law, but it had been offered first to all the other nations of the earth.

When it was offered to the sons of Esau, they asked: "What is written in it?" And they were answered: "Thou shalt not commit murder." "We cannot accept it," said they, "for our grandfather Esau was told that he would live by the sword."

The Holy Law was then offered to the sons of Ammon and Moab, and they wanted to know what was in it. "Thou shalt not commit adultery," they were told. They refused to accept it, saying: "We are the descendants of Lot's daughters and our very existence depended on an act of unchastity."

The Holy Law was offered next to the children of Ishmael. And they wanted to know what was in it. "Thou shalt not steal," was the answer. The Ishmaelites refused to accept it, for their ancestor had been told that his hand would be against every man.

And so it went with every nation.

"Remember, therefore," Moses was told, "that the gates are open for all the righteous on earth, and if any people is favored in the eyes of the Lord, it is so only because He is favored in their eyes, and they are faithful to His Commandments."

10. *The Six Hundred and Thirteen Articles of Faith*

God told Moses to build a Tabernacle. And Moses exclaimed:

"Your glory, O Lord, fills heaven and earth, how then can You dwell in a Tabernacle?"

"Not as you think, do I think," said God. "I can dwell in all the seven heavens, and I can descend into a square cubit."

Days passed, and Moses took his instruction in the Written Law and in the Oral Law. He learned the Decalogue and its interpretation. He studied the Six Hundred and Thirteen Articles of Faith, three hundred and sixty-five saying "thou shalt not" (one for each day of the year), and two hundred and forty-eight saying "thou shalt" (one for each bone in the human body). He was taught in full detail how to construct the Tabernacle and all its appurtenances. He was tutored in the selection and consecration of the High Priests, the preparation of the sacrifices, the burning of the sweet incense, the anointing of the oil. He was taught all the laws on how to treat workers; how to treat lepers; how to cope with adultery; how to know the clean from the unclean; the holy from the profane; how to worship; how to judge and how to punish the transgressors.

Finally, after forty days, Moses had received instructions in the entire of the Holy Law. He was about to leave Mount Sinai, when he turned to ask one more question:

"O Lord, what shall be the final decision if the Oral Law lends itself to diverse interpretations?"

"When the majority declare a thing permitted, it is permissible; when they declare it forbidden, it is forbidden. The voice of the majority of the people is My Voice."

"I understand," said Moses.

"But — " said the Voice.

"But what?" asked Moses.

"Thou shalt not follow a multitude to do evil."

The sixth hour of the fortieth day had come to an end, and Moses began to descend Mount Sinai.

What Moses learned in forty days on Mount Sinai no other man, however wise, could have learned in forty years. And the sages of all generations since his day still study what he taught and have not yet fathomed all he had to teach the world.

And the Law Moses received on Sinai shall endure forever.

11. *The Golden Calf*

On the sixth hour of the fortieth day on which Moses had left his people, Satan came to them and asked:

"Where is your leader, Moses?"

"He went up to the top of Mount Sinai to commune with God and to receive His Law."

"When will he be back?" Satan asked.

"He will be back at the end of forty days and at the beginning of the sixth hour."

Satan caused darkness to descend so that it seemed very late. Then he said to the people: "The sixth hour is already gone, and Moses is not here yet."

"We shall wait until Moses returns," said Aaron.

"But Moses is dead," said Satan.

"How do you know he is dead?"

Satan showed the people a vision of Moses on a bier. And the weak in faith began to doubt. Satan said to them that it was not good for people in a desert to remain without a god to protect them. The doubters agreed. First they went to Hur, son of Miriam, and asked him to make an idol for them to worship. When he refused, they killed him. Then, led by Satan in disguise, they went to Aaron and demanded that he make a god. Aaron feared that if he refused they might kill him as they had killed Hur.

"Go to your wives," said Aaron, "and tell them to give up all their earrings and ornaments, and I will make you an idol."

The women, just as Aaron had hoped, refused to part with their jewelry. But the ruse did not work. For the men took off their own rings and gathered them in a pile and brought them to Aaron saying: "Here is enough gold for you to make our god."

Satan, with the aid of some Egyptian sorcerers who had followed the camp of Israel, turned the gold into a calf, exactly like the one worshiped by the Egyptians. The people gathered around the Golden Calf and sang and danced and worshiped it. (And in that instant the sixty myriads of angels took the crowns away from Israel.)

When Moses came down and saw the great multitudes prostrating themselves before the Golden Calf, the tablets in his hands, which up to that moment had been light as a feather, turned as heavy as the dead. He looked up and saw that all the letters on the tablets had flown out, and in his hands remained two blank stones.

Moses flung the stones down, and they broke where they fell. Then he strode over to the golden idol, tore it from its pedestal and demolished it. The people stood aghast, knowing that Moses was alive and that Satan had tricked them, and they repented.

12. *Moses and Elijah*

One day Moses asked whether there was another man to whom was granted greater wisdom and greater knowledge than his, and God said that there was such a man, and that if Moses took enough barley bread and baked fish for a long journey and traveled toward the sea, he would meet his superior in wisdom.

"Where will I find him?" asked Moses.

"At the place where your baked fish come to life and swim away."

Moses assembled food in a basket and started out toward the sea. On the fourth day, as he rested on a rock near a spring, the last of his baked fish jumped out of the basket and into the water. Moses turned his head and there beside him sat a very old man.

"Why have you come here, Moses?" the old man asked.

"How do you know my name?" asked Moses.

"He Who sent me here revealed your name to me. My name is Elijah the Tishbite."

"I have come here, Elijah, to learn more wisdom from you that I may serve my God and my people better."

That day, and the day after, and the day after that Moses and Elijah spent in discourse, Moses asking questions and Elijah answering them.

At the end of the third day a sea gull flew in over the waves of the sea, dipped its beak in the water, then came to rest on Elijah's shoulder, cawing.

"The gull wishes me to tell you," said Elijah, "that knowledge is deeper than the sea, and wisdom greater than all the oceans. Yet your knowledge is as the wetness of its beak compared to the vastness of the ocean. Therefore let no man be proud and say: 'I have learned much and I am wise.' This, too, you shall teach your followers."

They continued their journey until they reached a village. Moses and Elijah were hungry and weary and asked the villagers for food to eat and a place to rest. The villagers refused them and Moses was angered. But Elijah said: "The fault is not with them whose hearts are from the beginning as the hearts of the wild beasts that look out only for themselves; the fault is with their teachers who failed to teach them to distinguish between good and evil."

For ninety days Moses journeyed with Elijah and learned much from him of goodness and humility. At the end of that time he returned to his people to tell them what he had learned from Elijah the Tishbite, and to lead them to their inheritance, the Land of Canaan.

13. *The Spies Are Cowards*

Moses and his people reached the borders of Canaan. Twelve men were selected, one from each Tribe of Israel, to go in advance and spy out the land.

When the spies returned after forty days, they reported that the land was indeed a land flowing milk and honey.

The vineyards, they said, bear grapes that require eight men to carry a single cluster from the vine. The black figs and the white figs are so large that a strong man can carry only one fig at a time. And the pomegranates are even larger and heavier.

"But," the spies ended, "the towers of their cities are like their fruit. And like their towers are their men. It is a land of giants, in whose eyes we were as beetles. Each man there is stronger than our God."

The people wept when they heard the report, and cursed the day they had left Egypt.

"These people are slaves, and unworthy of the Promised Land," God said to Moses. "But I will not turn them over into the hands of their enemies so that it may not be said I was powerless to protect them. Instead, for every day that the cowardly spies spent in Canaan, Israel shall wander a year in the desert. The transgression of the Golden Calf I have forgiven them; but the transgression of believing the cowardly spies as against My word I shall not forgive them. The slaves that left Egypt shall die in the desert. But their children I shall bring into Canaan and they shall inherit it as was promised to Abraham, Isaac and Jacob."

14. *Korah's Revolt*

When it became known that they were not going toward Canaan, but would wander about in the desert for many years, some of the people began to grumble against Moses and his brother Aaron. Under the leadership of a man named Korah the Levite, they questioned the authority of Moses and his brother; and Korah sowed dissension among the people. Moses humbled himself before Korah and begged him not to increase strife among the Children of Israel. But this act of humility only fed Korah's growing arrogance. He went out and began to dispute Moses's leadership openly.

God told Moses to separate himself from Korah and his followers and to warn the people to put a distance between themselves and the rebels. Then the earth opened like a mouth, and like a mouth it closed, swallowing up Korah and his family, and his two hundred and fifty followers and their families. They descended to *Gehinnom,* where the first half of each hour it rains fire, and the other half, snow falls. First they are burned, and then they are frozen; and that goes on forever.

The story is told of a merchant who traveled in the desert and met a man who asked:

"Would you like to see the place where Korah and his followers were swallowed up by the earth?"

Then the merchant was taken to a spot where there was a crack in the earth from which smoke issued. On the tip of a sword he placed wool steeped in water, and stuck it into the crack. When he withdrew the sword the wool was smoking.

The traveler lay down on the ground and listened and heard voices crying in agony:

"God is truth, and Moses is truth, and the Torah is truth!"

Those were the voices of Korah and his followers. But their cries avail them nothing. For there is no repentance after death.

15. *Aaron the Peacemaker*

Just as Korah sowed dissension, Aaron, brother of Moses, nurtured peace. When Aaron would learn of a quarrel between two men, he would visit one and say:

"My son, do you know how your enemy is behaving? He is beating his breast and blaming himself for the bad feeling between you. He really wishes to know how he can win you over and make you his friend."

Then Aaron would go to the other man and tell him the same thing. The next time the two men met, they would greet each other with smiles, shake hands, and become good friends.

16. *Aaron's Death*

During their long journey in the desert the Children of Israel learned to respect and obey Moses; and they came to love his brother Aaron.

One day, when they had reached the land of Philistinia, Aaron looked up and saw a beautiful green hill gilded by the rays of the setting sun. And he said to his brother:

"Let us and our sons go up to the top of that hill at sunrise and gaze upon the view before us."

The next morning they ascended the hill, and upon its side they found a cave which contained a bed, bearing the inscription: "This bed is ready for the man whose height is the same as its length."

One by one they stretched out upon it; first Moses and his sons, then the sons of Aaron, and it fitted none of them. But when Aaron lay down, an old man appeared at the entrance of the cave and said: "This bed fits you, Aaron, and I, the Angel of Death, have come for your soul in the name of God."

At these words all became sorrowful, excepting Aaron. He arose and kissed his brother and their sons, and said: "I am called in the name of God and I am ready."

The Angel of Death ordered all but Aaron to leave the cave. Later they returned and found Aaron upon the bed, as full of peace in death as he had been in life. They took him down and anointed him and dressed him in his robes as High Priest.

When the people learned that Aaron was dead, they wept and mourned for thirty days. They prayed for him five times each day, and after each prayer they wept for their loss.

17. *Balak, Son of the Birds*

Israel neared Canaan, and Moses asked the rulers of the land for permission to pass through their kingdoms. Some granted the permission and others refused. The King of Bashan refused. And Moses was obliged to wage war against him. That was no easy task, for the people of Bashan were like giants and a man eighteen feet tall was considered small amongst them. Their king was none other than the Giant Og, who could uproot a mountain with his bare hands and blow a fortress down with his breath. Yet Moses won the war against Bashan, for God was with him.

The King of Sihon also refused to let Israel pass through their land, and Sihon suffered the same fate as Bashan.

Then Balak, Son of the Birds, King of Moab, called in the wise men of the neighboring Kingdom of Midian, and said to them: "A strange people has come up from Egypt and they are very powerful. Even the Giant Og, King of Bashan, was conquered by them; and the sun stood still for them in the battle of Sihon. What shall we do to keep them from invading our kingdom?"

"Wherein lies the power of this people, according to your birds?" asked the Midianites.

King Balak had two birds, one made of gold and another of silver, which he could send out to the Cave of Secrets and learn anything he wanted to know. Balak sent out the golden bird in the name of the sun, and the silver bird in the name of the moon, and asked them to bring back the secret of Israel's strength. The birds flew to the Cave of Secrets, and soon returned.

"Israel is weak," the birds reported, "but Moses is strong. All the strength of Israel is in the words of their leader Moses."

"Our course is clear," said the wise men of Midian. "All we need is a sorcerer as great as Moses, to curse him and his people. We need only to get Warlock Balaam, Destroyer of Nations, to match his powers against Moses."

King Balak, Son of the Birds, dispatched messengers to Balaam the Great with gifts and coin, and invited him to come and curse the approaching armies of the Israelites and their leader Moses.

18. *Balaam's Ass*

Balaam was a sorcerer in Pharaoh's court whose fame had traveled throughout the world. His forebodings were heeded; his forecasts believed in; his astrology listened to as if he were reading from the Book of Laws; and, above all, his curses were dreaded by his enemies, and not without reason. For although Balaam was at the service of any ruler who could afford his services, he was nevertheless a man whom God did not ignore.

Balaam was a mercenary, but he was indeed very wise. He never permitted anyone to hurry him into a decision.

"Stay overnight," he said to Balak's messengers, "and I will give you my answer tomorrow morning."

While the messengers slept, Balaam consulted the stars, tested the winds, examined the entrails of a fish, suspended a ring, raked the ashes of a fire, walked around three times three in a circle, tasted three times three kinds of wine, and each time he received the same foreboding. The Israelites, he thought, must be blessed with a great blessing and my curses will not prevail against them. When the messengers awoke, he sent them back to Balak with the message that he had consulted the stars and he was told not to curse Israel.

The messengers returned to Balaam with even greater gifts, and promises of high honors, and a plea from King Balak to come at once and curse the Israelites and their leader Moses. This time Balaam could not resist the honors offered him. He saddled his ass and started out for Moab.

On the way an angel with drawn sword appeared and blocked the road. Although the ass could see the angel, the Great Balaam saw nothing. When the ass stopped in the road, Balaam began to beat it. After some time the ass turned his head to Balaam and started to laugh like a human being.

"What are you laughing at?" asked Balaam angrily.

"I am laughing at you," said the ass. "For you have eyes but cannot see what I see."

"If I had a sword I would kill you," said Balaam in anger.

"You are on your way to destroy a mighty nation with a curse," said the ass, "yet for me you require a sword!"

Then the angel revealed himself to Balaam and told him that he who shall curse Israel, that curse shall fall upon the curser. And the angel killed the ass so that those who heard it speak and laugh would not be tempted to worship it.

Balaam proceeded on foot and arrived before Balak limping, and blinded in one eye. And when Balaam was taken to the top of a mountain to curse Israel, he blessed them instead.

"If you cannot curse my enemies, Balaam, why do you have to bless them?" Balak demanded.

"I tried to curse them," said Balaam, "but the curses against the righteous and the faithful turn into blessings. I knew this would happen as soon as the ass spoke to me. For never before since Creation has an animal spoken with a human voice and uttered words of wisdom. That was indeed as a sign and an omen to me."

And Balaam limped back to his home in Haran.

19. *Moses Departs*

Forty years Moses lived in Egypt; forty years he lived in Midian; and forty years he led his people through the desert, from Egypt to Canaan, and from slavery to freedom. When Moses was one hundred and twenty years old, he knew his end was near. He had written down Laws in Books, and all that had happened to Israel since leaving Egypt he had written down in Chronicles to be remembered forever.

When his work was done, Moses called together the elders of the Twelve Tribes and their officers and all the people surrounding them. And when they were assembled, Moses announced that a new leader would lead them into Canaan.

"I, Moses, son of Amram, son of Ishar, son of Kohath, announce to you your new leader, whom you must follow: Joshua, son of Nun!"

Then Moses instructed his people for the last time. God, said he, was a Rock. The heart that rested upon the Rock need fear no evil, for God is like an eagle that flutters over its young and spreads its broad wings and carries its young upon its wing from danger. But they who are unmindful of the Rock, the sword without and the terror within shall destroy them. For God is Truth and He metes out justice to each according to his faith or faithlessness.

Moses blessed the people and said:

"Our Lord, God of our forebears Abraham, Isaac, and Jacob, these people whom You have consecrated with Your Commandments, save them in time of need and bless their inheritance; give them food in time of famine, courage in time of war, and joy in time of peace. And bear them up for ever!"

Later, when they were left alone, Moses blessed Joshua and said:

"My time has come. I do not want my body to be a hindrance to you and the people. Therefore I shall go up into the mountains and none will know the place of my grave."

And he started out alone for the top of Mount Abarim.

Word reached the people that Moses was gone and that their eyes would never see him again. They rent their clothes and wept. For although they had often complained bitterly and made his life miserable, as children at times make miserable the lives of their fathers, the people of Israel loved Moses, and when he left them the sound of their grief filled the Plains of Moab throughout the seven days of mourning.

On the eighth day after Moses had left them, the people looked up at the sky and recognized the face of Moses in the sun. Then they knew that their leader had not died but had ascended to heaven. And they were ready to follow Joshua ben Nun across the Jordan.

And that is how the Children of Israel came to the land of Canaan: from Adam to Noah, from Noah to Abraham, from Abraham to Joseph, from Joseph to Moses, and from Moses to Joshua, who led the people into the land of the Prophets.

CHAPTER ELEVEN

Job, the Afflicted

1. The Servant of God

In the days of Moses, there lived a Gentile king unlike any other king on earth. For although he had a splendid throne, he never sat upon it; although he had a crown of rubies and diamonds, he never placed it upon his head; and although he was entitled to be addressed as "Your Highness and Your Grace, Your Majesty the King," he asked his people to call him "servant." And they called him, "Job, the Servant of God."

When he was quite young Job, like Abraham, reached the belief in One God without anyone teaching it to him. By reasoning from his own existence, and the laws of the Universe which he could observe, he came to the belief in the Creator of the World. And Job reasoned that for a man's life to be worthy in the eyes of the Lord, it was his duty to shun evil and seek the good.

2. The Inn at the Crossroads

At the crossroads of his kingdom in the land of Uz, where lived also the Buzites, the kindred of Ram, Job built a large inn with a door at each of the cardinal points, so that a wayfarer could find an entrance at once no matter the direction from which he came. And over each door a white flag hung at all hours of the day and night as a sign that the inn was open and they who wished could enter without knocking.

Those who came to the inn found all the food they desired; and none who were hungry were ever turned away. The inn had many chambers to rest in, and a dining hall containing forty-two large tables constantly laden with food and drink. Twelve of the tables were reserved for widows, and twelve for orphans. And on a balcony in the hall musicians played to lighten the hearts of the bereaved and the weary. As each guest left he was given a gift and thanked for honoring the host, Job, with his visit.

The stream of guests at Job's inn kept fifty bakeries busy supplying the bread, and an even greater number of kitchens were kept busy preparing the other food and drink. Yet if a grateful guest offered to help in preparing the food, Job insisted on paying for the service. Job himself and his wife, Queen Zitidos, spent much of their time waiting upon their guests at the inn.

When Job heard of a man stricken with illness he would bring a physician to the home, and to the grieving wife he would say: "God has not abandoned you up to this time and He will not abandon you now. Faith is wisdom." Then, in the presence of a witness, he would pledge himself to care for the wife and children, should anything happen to the breadwinner.

Job ministered not only to the physical needs of people. When their hunger was stilled or their wounds healed, Job would teach them to sing in praise of God.

All the kings of the world marveled at Job and wondered how it was that the more Job gave away, the more his wealth increased. Whereas their sheep were devoured by wolves, Job's sheep killed the wolves. Whereas their crops took months to grow and were often destroyed by drought, wind, or hail, Job's crops ripened the day they were sowed.

It was Job's custom to give alms to the poor at the end of each day. And he would say to them: "Pray for my sons and my daughters not to fall into the ways of evil. For it is hard for the children of the rich to be humble. And without humility there can be no virtue."

Job was a humble man; and he is remembered to this day as the most generous man who ever lived.

3. Satan's Challenge

When the King of Uz came to believe in One God and went out to destroy the idols of Edom and Buz, Satan came to Job's door disguised as a beggar and demanded to see the king. Job, through his power of prophecy, knew it was Satan and refused to see him. He sent out the message to Satan: "You cannot eat my bread for it is forbidden to you."

Satan went up to heaven and complained: "No wonder Job loves God! He has been blessed with a good wife and children that do them honor; he has a throne and a crown; and his wealth multiplies without effort!"

And God said: "Satan, Satan! There is no one on earth like my servant Job. You may try him, but you must spare his life!"

"How can the vessel be broken without spilling the wine?" asked Satan.

But he was given no answer.

4. Job's Trials

Satan disguised himself as the King of Persia and came to the city where Job lived. He said to the inhabitants: "This man Job pretends to be generous, but see how rich he is with treasures that rightfully belong to you. Let us go and take from his storehouse what really is yours."

And the people listened to Satan and went and sacked Job's storehouse and reduced it to ashes.

At the same time a wounded messenger reached Job, blood streaming from his wounds. With his last breath he told how the wicked Queen Lilith had come at the head of an army, plundered the sheep and oxen, and killed Job's shepherds and herdsmen. Whatever she had left behind, the Chaldeans had taken away, and nothing remained of Job's great flocks.

More messengers arrived to tell of new misfortunes. And finally one came who told of a wind which had destroyed the house of Job's eldest son. The seven brothers and their three sisters and their families were gathered together at a feast, and all had perished in the disaster.

Job rent his clothes and threw himself upon the ground and said: "*I came naked into the world, and naked I shall leave the world:*

God has given and God has taken away; blessed be the name of God."

Job's trials had only begun. He found that the people who had benefited most from his generosity in the days of his prosperity, now that they had plundered his belongings, treated him with contempt.

"What have we done to deserve all this?" asked Zitidos, Job's wife.

"I can think of no sin grave enough to deserve such punishment," said Job. "Were I given the choice of physical pain instead of bereavement and poverty, I would have taken pain. But the choice was not given me."

At once physical pain was added to his other trials. Job was stricken with fifty different plagues. He was covered with festering boils from the sole of his foot to the crown of his head, and when the people saw him, they drove him from the city to live on the ash heap outside the gate.

5. The Humbled Queen

Zitidos, who had been a queen, now worked as a water carrier and a maid to earn her bread. When her master learned that she took bread home to her husband, he dismissed her. Then she and Job knew hunger as well as pain.

One day as Zitidos walked through the market place Satan came up to her disguised as a baker and offered to sell her bread.

"I have no money with which to buy your bread," said Zitidos.

"You may pay me with your beautiful hair," said Satan, and he gave her two loaves of bread for her two lovely braids.

As Zitidos reached home with her hair shorn off, Satan, in the guise of a neighbor, came up to her and said:

"Your sins and your husband's sins must be great indeed if you must buy bread with your hair!"

Zitidos ran in tears to her husband and pleaded with him: "For my sake, Job, blaspheme God that we may die, for I can bear this no longer."

Job knew that this was Satan's work and did not reproach his wife for her words but turned to Satan and said:

"Cowardly Satan! If you wish to engage me in battle, come forward. But do not hide behind a frail and grief-stricken woman!"

And Satan fled in grief greater than Job's.

6. *The Three Friends*

In the days of his prosperity Job had three friends who ruled in kingdoms three hundred miles distant from one another. Each of the kings had the likeness of the other three set into his crown. When misfortune befell one of them, his likeness in the crown faded.

One morning the three kings, Eliphaz, Bildad and Zophar noticed that the likeness of their friend Job had faded, and they knew that he must be in trouble. They started out immediately for the land in which Job lived and all met at the city gate. They went on together but could find no sign of Job's palace or his inn or any of his storehouses.

They had almost despaired of seeing their friend again when an old man led them out of the city and pointed to a figure seated on an ash heap. "There is Job," said the old man.

The three kings refused to believe the old man, and they came near and asked:

"Are you Job, our friend, a king equal with us in rank?"

"I am Job," he replied.

The three friends began to weep, and Eliphaz asked: "What has become of the splendor of your throne?"

Job answered: "The splendor of my throne is in heaven. Kings will perish and their glory will pass like a shadow across a mirror. But the throne in which I believe will last forever."

The friends sat down beside Job, wondering whether he was sane, and in silence they remained beside him for seven days and seven nights.

Then Job said to his friends: "I know your thoughts. You wonder whether I am sane. Remember, it was I who treasured up the words of His mouth. But can you answer these questions: Is man other than a handful of foam on the waves of a turbulent sea? Who created Paradise and Purgatory? Who created the righteous and the wicked? What is to hinder God from doing as seems good in His eyes?"

7. *The Heavenly Gift*

As the three friends talked with Job, they became convinced that he had sinned and brought down upon his head God's wrath. And at last they were ready to abandon him to his fate.

"You are not well," said Zophar. "Let us call our physicians to treat you."

"My afflictions are from God, and only He can heal me," said Job. "And my questions are of God, and only He can answer them. I have not sinned and God must have mistaken me for another and visited his punishment upon my head."

Then God appeared in a whirlwind and said: "Upon the head of every man there are thousands of hairs. And each hair derives its nourishment from its own sac. Not since the beginning of time has a single hair fed on the sac intended for another hair. How then could I have mistaken Job for another?"

There was silence. And God spoke again: "For every drop of rain that descends from heaven there is a mold in the clouds. If more than a single drop came from each mold the earth would become too moist to bring forth the crops. Not since the beginning of time have two drops of rain come out of a single mold. How then could I have mistaken Job for another?"

Job confessed his ignorance and said: "I abhor my words, O Lord, seeing that I am nothing but dust and ashes."

And God said to Job's friends: "You have blamed a man in his anguish. And you spoke not the truth about my servant Job. Lest he bring a sin offering for you, you shall be destroyed."

Whereupon they rose and Job prayed to God to spare his friends.

God then gave Job a girdle made of three ribands and told him to put it on. And as Job tied it about his waist his pain left him and his body cleared and was whole again. Even the memory of his afflictions had been wiped away.

Job returned to the city with his friends. There the three kings prepared a great feast for Job and each invited guest brought one sheep for Job to help restore his wealth. So great was the number of guests that in a few days Job had twice the wealth he had had before misfortune overtook him.

Job rebuilt the inn at the crossroads and again served the hungry and comforted the widowed and the orphaned.

8. Job's Bequest

Job's afflictions came upon him when he was seventy years old; and he lived one hundred and forty years after his trials were over.

Queen Zitidos died before God restored Job's health and wealth. Job married again and was again blessed with seven sons and three daughters.

His friends urged him to marry more than one wife. But Job said: "If God had intended Adam to have ten wives, He would have given him ten wives. He gave Adam only Eve and thereby indicated that each man should have only one wife."

At the end of his days he gathered together his sons and daughters and told them all that had happened to him and instructed them to put his record in a book. Then he divided his possessions among his children; and to each of his daughters he gave one riband of the girdle given him by God.

When his daughters put the ribands about their waists, their voices changed to the voices of angels. Jemimah, the oldest, whom Job called *Day*, took a cithern; Keziah, whom Job called *Perfume*, took a censer; and Amaltheas, whom Job called *The Horn*, took a cymbal. They played and sang together as an angel came down from heaven in a chariot to carry away Job's soul.

The Book of Job, the greatest single story in any religious literature, is about a desert sheikh, a prophet who was not a Jew, called "The Afflicted." The folk tales about Job are many (and in each this Prophet of the Gentiles is treated with tenderness and imagination) but none fully reflect the greatness of the Book of Job, "the

Matterhorn of the Old Testament," as Professor Charles Foster Kent calls it.

The remarkable part about the legends is the complete reverence with which this Gentile Prophet is regarded in Hebraic sources, particularly since nowhere else in the Old Testament do we encounter, so sharply portrayed as in Job, a questioning of the ways of God and the injustice of human suffering. (Only in the Apocrypha of II Esdras do we come across a strangely similar demand for an explanation why Jerusalem was destroyed for its sins, yet Babylon permitted to thrive though steeped in wickedness; and, like Job, Esdras questions Divine Justice.)

Historically, there is every reason to believe that Job belongs to the days of Abraham. Some of the names and the imagery in the Book of Job belong with the stories about Nahor and his sons; and the book itself is unquestionably of great antiquity and may have existed before the Five Books of Moses were gathered and edited. In the folklore chronology, however, Job appears as a councilor to Pharaoh and as a king in his own right, who lived in the days of Moses. For this reason the legends about Job and his kin are given here, after Moses and before Joshua ben Nun.

In Mohammedan lore the story of Job and his trials is told with many embellishments, but the main events are the same as found in the Book of Job. The valuable additions to the Job episode in Islamic lore are to be found in the legends about Job's kinsman, named Lukeman.

9. *Lukeman Al-Hakim*

Job's sister had a son named Lukeman, who became known as Lukeman Al-Hakim, meaning "Lukeman the Wise." For though Job's nephew was ugly to look upon, God had blessed him with wisdom the like of which was unknown before his day nor has been known since.

One day a band of robbers attacked Job's granaries and Lukeman tried to drive them off. But they were many and strong and Lukeman was alone and weak. They took Lukeman to a distant land and there sold him as a slave.

One day his master gave Lukeman a ram and asked him to prepare a tasty dish from the worst parts of the ram. Lukeman slaughtered the animal and prepared a dish from the tongue and heart, which the master greatly relished.

The next day Lukeman was given another ram and asked to prepare a tasty dish from the best parts of the animal. Lukeman slaughtered the ram and again prepared a dish from the tongue and heart, which again the master greatly relished. The puzzled master asked for an explanation. And Lukeman said:

"The tongue and the heart, when they are bad, are the worst parts of any living thing; but when they are good, they are the best."

The master realized Lukeman's wisdom and offered him his freedom, and it was not long before Lukeman returned to his native land to his uncle Job.

10. *The Reward of Wisdom*

When Lukeman was a very young man he was asked: "If you had the choice, which would you have: wisdom, or the power of prophecy?"

"Wisdom," said Lukeman. "For the prophet is despised until the day he dies; but the wise are rewarded in their lifetime."

"And how long would you want to live, if you had wisdom?"

"As long as seven generations of vultures," said young Lukeman.

(The vulture, some say, lives eighty years, and therefore Lukeman the Wise lived five hundred and sixty years; but others say that the vulture lives two hundred years, and therefore Lukeman lived from the days of Nahor and Abram to the days of Tobit and Sarchedonus.)

Since Lukeman had been granted wisdom and long life, he devoted himself to writing down ten thousand chapters of fables and proverbs, to be remembered forever by all mankind.

His fame spread throughout the kingdom; his proverbs were on everyone's lips; and King Sarchedonus appointed him Royal Cupbearer, Keeper of the Royal Seal, Chief Treasurer of the Kingdom, and Secretary of the Throne.

"From this day on," said the king, "your name shall no longer be Lukeman, but Ahiyakar — 'My Dear Brother' — and you shall be known as the Grand Vizier."

11. *Ahiyakar Adopts a Son*

Ahiyakar was sixty years old when he became Grand Vizier. He had wedded sixty wives, and had built sixty castles. But he had no son to inherit his wealth and wisdom. He then took his sister's infant son, Nathan, and adopted him as his own. As soon as the boy could walk and talk, Ahiyakar taught the boy booklore and wisdom. And the Grand Vizier proudly watched his adopted son grow like a cedar.

"My son," said Ahiyakar, "cast down your eyes and lower your voice, and look from beneath your eyelids; for if a house could be built by a loud voice, the ass would build two houses in one day."

"I understand," said Nathan in a gentle voice.

"My son, it is better to remove stones with the wise than to drink wine with fools."

"I understand," said Nathan.

"My son, when a rich man eats a snake, people say: 'He ate it as medicine.' But when a poor man eats a snake, people say: 'He ate it from hunger.'"

"I understand," said Nathan.

"My son, draw not near a woman who is a whisperer, nor to one whose voice is high."

"I do not understand," said Nathan.

"You will, when you grow older," said the uncle. Then he went on: "My son, the words of the liar are like fat sparrows; and only the fool eats them."

"I understand," said Nathan.

"My son, the flock that makes many tracks attracts many wolves."

"I understand," said Nathan.

"He whose hands are full is called wise; but he whose hands are empty is called foolish."

"I will remember that," said Nathan.

"My son, keep your tongue ever sweet: for the wagging tail of the dog brings him bread, but his barking tongue gets him blows."

"I will remember that," said Nathan.

"Above all, remember this, my son: Tarry not where there is contention. For strife leads to murder."

These, and all the adages of his ten thousand chapters, Ahiyakar taught his adopted son. And wherever the Grand Vizier went, he took young Nathan with him. Ahiyakar took Nathan to the king and asked that his adopted son be regarded as his heir in all he possessed in wealth and in office.

12. *The Wheel of Fortune*

Ahiyakar taught his nephew everything he knew; but, alas, he spared the rod and spoiled the boy with gifts and praise. Nathan began to consider himself as wise as his uncle, and wiser. He went about saying openly: "Ahiyakar is growing old and his wits are growing dim." When his arrogance went unpunished, the boy began to waste his uncle's fortune, abused the servants faithful to the Vizier, and even forced his attentions on Esh-Fagni, the Grand Vizier's favorite young wife.

Ahiyakar reproved him, and said: "My son, even if the swine grows a long tail, he cannot take the place of the swift stallion."

Nathan said nothing, but he began to plot against his uncle. In the name of the Grand Vizier he forged treasonable letters to Akhim of Persia and Pharaoh of Egypt, affixed the royal seal to them, then brought the evidence of treason to the king.

At first Sarchedonus would not believe that Ahiyakar would betray his country; but when he saw the evidence, he condemned Ahiyakar to death, and appointed Nathan to take his place.

Here the story of ingratitude and betrayal might have ended. But the swordsman who was ordered to cut off Ahiyakar's head, named Nebusemach, was the same Nebusemach whose life Ahiyakar had saved many years earlier. On the way to the execution, Nebusemach learned the truth from Ahiyakar and decided to save his life. With the aid of Esh-Fagni, the Vizier's faithful wife, he hid the condemned man in a dark cell, until the wheel of fortune should take a turn.

The wheel of fortune turned sooner than the swordsman expected. For when it became known in Egypt that Ahiyakar was dead, Pharaoh sent a letter to Sarchedonus, demanding an architect who could build a palace in mid-air, and answer his riddles. "If you send me such a man," said the letter, "we will pay you great tribute for three years. But if you fail us, then we shall exact like tribute from you."

Sarchedonus asked Nathan what should be done, but Nathan could not advise him.

"If Ahiyakar were alive," the king lamented, "he would have known how to deal with Pharaoh."

On hearing these words, Nebusemach the Swordsman fell upon his knees before the king and pleaded to be killed for his failure to execute the wise and good Ahiyakar.

"Speak on, good man unskilled in evil!" the king commanded.

The swordsman then related how he had saved the condemned man's life. They went to the hiding place and there they found a starved old man, dressed in rags, with hair unkempt and nails overgrown.

The king wept with joy to find Ahiyakar alive, and begged forgiveness. They returned to the palace. And as soon as Ahiyakar had regained his strength, he left for Egypt to answer Pharaoh.

13. *Ahiyakar in Egypt*

When Ahiyakar arrived in Egypt he did not reveal his name. Pharaoh and his nobles, all dressed in red, received the emissary from King Sarchedonus in the palace.

"What am I like, and what are my nobles like?" asked Pharaoh.

"You are like the Supreme God Bel and your nobles are your high priests."

The next day, Pharaoh and his nobles, all dressed in white, again received the emissary, and the king asked:

"What am I like, and what are my nobles like?"

"You are like the sun and your nobles are like your rays."

The next day, Pharaoh and his nobles, all dressed in black, received the emissary and he was asked the same question.

"You are like the moon and your nobles are your stars."

The following day, Pharaoh and his nobles dressed each in a

different color, and again they commanded Sarchedonus's emissary to answer the same question.

"You are like the month of *Nisan*, and your nobles are the flowers of spring."

"You are wise," said Pharaoh. "Can you tell me what is heavier than lead?"

"That is easy, my lord. A fool is heavier than lead."

"I see a pillar," said Pharaoh. "It has twelve cedars on its head. Each cedar has thirty wheels, and each wheel has two cables, one white and one black. What is it?"

"That is easy, my lord. The pillar is the year. The twelve cedars are the twelve months. The thirty wheels are the thirty days. And the two cables are day and night."

"You have told me four times what I am like," said Pharaoh. "Now tell me what your king and his nobles are like."

"My King Sarchedonus is like God in heaven, and his nobles are like lightning in the clouds. Woe unto him who incurs their anger!"

"Who are you to speak to me this way?" Pharaoh demanded.

"I am Ahiyakar, Keeper of the Seal of my king."

"But Ahiyakar is dead," Pharaoh exclaimed.

"I was supposed to be dead, my lord, but as you can see, I am not a corpse."

Pharaoh bestowed many gifts on Ahiyakar the Wise and sent him home with great honor.

And upon his return home, Ahiyakar meted out to his ungrateful nephew the punishment he deserved, for Ahiyakar believed in justice.

The Story of Ahikar *(a corruption of* Ahi-yakar*) is the most color-ful folk tale in the pseudepigrapha of the Old Testament. Its great antiquity, dating back centuries before Christianity or Mohamme-danism, is beyond dispute. Ahikar* (Achiacharus) *is mentioned in the many-centuries-old Apocrypha,* Tobit. *His story is retold in many variations in the* Arabian Nights. *The influence of Ahikar's story is discernible in the Psalms, the Proverbs, several of the Apocrypha, the New Testament, the Koran; and, as a fictional theme, in practically every national literature. The proverbs in* The Story of Ahikar, *the names, and the references to the month* *of* Nisan *are all Judaic. But the contents of Ahikar's story became widely diffused. According to Clement of Alexandria, the Greek philosopher Democritus incorporated the sayings of Ahikar in his writings. The proverbs and fables of Ahikar are also found in Aesop's fables. Mohammed refers to Ahikar and his ten thousand chapters of "pure wisdom" in the 31st Sura of the Koran.*

There are several versions of The Story of Ahikar, *in Arabic, Karshuni, Ethiopic, Armenian, Greek and Slavonic. The most interesting version is the Aramaic, taken from the Aramaic Papyrus discovered by Dr. Rubensohn at Elephantine in 1908, which is believed to have been written or copied in the 5th century B.C. This version, written in the first person, begins, startlingly, with:*

"In the twentieth year of Sennacherib, son of Sarhadum, King of Assyria and Nineveh, I, Ahikar, was the King's secretary. Sixty wives had I wedded: and sixty castles did I build them: and I had no son."

This would place Ahikar in the 7th century B.C. But in Mohammedan lore Ahikar is identified with Lukeman who, in turn, is presented as Job's nephew. Since Lukeman-Ahikar, according to legend, lived as long as seven generations of vultures, it is quite reasonable to place the story of Ahikar alongside the story of his uncle Job, nearly fifteen centuries B.C.

PART IV

The Promised Land

The legends of this section cover a period of over six eventful centuries, from Joshua ben Nun, successor to Moses, to Isaiah, the Prophet of Consolation. The conquest of Canaan and the rule of Judges (1451–1095 B.C.) came like the dawn after the night of slavery and migration; followed by the United Kingdom of Israel (1095–975 B.C.) under Saul, David and Solomon, who ruled, each in turn, for forty years. After that the kingdom was divided, and the Northern Kingdom lasted two hundred and fifty-three years before it was conquered and the people taken captive by the Assyrians in 722 B.C. Then the Prophet Isaiah warned the remaining Kingdom of Judah that the Promised Land was not in Canaan but in the heart of the people.

All the leaders of this period who fill the pages of Joshua, Judges, Samuel, Kings and Chronicles have been crowned in the lore with garlands of legends; and the garland of King Solomon surpasses them all, because, according to legend, given the choice, he chose *wisdom*.

CHAPTER TWELVE

The Conquest of Canaan

1. *The Miracle That Happened to a Hangman*

At his birth, Joshua ben Nun was thrown into the Nile, in accord
with the wicked law of that time in Egypt. Moses had been saved
by a princess; Joshua was saved by a whale, who swallowed the
child and then spat him forth unharmed on a far-off shore.

The infant was found by a childless couple who took him home
and raised him as their own son. But though they were kindly
people, they were very ignorant. And they raised Joshua in darkness of his origin and untutored in all other matters.

So ignorant did Joshua grow up that people called him "The
Fool" and the only work he could find was that of a hangman.

The law provided that the wife of the condemned belonged to
the executioner. But when Joshua approached the wife of the first
man he executed, two streams of milk began to flow from her
breasts. Joshua understood the sign — that this woman was his
real mother. And from her he learned the story of his birth.

Joshua left his home to join the forces around Moses and Aaron
who were then leading a revolt against slavery in Egypt. Moses
recognized in his new follower one who had found favor in the
eyes of God and, with the help of Metatron, the Angel of Study,
Joshua soon became the most learned man in Israel, next only to
Moses. He was no longer called "The Fool." The people treated him
with great respect and said: "Moses is the sun; Joshua is the moon."

2. *God Speaks to Joshua*

The day Moses departed, God came to Joshua and said: "Tomorrow I shall raise you in the eyes of the people and show them that

as I was with Moses, in his need, so will I be with you, in yours. I split the Red Sea for Moses; for you I will split the Jordan so that you may lead the people across to Canaan on dry land."

Joshua kept his eyes lowered to the Book of Deuteronomy in his hands, and when God had spoken, Joshua said: "Blessed is the Lord and Blessed is His Name!"

And God said to him: "Never go to war as long as it is avoidable. For even the most wicked on earth are in Our Image. When you must go into battle, the angel Michael, Guardian of Israel, will be at your side. Therefore be resolute and prepare to cross the Jordan. And may the Law never depart from your mouth."

"Amen!" said Joshua.

3. *The Good Rahab*

As a first step in conquering Canaan, Joshua sent two trusted messengers, Caleb and Phinehas, to cross the Jordan and spy out the strength of the city of Jericho.

Disguised as potters, the messengers entered the gates of the city. All day long they loitered in the market place asking the talkative women many questions. In the evening they looked for a lodging where none would suspect them of spying. The house of a harlot, the messengers knew, would be the best hiding place. Caleb and Phinehas therefore found their way to Rahab, a woman of forty, who had led the life of a harlot since she was twelve years and one day old, and whose dwelling was in a tower on the wall of the city.

When Rahab asked the messengers who they were and where they came from, Phinehas, who was a priest, could not lie to her. He revealed his identity and asked:

"Now tell us, what do the people of Jericho think of Israel?"

"They have heard how God has brought Israel out of Egypt with a mighty hand," said Rahab, "and that is the talk of the land. And the fear of Israel has sapped their courage."

As they talked, the king's men knocked on the door in search of strangers. Rahab quickly lowered Caleb and Phinehas through a window in the tower to the ground outside the walls of the city.

Then she opened the door to the king's men. There were two strangers in her house earlier in the evening, she told them, but they had gone and she knew not where.

(Because Rahab shielded the messengers of Israel; because she repented her way of life; and because she accepted the God of Israel, Rahab was rewarded. She later married Joshua and became the ancestress of eight prophets and the Prophetess Huldah.)

Caleb and Phinehas made their way back and reported to Joshua that God had already turned over the nations beyond the Jordan into their hands, for He had crushed their hearts with fear.

4. *The Longest Day in History*

The news traveled fast and the news traveled far. The Hittites, the Amorites, the Gibeonites, the Perizzites, the Hivites, the Gezerites, the Shimenites, the Jebusites, the Hepharites, the Kedeshites, and all the other Canaanites heard about the Twelve Tribes of Israel who had come out of Egypt and were on their way home to Canaan. These tribes, it was reported, had reached the River Jordan and were ready to cross and to conquer all the kingdoms between Hamath and the Orontes River, in the north, to the Sea of Sodom and Kadish Barnea, in the south.

The victories of the Ten Tribes over the Amorites, the Bashanites and the Moabites were recounted; and with each retelling their wonders were magnified. It was told how the leader of these tribes, named Moses, performed great magic and often destroyed his enemies by raising his hands heavenwards and uttering curses. It was told how the Great Balaam, Destroyer of Nations, was powerless against Moses and how his curses of Israel turned into blessings in his mouth. And it was told how Aaron, brother of Moses, could create peace wherever there was strife between neighbor and neighbor; and what he could do to bring amity between man and man, he could do to bring peace between nation and nation.

The strangest and most frightening story of all was told about the fall of the city of Jericho. Joshua the Conqueror, so the story went, led the Children of Israel to the edge of the Jordan. When the priests bearing the Ark stepped into the river, the waters piled up to a height of three hundred miles and Joshua led his people across on dry land.

In one day Joshua led the Twelve Tribes seventy miles inland and no one came to oppose them. Then they divided, six of the tribes going up to Mount Gerizim, and six to Mount Ebal. On each mountain an altar was built with stones taken from the bottom of the Jordan. And on each altar was inscribed in seventy languages:

Happy is the man who serves no idol.

Then the people marched on to the walled city of Jericho. They brought with them neither spears nor catapults, nor any of the appurtenances of war. When they reached the walls of the city they did not set up flails or ramrods. Instead, they surrounded the city, blowing a ram's horn and singing hymns. The walls of Jericho came tumbling down and the city stood defenseless.

"Alarm is a poor weapon," said the wise men of Gibeon. "The Israelites are strong because they are united. Let us unite fourfold, and we shall be unconquerable."

Forty-five kingdoms united under the King of Eglon and the Council of the Kings of Media. They sent messengers to Joshua ben Nun, warning that if he dared lead his people into their lands, the forty-five kingdoms, each with an army of trained and armed soldiers sixty thousand strong, would come out to destroy the Israelites.

The leaders of the Twelve Tribes were frightened by the message. Even Joshua the Courageous trembled at the thought of meeting in battle forty-five armies, each sixty thousand strong. Only Caleb, Joshua's adviser, rejoiced in the message.

"Those kings are trying to frighten us," said he. "That is a good sign. When one nation tries to frighten another with its greater strength in soldiers and arms, it is a sign that nation knows fear. They say they have each an army of sixty thousand men. Yet we know there are not that many men in the whole of Canaan. Behind their threat they hide their fear. And frightened fighters are not likely winners."

"Caleb is right," said Joshua. And he sent a message to the forty-five united kingdoms: "Now that you have challenged the lion and awakened his wrath, prepare to meet him in battle and to be destroyed to a man."

From each tribe Joshua selected one thousand men, and with this army of only twelve thousand he marched out to meet the enemy, singing songs and blowing trumpets as if victory were already theirs.

"Today is Friday," said Japheth, hero of the united kingdoms. "The Israelites, our enemies, keep the Sabbath holy. On that day they neither work nor fight. Let us spar with them this afternoon, and when evening comes we shall fall upon them and slay them at leisure."

The armies met in battle Friday afternoon. Joshua raised his right hand toward heaven, pronounced the Ineffable Name, and ordered the sun and the moon to stop in their orbits as long as his hand was raised.

The armies fought valiantly on both sides. But the soldiers of the united kingdoms fought only halfheartedly, waiting for an easy victory at sundown. After several hours of fighting they suddenly realized that the sun had not moved since the battle began. As time passed, they started to look at the sun instead of at their enemy. And though the superior numbers were theirs, the tide of battle turned against them.

Lest the Israelites become vain in their victory and claim it as their own, God sent down in broad sunlight showers of hailstones the size of rocks, and more of the enemy were killed by the hail than by the sword.

For thirty hours Joshua held up his hand, and for thirty hours the sun stood still. Panic-stricken, the enemy finally retreated in defeat, and the Council of Kings fled to a cave at Mekkedah.

Victory assured, Joshua lowered his arms and ordered his men back to camp to prepare for the Holy Sabbath.

5. The Deathless City of Luz

Joshua led his people to victory over the King of Bethel and the King of Jerusalem; the kings of Eglon, Gezer, Debir and Geder; the kings of Arad, Libnah, Hormah and Hepher; the kings of

Lachish, Kedesh, Shimron and Gilgal; and many other kings and rulers over the mountains and the valleys and the plains of Canaan.

When the wars were over and the land divided among the tribes according to the Will of Moses, Joshua asked Caleb and Othniel to help him find the place in which he could leave the Tablets of the Law, the *Urim* and *Thummin* and all the holy vessels and breastplates of the priests which Israel brought into Canaan.

There was only one place on earth where Moses could receive the commandments, and that was Mount Sinai; and there was only one place where Joshua could place the tablets, and that was in Bethel, meaning "the House of God." This Joshua knew, but he did not know how to get to Bethel.

"Bethel is now called Luz," the natives said to Joshua. And they told him how to reach Luz.

Joshua and his friends followed the directions and finally came to a walled-in city whose walls reached from earth to heaven. They circled the city seven times in search of a gate but could find none. Tired and puzzled, they sat down in an olive grove to rest. As they sat there, Joshua noticed that one tree seemed different from all the others. He rose, walked over to the tree, knocked upon its trunk three times with the knuckles of his right hand, and whispered: *"Hear thou Israel! The Lord our God is One God!"*

The tree opened like a gate, and Joshua and his friends entered. A steep stairway led them down into a dark cave; and from there they walked up into a gleaming hall filled with music; and a voice called to them: "Peace be with you!"

"Is this Luz, the Indestructible, or Bethel, the House of God?" asked Joshua.

"This is the place over which the Angel of Sorrow and the Angel of Death have no power."

"The place where there is no sorrow and no death is indeed the place for the Holy Law," said Joshua. "I shall bring the Tablets of the Law and all the holy vessels, so that the commandments may live forever for all mankind."

Joshua placed the Ark and the Tablets of the Law in Bethel, blessed his people and, after twenty-eight years as a leader in Israel, he died.

6. *The Judge Who Liked to Sing*

The Twelve Tribes settled in their allotted areas, each establishing its own laws, its own judges, its own seers, its own ways of settling disputes with neighbors. For many years they throve in peace. Only now and then a neighboring king would take offense at one of the tribes and try to molest its people.

King Jabin of Hazor was such a king. He envied the Ephraimites across the Waters of Merom and often came down with his armies to destroy his neighbors' crops and to provoke war.

In those days there lived a woman named Deborah who owned a vineyard and a large date orchard between Ramah and Bethel in Ephraim. God blessed Deborah with the gift of song and the power of prophecy. And the people selected her as a judge.

On given days, Deborah would sit under a date palm in an open field and whoever had a problem for a judge or a prophetess came to her there. She did not receive anyone in her home or in a tent so that none could ever cast aspersions upon her because she had been alone with strange men. While Deborah served her people, her husband Lapidoth cared for the vineyard and the orchard.

One day, as Deborah sat under her palm tree and people asked for forecasts on crops, advice in marriage and the settling of disputes, several hillsmen came running all out of breath to warn that King Jabin was again plotting to come down on Ephraim.

It was not Jabin that they feared so much as the general of his armies, the giant Sisera. When Sisera shouted, buildings crumbled and trees were uprooted. When he dived into a river, the river overflowed its banks. It took nine hundred asses to draw his chariot. And his beard was as large as a net in which fish are dragged. There was not a nation that did not fear him. He had only to shout and his enemies surrendered. No wonder the Ephraimites feared him!

When Deborah heard the news she sent for Barak, son of Abinoam, head of the armies of the Tribe of Naphtali, and said to him:

"Barak, word has come that the tyrant, King Jabin, is restless again and has sent Sisera and his chariots against Ephraim and Naphtali."

"What can we do against Sisera?" Barak asked in despair.

Deborah did not answer his question but asked one of her own: "Do you, Barak ben Abinoam, believe in the Lord our God?"

"Of course, I do. Why?"

"Because I want you to gather all the brave men of Ephraim and Naphtali and march them against Sisera and his army before he reaches our land. Meet him at Lake Kishon where he will be encamped, and destroy his army to a man."

"That is not so easily done," said Barak.

And Deborah answered: "One measure of faith will tip the scales against a mountain of force. And God promises to deliver into our hands Jabin's armies, even Sisera, to destroy them."

Barak hesitated, then he said, "If you will go with me, I will do as you say."

"I will go with you, for I know no doubt since the Lord has spoken. But it will not be to your glory, Barak, if it is said that you needed the help of a woman to go against Sisera."

Deborah rose from her seat under the palm tree, and with Barak and Lapidoth, her husband, ran through the land, calling:

"He who is strong of heart and believes in the One God, follow us to banish our enemies and to destroy Sisera, the foe of Israel!"

Their followers grew into a mighty army of ten thousand men and they swept over Sisera like a cyclone. God was with them, and Sisera's men were defenseless. Sisera ran from the field of battle and hid in the home of Jael, the wife of Heber the Kenite.

Jael was at home alone, and Sisera tried to make love to her. Jael put him off, for she was a woman of virtue, and when Sisera asked for water to quench his thirst, she gave him warm milk to make him sleepy. And God sent an angel as a witness that Jael did no wrong though alone with a strange man of evil repute. When Sisera lay down to rest, Jael took in her left hand a tent peg and in her right hand a hammer; she tiptoed to Sisera, who lay sleeping, and drove the peg into his temple until it went through and into the ground.

Barak, who had been pursuing Sisera, came to Heber's house. Jael opened the door to him and said:

"Come and I will show you him whom you seek."

And she led Barak to Sisera, who lay dead with the tent peg through his temple.

The war was over, Deborah and her husband returned to Ephraim. Lapidoth went back to his work in the fields, and Deborah again sat under the date palm prophesying and judging. And when she had time, she composed a song in praise of the One God; and a blessing for Jael, who killed Sisera. She described how, when Jael struck him in his sleep, Sisera awoke too late, and bowed down at her feet; and where he bowed, there he fell dead. And she implored God to bless Jael above all women, even above Sarah, Rebekah, Rachel and Leah, for Jael was not of Israel yet carried out God's will. And she prayed that the faithful who are forced into battle by evildoers shall come out of battle like the sun at sunrise, full of strength, and know peace all their days thereafter.

7. *The Man Who Refused to Be King*

The Tribes of Israel appealed to God when their needs were great; but when all went well with them in peace, they neglected God and were willing to listen to the priests of strange idols.

Only a few years after Sisera's death, Israel began to listen to the Midianite priests and their sorcerers. They even taught their children to worship their own images reflected in water.

When God's patience was exhausted, He delivered Israel into the hands of the Midianites and filled their hearts with fear.

At that time there lived a man in the town of Ophrah, in the land of Menasseh, named Gideon ben Joash. He was a good man who was very humble about his own affairs, but very ambitious for Menasseh, his tribe, and Israel, his people.

One day as Gideon rested under an oak tree, an angel of the Lord came to him and said: "Gideon, God commands you to leave your land and go out to lead your people. And God will be with you."

And Gideon replied: "When Moses was asked to lead his people he was given a sign."

The angel then drew water from a rock in the field; one half of the water turned into fire; and the rest turned into blood. The angel poured the blood on the fire, yet the fire was not extinguished, nor did the blood dry out.

Gideon understood the signs: water meant peace; and blood meant war. Just as blood failed to extinguish the fire, so war failed to extinguish the causes of war.

"I will obey," said Gideon, "for God has spoken."

Gideon and a number of young men of his tribe went through the land, calling:

"All who cherish the memory of Mount Sinai, gather at the Well of Herod!"

When Gideon reached the well he found thirty-two thousand young men waiting for him.

"Those of you who are afraid," said Gideon to the gathering, "those of you who have brides, and those of you who have wives and children — return to your homes!"

Twenty thousand departed.

"Those of you who are not perfect in vision, or who are slow in movement, or who have been in battle before — return to your homes!"

Seven thousand more departed.

"Those of you who are not prepared to meet the enemy alone and without a weapon, if need be, yet remain brave at heart — return to your homes!"

Another three thousand departed.

Then Gideon took the remaining two thousand down to the banks of a river for the final test. Each man was told to kneel with his hands behind him and lap up the water like a drinking animal. All tried, but only three hundred succeeded.

With this handful of three hundred men Gideon prepared to battle an enemy as numerous as the grasshoppers. Each of his men was given a trumpet, a sword and a torch. Late at night, when the enemy camp lay deep in sleep, Gideon and his men lit their torches and, with a loud blowing of trumpets, rushed down upon the enemy, shouting:

"For God and for Gideon!"

The enemy, believing that Gideon and his daring band were the vanguard of a large army, fled in panic. Gideon and his men drove them out of Canaan and did not stop until the last of the enemy was across the Jordan or had fled to the desert — yet they had not shed one drop of blood.

When Gideon returned victorious, he was asked to become king of the Tribes of Israel.

"The tribes should unite," said Gideon, "but their king should be the One God."

Then Gideon returned home and spent the rest of his days on his farm.

8. *The Bramble That Would Be King*

Gideon had two sons: one was as good as his father but not as brave; and the other was as brave, but, alas, not as good.

The brave son, Abimelech, decided to unite the Tribes of Israel into one kingdom, with himself as king. His older brother, Jothan, thought it was a good idea to unite the Twelve Tribes, but he was not at all certain his brother was the man fitted to rule over them.

When the people came to Jothan and asked him whether he would support his brother as King of Israel, he replied in his own way, which was by way of a parable:

"The trees once decided to choose a king and they went and asked the olive tree to reign over them. But the olive tree refused, saying that he was too busy growing olives to waste time in ruling others. The fig tree gave a similar answer. And so did every tree bearing fruit and every bush bearing berries or flowers. Finally they came to the prickly bramble bush and asked: 'Will you be our king?' The thorny little bush accepted and at once commanded all the trees to obey him, or be devoured by fire."

The people listened to Jothan and understood what he meant. But when they refused to recognize Abimelech as their ruler, he organized an army of outlaws and tried to force his authority over Israel.

One day a brave woman threw a stone at the would-be king and broke his skull. Abimelech commanded his armor-bearer to draw his sword and slay him so that no one could claim that Gideon's son was killed by a woman.

And so died the bramble that would be king.

9. *The Chief Freebooter of Ledja*

There was once an indiscreet man who had a mistress and she gave birth to a son. The man's name was Gilead and the name of his illegitimate son was Jephtah.

Jephtah grew up to be a brave and wise man, but Gilead's other children would have nothing to do with him and informed him that he would not be allowed to share in his father's inheritance. When he was still young, Jephtah ran away from home and fell in with a group of brigands. Because of his courage and shrewdness, he soon became their leader. But though the leader of a band of outlaws, his heart remained true to the interests of his tribe, Menasseh, even though the people called him "Chief Freebooter of Ledja."

When the Ammonites made war on Menasseh, the elders of the tribe came to Jephtah and asked him to lead the war against their enemy.

"You drive me from town to town, and call me a 'freebooter,' why then do you come to me now?" asked Jephtah.

"Because you are the bravest man we have and we know that you have remained true to your people," said the elders.

"If I win the war against the Ammonites, will you make me a judge in Israel?" asked Jephtah.

"We will," the elders promised.

Jephtah gathered an army of brave men and went out to meet the enemy. On the way he made a vow: "O Lord, if You will deliver the enemy into my hands, whatsoever greets me first from out the gates of my house, that will I offer up as a sacrifice and as a burnt offering to You!"

And God said: "Jephtah vows to sacrifice whatever greets him first upon his return home. What will he do if a dog should come out of his gate? For the sake of the prayers of Israel, I shall give Jephtah victory in battle; but for his thoughtless vow he shall be punished."

And so it happened.

Jephtah crossed the Jordan and defeated the Ammonites, then returned home a victorious hero. The people came to greet him with music, and shouted his praise. They no longer called him "Freebooter" but "Our Hero" and "Our Wise Judge." The women danced in the streets and sang:

> *Our enemies came down upon us,*
> *The Ammonites were down upon us,*
> *But Jephtah, son of Gilead, arose*
> *And drove them into the sea!*

Jephtah rode ahead of his army, happy and proud. But his joy vanished as he reached the gates of his house. For the first to come to greet him was his only child, his daughter Seelah.

Jephtah fell to the ground and wept. His daughter ran to him and put her arms around him and tried to find out the cause of his tears. Then Jephtah told her of his vow.

Seelah argued that human sacrifices were not acceptable to God and he had only to arrange for a vicarious sacrifice.

"Only the High Priest Phinehas can rule on that," said Jephtah.

But the High Priest was too proud to come to Jephtah, whom he still considered a brigand; and Jephtah was too proud to go to the High Priest, now that he was a judge.

And because of their pride, Seelah died.

Then God punished both Phinehas and Jephtah. The holy spirit departed from the High Priest and he died in shame. And Jephtah was doomed to die a horrible death, soon after his daughter's sacrifice.

10. *The Faithful Ruth*

In the days when the Twelve Tribes were ruled by Judges, there lived in Bethlehem a man named Elimelech and his wife Naomi, with their two young sons, Mahlon and Chilion. When the sons were still very young, famine ravished Canaan, the sixth famine since the days of Adam. Naomi was generous, but her husband grudged the poor the bread given them by his wife. He therefore took his family and moved away to Moab. When the boys grew up, they married two Moabite sisters, Orphah and Ruth.

Elimelech and his two sons died in an epidemic that swept the land, and Naomi prepared to return to her kinsmen in Canaan. She advised her daughters-in-law to return to the home of their parents.

Orphah accompanied Naomi four miles on her way to the border of Moab. There she kissed her mother-in-law and turned back to her father's home.

(Upon her return Orphah attached herself to a Philistine giant warrior and abandoned herself to an immoral life. Because she followed Naomi four miles, she was rewarded with four giant sons; and because she led an immoral life, her grandsons, the giants Yishbi and Goliath, grew up like wolves and drenched their land in blood.)

Ruth refused to join her sister, saying she had come to love Naomi more than her own mother; and Naomi's religion, more than her own religion.

"Where you go, there I will go," she said to Naomi, "and where you live, there I will live. Your people are now my people, and your God is my God."

Naomi and Ruth reached Bethlehem at harvest time, and Ruth went to work in the fields of one of Naomi's relatives, named Boaz. When Boaz came to the field to watch his reapers he noticed Ruth. He admired her grace of movement, her comely face, and her modest behavior among the reapers and the gleaners. He inquired about her and was glad to learn who she was and that she had come to believe in the One God.

Boaz said to Ruth: "I have had a vision, and in the vision I saw that kings and prophets will come from your offspring."

Ruth told Naomi of Boaz's vision and that she had found favor in his eyes. And Naomi instructed Ruth in the ways of her people. She anointed her with sweet-smelling oils, dressed her in fine raiment, and sent her to join Boaz after he had eaten and was merry from drink.

When they were left alone, Satan came to Boaz and tempted him, saying: "You have no wife and Ruth has no husband. She came to you because she is lonely. You will commit no sin, for she is not a married woman."

Boaz struggled with Satan. And for the strength of his will, he was rewarded.

11. *Nathan the Rich*

The story is told of a rich man, named Nathan, who fell in love with a married woman named Hannah. Nathan longed for Hannah until he became very ill; but the doctors knew of no remedy that would cure him.

Hannah's husband was put in prison for debt and Hannah worked to support herself and to buy food for her husband in jail. Each time Hannah came to visit her husband, he urged her to borrow money from Nathan for his release from prison, and Hannah refused. Then her husband accused her of waiting for him to die in prison so that she would be free to marry Nathan the Rich. Hannah prayed, put on her best garment, and went to ask Nathan for a loan.

When Nathan was told who had come to see him, he sent all his servants away. Then he said to Hannah:

"You can have all the money you want. But do you know what I shall ask in return?"

"I am in your hands," said Hannah. "But can you not imagine that I have already submitted to your will, and thereby conquer your desires? I pray you, do nothing you would soon regret."

Nathan gave Hannah the money without touching her hand, and sent her home without as much as looking at her. But when Hannah's husband was released he would not believe his wife and spread rumors about Nathan the Rich.

One day a great teacher saw Nathan riding on a horse, a crown of light about his head.

The teacher said to Nathan: "Hannah's husband is spreading rumors that you multiply evil. Yet I see by the light about your head that you will inherit a share of the World to Come. What have you done to deserve it?"

"I have conquered my desires," said Nathan, and told him what had transpired between him and Hannah.

The teacher invited Nathan to become his pupil.

Hannah's husband came to the House of Study, and saw Nathan the Rich at the teacher's right hand. And he asked: "Why is Nathan so honored?"

The teacher answered: "Because he is a man who is master of his evil impulses."

Hannah's husband then realized his wife had told him the truth and he trusted her ever after. And Nathan the Rich became known as Nathan the Learned.

In a like manner Boaz was tempted on the night Ruth came to lie at the foot of his bed, and he conquered his desire.

And God blessed Boaz and Ruth. When they were married He rewarded them with offspring from whom issued King David, the Prophet Daniel and the Three Pillars of the World, Hannaniah, Mishael and Azariah.

This device of a story within a story to demonstrate a moral principle is frequently encountered in the lore of the Old Testament.

12. *The Weakness of a Strong Man*

In the days of the Judges there lived a childless man named Manoah the Danite and his wife Zelalponit. They had given up all hope of having any children, when an angel in the guise of a young man came to Zelalponit in the fields and said:

"Within a year you will have a son. Name him Samson and bring him up as a Nazarene. His hair must never know shears, nor his palate the taste of wine. And he will grow up to be a great man."

As the angel foretold, Zelalponit gave birth to a boy, and the child was named Samson. From early childhood he showed super-human strength. At twenty years of age he became a judge in Israel. Samson measured sixty ells between the shoulders. To demonstrate his strength he once lifted up two mountains, rubbed them against each other and turned them into dust.

Though Samson was the greatest giant that ever lived, excepting Goliath, the secret of his strength was not in his shoulders, though they were broader than a river, nor in his arms, though they could uproot mountains, nor in his feet, though he could walk a thousand leagues without tiring. His strength resided in seven golden hairs which were braided, one each, into the seven braids of his hair, that had never been touched by shears. When the spirit of God was upon him, Samson's hair vibrated, making a sound which could be heard many miles away, and which struck fear into the hearts of the enemies of Israel.

Even greater than his physical strength was Samson's goodness of heart. He was as humble as he was strong; and as unselfish as he was humble. All his days he devoted to the battles of his people, yet he never expected nor accepted a reward. When the enemies of his people dared raise their heads, he would lay their cities waste with the jawbone of an ass; or he would tear a city apart and carry off the great gates on his shoulders.

Samson never drank. He kept the Sabbath holy. He honored his parents. He fulfilled daily all the Six Hundred and Thirteen Articles of Faith. Yet he had one weakness; and that weakness was his undoing: He loved beautiful women.

Samson had been a judge in Israel for twenty years when he fell in love with a woman in the Valley of Sorek, whose beauty was unequaled in five kingdoms. Her name was Delilah and, though she was a harlot, her beauty was so great that she was known as the Daughter of Dagon, whom the Philistines worshiped.

The Lords of the Philistines, hearing of Samson's great love for Delilah, came to her and promised to build her a palace and give her great wealth if she could learn the secret of Samson's strength, and part him from it.

Delilah was beautiful and she was wise in the ways of men. When Samson came to her, she told him she could not love him until he told her the secret of his strength. For a long time Samson put her off. But in the end he told her. Delilah lulled him to sleep upon her knees, and cut off the seven locks of hair in which were entwined the seven hairs of gold.

The Philistines fell upon Samson, whose strength had departed from him, gouged out his eyes, and put him to hard labor in a prison. And a great festivity was proclaimed to celebrate Samson's downfall and Delilah's triumph.

Thousands gathered in the Temple of Dagon, in the city of Gaza, to praise Delilah and to mock the blinded Samson. The giant was led, helpless, into the center of the temple.

Delilah called out to him: "Samson! Renounce your God and worship Dagon, who delivered you into our hands, and I will ask the Five Kings to grant you your freedom."

Samson wiped his face and forehead with the open palm of his hand, and trembled. For as his fingers swept across his shaven head they were pricked, as if by fine wires — the seven golden hairs had begun to grow again.

"What is your answer, Samson?" Delilah taunted.

Samson turned to his guard and said: "Lead me to the pillars, that I may lean upon them."

The guard led him to the pillars upon which the roof of the temple rested. There Samson stood for a moment in silent prayer. Then he straightened out his wide shoulders, gripped the pillars supporting the heavy roof and shouted:

"*Hear thou Israel!*"

His voice struck horror in the hearts of the thousands in the Temple of Dagon, for it sounded like the Samson of old.

"The Lord our God is One God!" Samson shouted.

Then he tugged at the two pillars with all his might. Before the worshipers knew what was happening they were buried under the roof; and in his last act, Samson the Danite destroyed more Philistines and idolaters than in all his twenty years of warfare with them.

So died, for a sin of his own, the Nazarene Samson, last but one of the judges in Israel.

CHAPTER THIRTEEN

King Saul

1. *Hannah's Vow*

The story of the first king in Israel begins, as might be expected, with the story of a prophet.

In the days of the Judges there lived a man named Elkanah and his wife Hannah. Each year they made a pilgrimage from their home in Ramah to the House of Worship in Shiloh, to offer sacrifices and to pray for a son. When ten years passed, and Hannah still remained childless, she urged her husband to take a second wife and fulfill God's Law.

Elkanah loved Hannah and could not bear the thought of another woman in his house. But when he could delay no longer without transgressing the Law, he married the beautiful Peninnah, and within a year she bore him a son.

Year after year Peninnah gave birth to a child until she had eight children; and with each new child life in Elkanah's house became more difficult for Hannah. For as Peninnah's family multiplied, her arrogance toward Hannah increased.

Hannah grew thin and sad and wept many tears. When Elkanah found her weeping, he would say: "Why do you cry, Hannah? You know that I love you more than ten sons!" But Hannah was not comforted.

When her grief was greater than she could bear, Hannah went alone to Shiloh, and in the House of God she sank down into a corner and prayed:

"O God, Creator of the Universe! You have made the angels and You have made Adam. Angels have no children, they know no sorrow, and they live forever in heaven; Adam's children propagate, they know sorrow, and they die. But You have made me unlike either. I have the substance of a woman, yet not the essence.

You have given me breasts but no child to feed at them. Grant me a child, O Lord, and the day he is weaned I shall bring him to the House of Worship to serve You all the days of his life."

Hannah's prayer went on and on. She sat with eyes closed, lips barely moving, the words voiced within her heart only, her head nodding as she prayed. The High Priest Eli noticed her and thought she was intoxicated. He came over to reprimand Hannah and to remind her that it was forbidden to pray when drunk.

"My lord," said Hannah, "you see a woman deep in sorrow asking God for His blessing." Then she poured out her heart before Eli.

"Go home in peace," said the High Priest. "And may the God of Israel grant your prayer."

2. Samuel in Shiloh

On the way back from Shiloh, Hannah's husband came out upon the road to meet her and she told him of the vow she had made. And within the year Hannah gave birth to a son, whom they named Samuel, which means "God lent him to me."

When the time came for Samuel to be weaned, Hannah delayed and delayed, saying that the child was still too frail. Yet it was clear that Samuel was no ordinary infant. He began to speak before he could walk; and discoursed on the commandments before he was two. The weaning could not be put off any longer. On his second birthday Hannah took her son to Shiloh, as she had vowed, and placed him in the hands of Eli.

"My lord, take good care of my son, for he is so young, and not as strong as other children," she said to the High Priest. "Punish him not harshly when he errs. Remember that he was only lent to me and he belongs to God."

Hannah left her child and returned home. Six more children were born to her, but Samuel was always first in her heart. All through the years she thought of him, longed for him, and made small garments to take up to him during the annual pilgrimage to Shiloh. And each year Hannah marveled that the garments were too small because he had grown so much during the time she had not seen him.

3. *Samuel and the Stargazer*

Samuel was still very young when his fame as a prophet traveled throughout the land and sages of other nations came to consult with him, to match their powers of prophecy with him, and to do him honor.

One day Samuel was crossing a field with the stargazer Abaleth. Abaleth pointed to a man in the distance gathering wood, and said: "I see by the stars that that man will not return home. A snake will bite him and he will die."

"It is true that the man was destined to die," said Samuel. "But if he has done one good deed today, he shall be saved from death."

Later that day the man crossed their path bearing a load of wood in his arms. Unnoticed by the woodcutter, a dead snake lay coiled around one of the logs.

"What good deed have you done today?" Samuel asked the woodcutter.

"I cannot think of any," said the man. "Excepting that there were several of us working in the forest. We put our bread together and shared it at mealtime. There was one man who had no bread, but I pretended I had gathered his part with mine and I shared my food with him."

"You see," said Samuel to Abaleth. "A man's fate may be written in the stars, but charity saves from death."

4. *"We Want a King"*

As far back as Samuel could remember the people had come to him, demanding: "We want a king! We want to be like other nations!"

"The honor of Israel is that it is unlike other nations," Samuel would reply.

"Honor wins no battles," the people would say.

"You are strong in the eyes of God."

"But we are weak in the eyes of our neighbors," the people countered.

"A king will send your sons to war; he will take your daughters to keep his house; he will levy taxes on your land; and he will demand tithes of all your crops," Samuel warned.

But the people were determined. They had tired of the brigands who harassed them, and the division of the tribes. They wanted their domains united under a worthy king. When Samuel continued to argue against them, they reminded him: "On Mount Sinai Moses was told that the voice of the people is the Voice of God!"

Then Samuel relented and said: "If I can find one worthy to be king I will bring him to you and anoint him."

5. *King by Accident*

The first king in Israel was the son of a Benjamite farmer and he was chosen king quite by accident. It all happened in this way:

Old Kish ben Abiel had a farm and he discovered one day that several of the asses had broken out of their corral and had strayed off. Kish sent his son, Saul, with a slave named Rabaal, to find the lost animals.

All day long Saul and Rabaal searched for the asses. Toward evening they met several maidens who had come to draw water from a nearby well. Saul and Rabaal asked them whether they had seen the stray animals. Saul was tall, taller by a head than any other Benjamite, and as handsome as he was tall. The maidens did not answer his questions, saying "yes," or saying "no," but tried to engage Saul in conversation to learn who he was and where he had come from. At last they advised him to consult the Prophet Samuel who lived nearby.

"Ask him," they said, "for he knows everything."

Saul and Rabaal went to Samuel's home and told him of their search and their failure.

"I am hurrying to the House of Worship where others await me," said Samuel. "Remain here and rest from your long day's search. When I return, I will tell you where your father's animals are to be found."

Samuel went on to the House of Worship and announced that he had found the man to be King of Israel. When the people asked for his name and who he was, Samuel said:

"He is a farmer's son, who came here with his servant in search of his father's stray asses. When I asked him his name, he said, 'My name is Saul, the son of Kish, and we come from Gibeah.' He did not tell me that he is a descendant of the illustrious Aphiah. Nor did he mention his exploits in the war with the Philistines. Nor did he tell me that when Goliath captured the Tables of the Law, it was he, Saul, who marched sixty miles from his camp, recaptured the Holy Tablets and returned them to Shiloh on the same day. When I detained him, he said, 'We want to return home as soon as we can for our father might be worried.' When he said 'our father' I thought the man with him was his brother, but I learned that his companion was a slave. Saul comes from the smallest of our tribes, and he is the humblest of our youth. Such is he whom I have chosen as our king."

"A youth! And a farmer's son!" the people grumbled.

"If you want a graybeard who will parade in costly robes like a peacock, choose not Saul," Samuel silenced them. "But if you want a king who will march ten leagues ahead of his army in battle and lead you to victory over our enemies, there is no man this side of the Jordan or across it to surpass him."

Then Samuel sent for Saul. When he arrived at the House of Worship, the prophet said:

"In the name of our God in heaven, and in the name of the assembled leaders in Israel, you are welcomed here and we bless you to be honored among the rulers of the earth."

And the assembled shouted: "Long live King Saul!"

Samuel anointed Saul with consecrated oil, blessed him, and kissed his forehead three times.

After the ceremony was over, the newly elected king walked out of the assembly followed by the prophet. And when they were alone, Saul whispered to Samuel:

"It is growing late and my father will be troubled about us. Could you tell me where we may find the lost asses?"

6. *Taluth, the Water Carrier*

According to Mohammedan lore, Saul was not a Benjamite but an Egyptian, called Taluth. Though he was the handsomest youth in the land, Taluth was very poor and earned his living by drawing water from the river, which he poured into goatskins, loaded onto the back of an ass, and sold to the housewives.

One day Taluth's ass strayed, and he feared that he might not be able to earn his bread. Taluth went to Samuel the Seer and implored him to pray to God for the return of the animal.

"My son," said Samuel to the water carrier, who was taller and comelier than any man he had ever seen, "Allah gave me a rod from the Garden of Eden, saying, 'He who is in height the length of this rod shall surely be King of Israel.' I have set it against many youths, but none measured up to its length. Now let me try you against it."

Taluth stood up against the rod and he exceeded its length by a hair's breadth.

Samuel rejoiced and brought Taluth before the people in the House of God and announced that he had found the man to rule over them.

There were some in the multitude who grumbled: "Shall the scepter of Judah be given to an Egyptian? Shall a water carrier from the dregs of his people rule over us?"

Samuel silenced them and said: "Allah has spoken! And let this be as a sign to you that Allah is with him. For he will go now and bring back the Ark of the Covenant from the mighty hands of Amalek who captured it."

Taluth then assembled eight hundred thousand foot soldiers and ten thousand riders and led them against Amalek. The heat of the desert was great and the warriors were parched with thirst. Taluth led them to the Jordan and said:

"Each soldier who falls upon his knees and takes up water in the palm of one hand and drinks no more, he shall follow me; for he shall thereby prove that he can endure hardships and will not retreat before the enemy. But he who drinks to his fill must return home; for his heart is not in this war."

Of all the men in Taluth's army only three hundred passed the test. With these he fell upon the enemy and vanquished him.

When Taluth returned in victory, the Children of Israel rejoiced and shouted:

"Long live our King Taluth!"

7. David Meets Saul

In the days when Saul was king, there lived a widow in Hebron named Rinoh, which means "song." But after her young husband died, there was no song on Rinoh's lips nor gladness in her heart.

And her friends said to her: "You are young, Rinoh, and cannot live forever with your sorrow. God does not sustain the living with the dead. Return to your parents for a while and when your grief has subsided you will be able to come back and build your life again."

Rinoh followed their advice, sold all her possessions and placed the gold coins she received for them in two jars filled with honey.

She left the jars of honey, in the presence of witnesses, with her husband's best friend, Baal-Perez, to keep in safety until her return. Then Rinoh left for Gildad.

One day Baal-Perez needed honey. "I will borrow Rinoh's honey," he said to himself, "and refill the jars after the holiday." But as he poured the honey, he noticed the gold pieces. "God has made me rich by a miracle," thought Baal-Perez. He emptied the two jars of honey, took the gold coins, and the next day refilled the jars with honey he had bought in the market place.

Some months later Rinoh returned to claim her two jars of honey. She soon discovered that the money was gone, and brought Baal-Perez before King Saul and his judges. Baal-Perez produced the witnesses who testified that, in their presence, Rinoh left two jars of honey and that the same two jars of honey had been returned to her in their presence. King Saul and his judges could not find Baal-Perez guilty.

A few days later, as Rinoh walked along the outskirts of the town, she passed a group of children playing, and heard one of the boys say: "Come, let us play the trial of Rinoh and the two jars of honey." Rinoh stopped to listen.

The redheaded boy who had proposed the game acted as judge and, after listening to the story presented by the child representing Rinoh, he said: "If Rinoh tells the truth, then Baal-Perez must be lying. If he really is a thief, he did not know how much money there was in the jars. He might have refilled them in haste while a coin still stuck to the bottom or the side. Break the jars and learn the truth."

Rinoh kissed the boy judge and ran to King Saul to tell him what she had heard the boy judge say. The jars were broken and three gold pieces were found at the bottom of each jar. Baal-Perez confessed and returned the widow's money.

"What was the boy's name?" King Saul asked Rinoh.

"He said his father's name is Jesse and that his name is David."

"Blessed is Israel to have such children!" said the king, and asked that David be brought to him.

And that was how David ben Jesse, age ten, met King Saul and the Prophet Samuel.

8. *David and Goliath*

David found favor in King Saul's eyes, and he was invited to spend much time at the court. Soon the king discovered that young David played the harp better than any of his court musicians. King Saul appointed David his armor-bearer and, when his spirits were low, David sat at his feet and played for him.

One day David's music failed to cheer the king.

"What troubles my lord?" asked David.

"The Philistine, Goliath, son of Orphah," said the King. "He is a giant stronger than Samson, and he is as impious as he is strong. He blasphemes the name of the Lord, and has challenged the God of Israel to a contest of strength. As King of Israel it is my duty to fight him, but I am no match for Goliath."

"Let me fight him," David pleaded, "and I shall slay him!"

"You?" said Saul in astonishment. "You are as a gnat beside the mountain Goliath!"

"My lord," said David, "one day when I tended my father's sheep, a lion came to steal a lamb from the flock. I bearded the lion and slew him — as I would slay Goliath the Impious!"

"You have not convinced me," said the king.

"Another day," David went on, "I came to my father's field, and there was a hill where no hill had been before. I climbed to the top and discovered two great horns. I knew then that I was upon the fearful Beast Reem that causes the King of Beasts to tremble. Yet I knew no fear of the mammoth, for I know only one fear: the fear of the God of Israel."

Young David told King Saul of other marvelous encounters, in which victory was always on the side of his faith in God. Finally the king consented to let the stripling David challenge the giant Goliath.

When King Saul tried to equip David with armor and sword, he refused them, saying:

"My shield and my sword is my faith in the Lord; I shall need no other."

He took only his shepherd's sling, and in his shepherd's pouch five smooth stones gathered from the bottom of a brook, and went out to meet the challenger of Israel's God.

Like a mighty oak, like a mountain of strength, Goliath descended in scorn upon David. Six cubits and a span in height was he; and his arms alone weighed five thousand shekels of brass. But as he neared, the giant realized too late the magic power of David's eyes. For when their eyes met, Goliath became rooted to the ground like a tree. Only his tongue still moved freely.

"Am I a dog that you come to me with a stick and stones?" shouted Goliath. "Come, and I will feed you to the scavengers of the field and sky."

"Curse on," said David, "as long as there is still breath in your belly."

As David took out the five stones, they turned into a single stone; and he knew that God was with him. He placed the stone upon his sling and let it fly. The stone pierced Goliath's forehead. And an angel dropped Goliath face downwards so that the image of Dagon, on the amulet around the giant's neck, lay in the dust; and Goliath's head lay between David's feet.

All the people in Israel rejoiced and sang in praise of David's victory over the giant Goliath. But King Saul was sad, suspecting in his heart that he who had come to court as a shepherd boy would gain the favor of the people, and remain to claim the throne.

9. *Reason for Madness*

One day young David saw an unkempt madman running through the market place with a group of urchins chasing and mocking him.

"O Lord," said David, "I wonder why You created madness, which makes one in Your Image the laughingstock of children. As I wonder why You created the ugly spider and the vicious wasp."

That same evening as David played to the brooding king upon his harp, Saul fell asleep and dreamt that young David boasted he would soon take Saul's place as King of Israel. Saul awoke and in a fit of fury threw his javelin at the youth. The javelin missed its aim, and David fled to hide in the hills.

David hid in a cave one day to elude the king's men who had been sent to capture him. A spider came and spun a web across the entrance. When the soldiers pursuing him reached the cave, David heard them say: "He cannot be hiding here for the entrance is covered with cobwebs." And they went away.

The next day the fleeing David fell asleep in a field. He was awakened by the sting of a wasp, and just in time, for Saul's soldiers had discovered his trail.

After some time David reached Gath, ruled by Achish, King of the Philistines. Immediately Goliath's brothers petitioned the king to behead David and avenge their brother's death.

David prayed to God to save him. And God granted him a sign that his prayer would be answered. When David came before the king he appeared like a raving lunatic. The king, whose wife and daughters were lunatics, shouted: "Do I lack madmen in my household that you have brought another to me? Send him away!"

And so David's life was spared, and he prayed: "O Lord! How wondrous are Your ways! You can make a spider defeat an army; and a wasp destroy the plans of evil men! And You can use madness as a measure of mercy."

10. *Because of Agag a Crown Is Lost*

During Saul's reign of sixteen years, he led his people against the Ammonites, the Philistines and the Amalekites, and each time he led them to victory.

Before Saul entered into the battle with the Amalekites, the Prophet Samuel came to the king and told him that so wicked were the Amalekites that it was God's will that the enemy should be completely destroyed.

But Saul, victorious over the enemy, allowed his men to spare many of them and their King Agag. Samuel came to him and said:

"There is no man to compare with you in humility, Saul. That is a virtue. There is also no one to compare with you in kindness. That, too, is a virtue. But it is not a virtue in a ruler who must wage war. Therefore, Saul, the kingdom shall not go to your off-spring, but it shall pass to another."

And that was how a crown was lost because of the kindness to King Agag.

11. *And So Died the First King*

The Prophet Samuel went to the house of Jesse, son of Ruth and Boaz, as God had commanded him, secretly to anoint one of his sons King of Israel. Samuel tried to pour the anointing oil on the head of Eliab, Jesse's oldest son, but the oil would not flow out of the horn. Nor would the oil flow when he tried to anoint the other brothers. Only when the youngest, David, approached, did the oil flow. It flowed in a constant stream, and the drops which fell on David's shepherd cloak turned into diamonds and strands of pearls. Everyone present then knew that David was God's choice as the next King of Israel.

Not long after the anointing of David, the Prophet Samuel died. And throughout Israel old and young mourned him. But none mourned him more than Saul. For Saul's rule was secure only as long as Samuel remained alive; the prophet interceded for the king each time he offended the Lord. Saul understood that Samuel had been taken away so that he could no longer intercede for the king; and he wondered how he could rule without the prophet's constant advice. He tried to communicate with Samuel through witchcraft, but to his question how to save himself, the king received the answer from Samuel's spirit:

"If you accept God's judgment, you will be united with me by tomorrow."

King Saul accepted the judgment. The next day he calmly gathered his three sons and with them went into the battle in which all four perished.

And a voice came down from heaven, saying:

"Saul was worthy of My crown, for he accepted cheerfully the punishment that was meted out to him."

So died the first king in Israel, a hero and a saint. And when his soul ascended to heaven, the angels sang in welcome and called him, "Saul, the Elect of God."

CHAPTER FOURTEEN

King David

1. David Acquires Jerusalem

In the days of King Saul Jerusalem was a twin-city, one part belonging to the Jews and the other to the Jebusites, who called their city *Jebu*. When David became king, he went out to acquire Jebu, knowing that since the days of Adam, Noah and Abraham it had been destined to become *Zion*, the site of the Holy Temple and, in the days to come, the dwelling place of the Messiah.

But when David approached to take Jebu, the Jebusites came forward with brass tablets on which were clearly engraved the agreement between the sons of Heth and Abraham that they would never be forcibly dispossessed of their city.

David then said to the Jebusites: "Build a high wall around your city and leave no gate for anyone to enter. If I can enter it without force, you shall treat with me peaceably and sell me your part of Jerusalem."

The Jebusites agreed and built a gigantic wall around their city, without a gate or an opening in it anywhere.

David came nigh, and the walls lowered themselves so that he could step over them as one crosses a threshold; then they rose again ten times the height of a full-grown cypress. When the Jebusites saw the wall lower itself for David, they knew it was God's will that Jebu should be joined with the rest of Jerusalem. But the heart of their king had hardened and he refused to abide by the agreement to part with the city peaceably.

Meanwhile word had come to King David that the Philistines were gathering in the Valley of the Giants to march on Israel. David assembled his armies and went out to meet the enemy.

He arrayed his men on the battlefield among a grove of mulberry trees, and commanded them to remain silent, until he gave the word to attack. They stood there waiting for a long time, and the great armies of the Philistines came nearer and nearer. David's men began to plead in whispers that it was time to attack, but the king restrained them. They saw the Philistines appear in an open field; they could hear the sound of the marching feet and the rumble of voices coming nearer and nearer; and soon they could almost hear the breathing of the enemy. Still David held them back.

When the enemy was only four ells away, the king loosed the attack. So startled was the enemy that the men fled in confusion and defeat.

After the battle King David returned to treat with the Jebusites. The report of David's prowess in warfare had reached the king of the Jebusites. His heart softened, and he sold Jebu for six hundred shekels in gold.

Then David gathered a multitude and transferred the Ark from Geba to Jerusalem. As the Ark was carried into the city, David danced before it with his people. Then he began to sing. (David's voice was so sweet that wild beasts left their lairs and came out to listen; birds fell from the air, and water ceased to flow; people forgot their hunger; and the suffering, their pain. In their ecstasy his listeners often did not notice what they were doing and recognized no danger. Most ecstatic were the young women, to whose ears David's voice was as the voice of an angel.) And now that he sang before the Ark great numbers gathered to dance with him in the celebration.

Queen Michal saw the king through the palace windows and was distraught and ashamed. When he returned home she mocked him, saying:

"How the King of Israel displayed his talents today before the serving-girls!"

"My esteem has not been lowered in the eyes of my people," David replied. "For they know that I rejoiced before God at the wedding of the Ark and the people of Israel in the City of Jerusalem."

2. *How David Saved the World*

When King David's workmen began to build the House of God, they dug the drain for the altar very deep and inadvertently lifted the shard on the Mouth of the Abyss. Instantly the Waters of the Deep began to rise to flood the earth. David knew that unless the Mouth of the Abyss were sealed again, the world would be destroyed. He also knew that only a stone with the Ineffable Name upon it could seal the Abyss.

He asked his councilors whether it was permitted to use the Ineffable Name for such a purpose. His councilor Ahithophel refused to advise him, but the others replied:

"Since it is permitted to erase the Ineffable Name, if necessary, to create peace between husband and wife, it must therefore follow that the Ineffable Name may be written to make peace between the Abyss and the world and to to save all mankind."

David lowered the stone with the Holy Name on it sixteen thousand ells, and tightly sealed the Mouth of the Abyss. But it was soon discovered that the earth below had lost its moisture and even the rains were not enough to grow the crops. King David then composed fifteen psalms, and as each psalm was completed, the Waters of the Deep rose one thousand ells. When the Waters reached within a thousand ells of the surface of the earth, he offered thanks to God, Who keeps the ground always moist enough for the crops, and does not allow the Abyss to sink one iota below, or rise one iota above, one thousand ells.

The legend of how King David saved the world from another flood appears in many forms and is attributed to various saints, yet all are based on the eloquent psalmic exclamation: The waters saw You, O God, the waters saw You and were afraid! (*Psalm LXXVII: 16*).

3. *The King Spearmaker*

According to Arabic lore, from the day David was crowned, he vowed to serve the people and sought to carry out their will. He knew that, once he was on the throne, no one would tell him his faults, nor would anyone in the court inform him of the displeasure of the people. The king therefore disguised himself as a beggar once each week and wandered through the market places and villages, asking:

"What think you of King David?"

And each man questioned told what was on his mind or in his heart, yet no one ever recognized the king.

One day King David, disguised as a beggar, met a very old man in a distant village, and asked:

"What think you of King David?"

"He is a just king," the old man replied, "but he profits too much from the treasury of the kingdom. If he were truly righteous he would know that the treasury is for the people; and no one may justly benefit from it — not even the king."

"What can the king do?" asked David.

"He, like all the people, should eat only the bread he earns with his own labor; for no man has a right to the bread of another," answered the old man, who was really the Angel Gabriel.

King David returned home. And after that day he spent several hours daily making spears, so that the bread he ate was earned by his labor and not taken from the people's treasury.

4. David's Councilor

The most honored man in King David's court was a youth named Ahithophel. Though many years younger than the king, he was the Royal Councilor and the king's tutor. Ahithophel was so wise that his forecasts were always the same as those given by the oracles of the *Urim* and *Thummin;* and his knowledge exceeded his wisdom.

The king made no move without his Royal Councilor, and he drank of Ahithophel's knowledge as the thirsty drink at a fresh spring. But the councilor had one fault that outweighed all his virtues and in the end caused his undoing: Ahithophel was insincere. Because King David was humble, the councilor became proud; and because the king sought his advice often, the councilor often tried to withhold it.

The councilor grew vain and began to dream of kingship. "I know more and am wiser than David," thought he. "Why should not I be King of Israel." He began to plot a rebellion against David, and his scheming found a willing ear in Absalom, David's son. The councilor encouraged Absalom to rebel against his father and to plot his destruction, hoping that when Absalom carried out his plan, the people would reject the murderer and select Ahithophel to rule them.

But on the day the shard on the Mouth of the Abyss was disturbed by David's men, Ahithophel permitted his ambition to blunt his wisdom. For when David asked his councilor what to do to prevent another flood, Ahithophel remained silent, thinking: "Now David will be drowned for he does not know what to do to save himself. And when he is dead, I shall close the Mouth of the Abyss with the Ineffable Name and become king in his place." David understood Ahithophel's silence. And when the emergency was over, the king rebuked Ahithophel for endangering the world because of his personal ambition, and cursed him to die by his own hand. The curse was fulfilled. At the age of thirty-three Ahithophel hung himself.

Ahithophel's great knowledge died with him, excepting what he had written down in the *Book of Fortunes*.

5. *General Joab*

Ahithophel, as long as he was faithful, was King David's left hand; General Joab was his right hand. What the general lacked in learning, he made up tenfold in goodness and sincerity.

King David never went to war without Joab at his side. And often Joab insisted on going to war without the king, so that David would have time to study the Holy Law.

Once Joab led his armies against the capital of the Amalekites, whom Saul had failed to destroy. They besieged the city for six months, and in the end had made no breach in the walls. The soldiers asked Joab to give up the campaign and let them return to their wives and their homes.

"If we abandon the siege of the city," said Joab, "we will earn the contempt of the enemy, and it will embolden him to pursue and destroy us."

"What shall we do?" asked the men.

"When night comes, hurl me across the walls. Then wait for forty days. If I do not appear to you by then, you may return home."

Joab was supplied with one thousand gold coins, and hurled across the walls from a sling. He landed in the courtyard of a widow and her daughter.

"I am an Amalekite," Joab told them. "I was taken captive by the Israelites and they flung me over the wall in order to kill me."

He showed the gold coins to the widow and her daughter, and they believed his story. He gave them some of the coins, and they convinced their neighbors.

Joab put on Amalekite clothing and walked about the city undetected. Within ten days Joab had learned the plans of the city and the habits of its people.

Joab found a master swordmaker and ordered a sword, larger and stronger than any the armorer had ever forged. When the sword was completed, Joab took it in his hands to test it, and broke the sword as if it were a shard. Three swords the armorer forged, each stronger and larger than the first, and Joab snapped each in turn. At last the armorer forged a sword sharp as a razor and so strong that even Joab could not break it.

"Whom would you like me to slay with this sword?" Joab asked the swordsmith.

"General Joab," came the answer.

"I am he," Joab replied, and pierced the smith before he could utter his astonishment.

Then Joab went out and on his way met five hundred Amalekite warriors. He engaged them in battle and slew them all. A rumor raced through the streets that the King of Demons, Asmodeus, had invaded the city. Panic struck the people in their homes. Warriors left their posts; and terror reigned in the streets.

Joab climbed a high tower on the walls of the city and commanded his men to storm the gates. And when the city was captured, all the idols and their temples were destroyed, and the high priests were slain. Joab and his men returned to Jerusalem, taking with them the Amalekite king, with a crown of pure gold upon his head. They brought him to King David as a token of their victory.

6. *David and Satan*

King David devoted his days to the service of his people; and his nights, to study and prayer. Over the head of his bed he hung his harp in such a manner that when the north wind blew at midnight through his chamber window, the strings began to vibrate and sing. The king would leave his bed and spend the rest of the night composing psalms.

One night, when he had completed the Book of Psalms, David exclaimed: "Is there another creature on earth who devotes so much of his time to the praise of God, and to proclaim His wonders?"

A frog in the pond outside his window responded: "From sunset until sunrise I sing in praise of my Creator, and I have composed more psalms than in your psalter."

Still proud of his Book of Psalms, David addressed himself to God:

"The people always say 'God of Abraham, Isaac and Jacob' and they never say 'God of David.' Why?"

"Because Abraham, Isaac and Jacob were tried and their faith was not found wanting," said God.

"Then try me, too," David pleaded.

"It shall be as you ask," said God. "And I shall grant you what I did not grant the Patriarchs: for I will tell you in advance that you will be tried through the temptation of a woman."

One day as David sat in his chamber writing a psalm, Satan came into the room disguised as a bird. Its feathers were of pure gold, its beak of diamonds, and its legs of glowing rubies. David dropped his book and tried to catch the bird which he thought had come from the Garden of Eden. But the bird flew out of the window and settled upon the low branch of a tree in a neighboring garden. And under the branch of the tree a young woman was washing her hair.

The king was dazzled by her beauty. Nor could he keep the thought of her out of his mind. When he learned that she was Bath-sheba, the wife of a soldier who was away at war, David sent word to Joab to place that soldier in the thick of battle and to abandon him. After word came that the soldier was dead, David married Bath-sheba, though the king already had ninety-nine other wives.

For this sin David was to repent twenty-two years. Daily he mixed ashes with his bread; daily he wept an hour before he touched food. His son, Absalom, rebelled against him and sought to kill him. And still David's penance was not yet at an end.

7. *The Poor Man's Lamb*

The Prophet Nathan came to King David and said: "There were two men in one city. One was rich and the other poor. The rich man had many flocks and herds, but the poor man had only one ewe lamb which he raised as tenderly as a daughter. Until one day a guest came to visit the rich man. And he, who owned so much, spared his own flock, but killed the poor man's lamb to entertain the guest. Now, tell me, King David, what shall be done to such a man?"

And King David replied in anger: "The man who has done such a thing deserves to die!"

"You are that man!" said Nathan. "For you have been anointed King of Israel, and given wealth, and you have taken to your bosom ninety and nine brides. And you could have whatever your eye saw and your heart desired. Yet you have caused the soldier, Uriah the Hittite, to be slain by the sword of Ammon, that you might take his wife. And you have done this as if you thought that God is deaf and cannot hear, or blind and cannot see. How you have despised His commandment!"

"I have sinned," said David. "I have sinned against the living God!"

"By your sin you have given occasion to the enemies of Israel," said the Prophet Nathan. And he departed from the king's house.

8. *David in the Desert*

David went into the desert to repent. For three years he remained there, and he wept more tears than all of mankind before him. At the end of that time God came to him and said:

"You shall not be forgiven until Uriah has forgiven you."

King David went to Uriah's grave and called: "Uriah, Uriah! Forgive me for my sins against you."

And Uriah called back from the grave: "Who are you to disturb my peace?"

"I am David, and I have come to beg you to forgive my sins against you."

"It is not for me to forgive you," answered Uriah, "but for God to judge between us."

David left the grave, bowed deep in sorrow.

Uriah went up to heaven, and there he saw a palace of great splendor, full of beautiful women, with eyes as black as ravens, preparing for a great feast.

"For whom is all this honor intended?" asked Uriah.

"For him who forgives his brother even though he has been wronged."

"I forgive David his sin against me," said Uriah.

David was told that he was forgiven by Uriah, and he returned home to rule his people, who had felt bereft as long as the king was away.

9. *Gad's Offer*

The Prophet Gad came to King David and said: "You have sinned; and you have sinned again. Yet when the kingdom was stricken with famine, you did not search your heart, but sought the fault in the people. The first year of the famine you suspected the people of idolatry, for which famine is a punishment; but when you investigated, you found out that you were wrong. The second year of the famine you suspected the people of lewdness, for which hunger is the punishment; but when you investigated, you found out that you were wrong. The third year of famine you suspected the people of lacking in charity; but an investigation proved you wrong again. Yet at no time did you blame yourself, nor say: 'The gold and silver I acquired shall be used to feed the hungry.' You saved your wealth to build the Temple. Therefore the Temple shall not be built by you, and you shall still be punished for your transgressions. Which, therefore, do you choose as your punishment, famine or oppression by enemies?"

"I am as a sick man who is asked by his physician whether he chooses to be buried next to his father or next to his mother," said David. "I want neither famine nor the victory of my enemies, for in both cases the people would suffer for my sins. I would rather have a plague that would afflict only me."

As he spoke, an angel afflicted the king with trembling and with cold. His hand could no longer carry the food to his mouth; and he was always chilled as if the marrow of his bones had turned into ice.

10. *David's Death*

Once, in his prayers, King David pleaded with God to reveal to him the day of his death.

"No man may know the time of his last hour on earth," he was told. "But this much you may know: Adam granted you seventy years of his life when you were born, therefore you shall die when you are seventy years old. And the day of your death shall be on a Sabbath."

"Let me die on a Friday," David pleaded, "for I do not wish to die on the Holy Day."

"No man may die before his time for whatever reason," he was told.

"Then let me die on Sunday, following the Sabbath, my last Sabbath on earth."

"Nor can that be granted. For your son Solomon shall rule after you, and no one may rule for another, even to the extent of one day."

After that day David spent every Sabbath in seclusion, praying

and studying the Law. As long as he was in the midst of prayer
and study, the Angel of Death could not cross the threshold into
his chamber.

But one Sabbath day the king heard a great commotion in his
garden and hurried out of his chamber to see what was happening.
He followed the sound, not knowing it was the Angel of Death,
and fell down a stairway. And where he fell, there he lay dead.

David's body could not be moved because it was the Sabbath.
Solomon commanded several eagles to spread their wings over his
dead father and protect the body from the rays of the sun.

11. *King David in Heaven*

When King David's spirit departed from him it went directly
to Paradise. The sun, the moon and the stars, the angels and the
seraphim greeted him. A great throne of fire waited for David,
placed in front of the Throne of Glory, and there the angels seated
him to lead in the praise of God.

And when the Judgment Day arrives, David will be seated opposite God at the banquet for the righteous. Then God will take
the cup of wine and say to Abraham:

"Pronounce the blessing over the wine, for you are the pious of
the world!"

And Abraham will reply: "I am unworthy, for I am also the
father of the Ishmaelites who have kindled Your wrath."

Then God will say to Isaac: "Pronounce the blessing, for you
were bound up as a sacrifice upon the altar!"

And Isaac will say: "I am unworthy, because the children of my
son Esau have destroyed the Holy Temple."

Then God will say to Jacob: "Pronounce the blessing, for your
children brought forth the Twelve Tribes!"

And Jacob will say: "I am unworthy for I was married to two
sisters, and that was later prohibited."

Then God will turn to Moses and say: "Pronounce the blessing,
for you received the Tablets of the Covenant!"

And Moses will say: "I am unworthy, for I was not found worthy to enter the Holy Land."

And God will say to Joshua: "Pronounce the blessing, for you were found worthy to lead Israel into the Holy Land!"

And Joshua will answer: "I am unworthy, for I had no son to follow me!"

Then God will turn to David and say: "Take this cup and sing the blessing, for you are the sweetest singer in Israel!"

And David will take the cup and pronounce the blessing. Whereupon the angels will open the gates of heaven and allow the wicked to ascend from *Gehinnom* to Paradise.

CHAPTER FIFTEEN

King Solomon

1. *Solomon's Wish*

When Solomon was still a small boy, God came to him in a dream and asked:
"If you were given only one wish, what would you choose?"
"Wisdom," Solomon replied without hesitation.
"Why would you choose wisdom?"
"Because without wisdom no treasure is of value; and no pleasure, sweet. Without understanding one cannot tell good from evil, and cannot follow in the ways of God."
"You have chosen well," said God, "for all good things come with wisdom and all treasures are in her hands. But you must promise never to use your gift for anything but peace; and that at the end of your days you will record the value of wisdom in a book so that all succeeding generations will know it is the breath of the power of God."
And Solomon promised.

2. *The Price of a Boiled Egg*

Solomon was eight years old when two men came before his father, King David, for judgment.
"Six years ago," said one man, "we were working in a field. This man, the defendant, was hungry but had no food. He asked me to give him a boiled egg and promised under oath and before witnesses that he would repay me its worth at any time I demanded payment. I demand it now. And I estimate its worth as follows: Had I hatched the egg, I would have had a chicken. Within one

year the chicken would have hatched at least a dozen more. I therefore conclude that this man owes me the price of 12×12×12×
12×12, or 248,832 chickens. And that is what I now demand."

The defendant argued: "He gave me only one egg and now he
demands a fortune and threatens to take all my possessions and
sell me and my sons into slavery."

"You promised under oath and before witnesses to repay this
man the full value of the egg at any time he demanded payment,"
said the king. "There is nothing I can do but award him the judgment."

Solomon, who sat beside his father, asked for permission to
speak.

"You have ruled justly," said the boy. "But you have not set the
time when payment should be made. Therefore I suggest that the
complainant be given some boiled beans to plant in his garden.
And as soon as the boiled beans sprout, payment for the boiled egg
should be made, as ruled."

3. *It Takes a Thief*

In the days when Solomon was very young, three merchants
went on a distant journey. Each night, when they stopped at an inn,
they jointly hid their money so that if a thief reached them in the
middle of the night he would not be able to rob them, for only
the three merchants knew the hiding place. But one morning, when
they came to the hiding place, the money was gone. And each accused the others of the theft.

The merchants brought their case before King David. After
lengthy deliberation the king said: "Clearly one of you is the
thief. But I do not know how to uncover him."

Young Solomon, who was at his father's side, then asked: "May
I tell these men a story?"

"Tell it, my son," said King David.

"There was once a young girl and a boy," Solomon related, "who
lived next door to each other, and in their childhood vowed that
when they grew up neither would marry without the other's consent unless they married each other. In time the boy moved to dis-

tant parts, and when the girl grew up she became engaged to a
man she loved. But she refused to marry until she first obtained
the release from her childhood vow. The girl and her betrothed
traveled to the distant home of her childhood companion, bearing
gold and silver as gifts. The youth released the girl from her vow
and refused to accept any gifts, saying that though he still loved
her, he wanted only her happiness. On the way home the girl and
her companion were waylaid by an old bandit who wanted to rob
the young man of both his betrothed and his money. The girl told
her story to the bandit and pleaded: 'For my sake a young man
controlled his passion and sacrificed his love; cannot you, an old
man, do likewise and receive your reward from heaven?' The thief
was moved by her plea and let them go, touching neither the girl
nor the money."

Solomon paused a moment, then asked the three merchants
before the court: "Which of the three acted most nobly?"

"The girl," said one merchant, "because she was faithful and
did not forget her vow."

"The boy," said the second, "because though he still loved the
girl, he released her from her vow for the sake of her happiness."

"The thief," said the third, "for he could have released the girl
and still have kept the money."

Solomon pointed to the third merchant, saying: "There is the
guilty man. For it takes a thief to admire a thief!"

The man was questioned further and he finally confessed his
guilt.

4. *The Wise Are Not Proud*

Even before Solomon became king he had learned all the languages of man and beast and demon. Since he knew their tongues,
Solomon befriended many strange animals. The lion, prince of
beasts, carried him on his back wherever Solomon wanted to ride;
and the eagle, prince of birds, carried him on his wings wherever
Solomon wanted to fly.

Soon after he became king, Solomon started out on a long journey upon the eagle's wings and, while flying high among the clouds,

exclaimed with pride: "Although I am only twelve years old, I am already a king. And there is no one among mortals as wise as I am, or as full of knowledge and power!"

Whereupon a great storm arose that darkened the skies and threatened to destroy eagle and rider.

"Ruach!" Solomon commanded the gale. "Stop blowing!"

But the wind replied: "I shall stop when you stop boasting of your wisdom and acknowledge that wisdom and power is from the Lord. He gives it and He can take it away."

Solomon repented the folly of his pride and prayed for forgiveness. The storm ceased at once, and the sun shone again.

The eagle and its royal rider flew on until they came over the desolate Valley of the Ants. When the ants saw them coming, they ran to their hiding places for fear of being trampled by Solomon if he alighted in the valley. Solomon asked the eagle to come down gently so that none of the ants would be harmed. And of the ant that had given the order to the others to hide, Solomon asked: "Who are you?"

"I am the Queen of the Ants," the insect replied. "Who are you?"

"I am King Solomon, the wisest man on earth," said he with pride. "Tell me, is your power in your kingdom as great as mine in my kingdom?"

"If you will lift me up on your finger, I will give you your answer," said the Queen of Ants.

Solomon lifted the queen to the level of his eyes, and she said to him: "My power is much greater than yours, for the needs of my subjects are very few; and their industriousness very great."

Then Solomon asked the Queen of Ants many questions; and all her answers pleased him. At last he set her down on a rock and was ready to depart, when the queen said: "I should like to give you a gift by which to remember my kingdom." And she gave King Solomon the greater part of the leg of a locust.

Solomon accepted the gift with humility and mounted the eagle, humbled by the wisdom he had learned from the ant.

From the Valley of the Ants they flew great distances until they came over a craggy island. Here, on the top of a steep cliff, they saw a lofty palace built of shining gold. Solomon asked the eagle to descend near the palace. To his great surprise, there were no guards near it. He walked around the palace three times, but could find no door or gate to enter. The eagle carried Solomon up to the top of the roof, but the king could find no entrance there, nor any sign of life.

Solomon then summoned Ramirat, Prince of Demons, and bade him find someone on the island who could tell him how to enter the palace. Ramirat left, and soon returned with an eagle seven hundred years old.

"What is your name?" asked Solomon. "And do you know who lives in this palace?"

"My name is Elnedod and I have lived here all my life," said the eagle, "yet I have never seen anyone enter or come out of this palace. But I have an older brother who may know."

Elnedod left, and soon returned with an eagle nine hundred years old.

"What is your name?" asked Solomon. "And do you know how I can enter this palace?"

"My name is Eleof and I have lived here all my life," said the eagle, "yet have I seen no door open or close in this palace. But I have an elder brother who may know."

Eleof left, and soon returned with an eagle thirteen hundred years old.

"What is your name?" asked Solomon. "And do you know where the door is that leads into this palace?"

"My name is Eltamar, and I do not myself know where the entrance may be. But when I was very young, my father once told me that on the west side of this palace there is an entrance which the sands and dust of the ages have covered."

Solomon commanded the winds to clear the dust and the sand on the great west wall, and soon he saw a locked gate bearing the inscription:

"No man may enter this palace unless he is a king or prophet. If any such desire to enter, let him dig near the right side of the gate until he finds a chest, and in the chest he will find the key that will open this palace to him."

Solomon unlocked the gate and entered. And he beheld such splendors as no human eye ever beheld before or since. The palace had many halls and chambers, paved with gold and silver, adorned with rubies, emeralds and pearls. In the resplendent halls, each more beautiful than any the king had ever seen or dreamt of, were tablets of gold upon which were inscribed the wills and testaments of the palace occupants of long, long ago.

One tablet read:

"I, Sheddad, son of Ad, reigned over a million provinces, rode on a million horses, ruled over a million vassals, slew a million warriors in fair battle. Yet I could not oppose the Angel of Death."

In another hall, on another tablet, was written:

"How much wisdom I have acquired! How much good food I have eaten! How many stimulating drinks I have consumed! How many fine robes I have arrayed myself in! How much I caused others to fear me! And at last only I was frightened, for my time came to lie beneath the earth!"

Solomon wandered through all the empty halls reading the tablets, each repeating in its own way the vanity of pride and the barrenness of worldly possessions. At last he was ready to leave. And as he went out of the palace, over the door leading to the last gate, he read above the door the words engraved in gold:

"Hurry not, son of man, but walk with dignity, for the world is given from one man to another. And the world endures forever."

Solomon mounted his eagle and flew straight home.

There are innumerable stories of this nature illustrating the wisdom of the young Solomon.

5. *The Site of the Temple*

Solomon's forty-year reign is remembered for many achievements; but the crowning success of his life was the building of the Holy Temple. Yet the site of the Temple was not revealed to Solomon for a long time.

One night Solomon walked across a field belonging to two brothers. One of the brothers was unmarried and poor, and the other had a large family and was rich. That night the king saw that under cover of darkness the rich brother was carrying grain to the poor man's granary, saying: "He is poor and I am rich and he should have some of my grain." And the poor brother was carrying grain to the rich man's granary, saying: "I am alone and he has a large family; he has need for more grain."

Solomon realized that he had at last found the site for the Temple in this field, which was the scene of so much brotherly love.

6. *The Building of the Temple*

For four years Solomon planned the Temple. And when the plans were perfect in every detail, the building began. The building of the Temple started when Solomon was sixteen years old; and he was twenty-three when the building was completed.

The materials for the Temple came from many parts of the world. Wood for the doors was brought from Egypt. Solomon sent Nickmar, the supervisor, to bring the wood to Jerusalem. On the way back a storm arose at sea and the passengers of the ship demanded that the cargo of wood for the Temple be thrown overboard. But when Nickmar demanded to be thrown overboard with the wood, the sea calmed and the cargo arrived safely in Jerusalem.

The stones for the Temple were needed in such large slabs that no human hands could transport them. Angels, disguised as workmen, carried the stones hundreds of miles to Jerusalem. Then the problem of cutting the huge stones arose. It is forbidden to use iron tools in the building of a holy place; and the only other way to cut and fit the stones, Solomon knew, was with the aid of the *shomeer*.

7. *What the Shomeer Was Like*

The *shomeer* was one of the Ten Wonders of the World created on the Sixth Day, expressly for the building of the Temple.

According to some sages, the *shomeer* was a worm the size of a grain of wheat, that had the power to hew down trees and split mountains into slabs of stone. These sages said that the *shomeer* was kept in wool, in the Garden of Eden, until Solomon was ready to build the House of God. Then an eagle was sent to carry it to the builders.

Other sages claim that the *shomeer* was a blue stone, the size of a small jewel. And wherever it was placed, and the Ineffable Name whispered, the rock beneath would break into the desired shape and size. With the *shomeer* the names of the Twelve Tribes were engraved on the precious stones used by the High Priests. But the hiding place of the *shomeer* no one knew, excepting Asmodeus, King of Demons, who lived in the Mountains of Darkness.

8. *How Solomon Obtained the Shomeer*

Solomon dispatched seven messengers to the Mountains of Darkness. The messengers bore chains, on which were engraved the Ineffable Name, with which to bind Asmodeus. They traveled seven months into the Mountains of Darkness, until they found the well where the King of Demons came to quench his great thirst. From their hiding place nearby the messengers saw the demon approach the well, inspect the seal, open it, drink seven hundred barrels of water, then seal the well again.

After Asmodeus left, the messengers drilled an underground passage to the well and replaced all the water with wine. Then they hid again and waited.

The next day Asmodeus came again for a drink. He began to sniff about, suspecting that something was wrong. He inspected his seal on the well; it had not been broken. Then he opened the well and drew out a bucket of wine.

"I will not drink this!" shouted the demon, and the mountains shook as if by an earthquake. "There is a king in Israel who said: 'Look not upon the wine that it is red and sparkles in the glass, in the end it shall bite you like a snake and sting you like an adder!' I shall not drink this wine!"

Asmodeus sat down near the well, and the messengers waited patiently. For seven days they waited. And all this time the demon's thirst burned in his bowels like a thousand fires and his tongue stuck to his palate. When the King of Demons could bear the pain no longer, he drew bucket after bucket of wine to quench his thirst, and soon fell into a drunken sleep.

The messengers came out of their hiding place, chained the

demon with the chains bearing the Name that renders demons powerless, and took him prisoner before Solomon. The king promised Asmodeus he would be released if he would reveal where the *shomeer* was hidden.

"The *shomeer* was given to the Keeper of the Abyss," said Asmodeus. "The Keeper of the Abyss gave it to the mountain cockerel Nagar-Turoh, and Nagar-Turoh has it now."

"Where is Nagar-Turoh?" asked Solomon.

"On top of the highest mountain on earth. From time to time the bird takes the *shomeer* and places it on a high mountain. The mountain splits and forms a canyon. The bird plants wild fruit trees in the crevices so that her young may never be in want of food. Find the nest of the Nagar-Turoh and you will find the *shomeer*."

Solomon released Asmodeus, as he had promised, and sent messengers to the nest of the mountain cockerel. The messengers placed a heavy slab of stone over the bird's nest, and when Nagar-Turoh returned with food for her young, she could not get in. She flew away to the hiding place of the *shomeer* and brought it in her beak to split the stones which rested upon the nest.

Some of the messengers rushed out, blowing trumpets, and frightened the cockerel away, while others picked up the *shomeer* and carried it to King Solomon.

9. *What Happened to the Shomeer*

Not only could the *shomeer* hew trees, split enormous rocks, engrave names on precious stones, and melt brass and copper, but it also brought good fortune to all who used it.

One hundred and fifty thousand workers were engaged for seven years in building the Holy Temple, yet during all that time not one worker was hurt, not one became ill, and not a tool was lost or broken. And all the workers on the Temple were blessed for the rest of their days, and their tools were blessed with them.

When the Temple was completed, Solomon arranged great festivities, knowing that the completion of the Temple also marked the true completion of Creation.

Before the festivities began, Solomon returned the *shomeer* to Nagar-Turoh; the mountain cockerel gave it back to the Keeper of the Abyss; the Keeper of the Abyss buried it in the Bottomless Sea. And from there no one can obtain it excepting the Creator Himself.

10. *The Throne of Solomon*

The Temple completed, Solomon started on the Palace of the Kings. And in the palace he built a throne, second only to the Temple in its splendor.

The throne upon which Solomon sat in judgment was made entirely of ivory, overlaid with gold from India and decorated with rubies and emeralds and other precious stones. Twelve golden lions and twelve golden eagles flanked the throne, golden lion against golden eagle, and six great steps led up to it. On the first step crouched an ox facing a lion; on the second step a wolf faced a lamb; on the third, a leopard faced a goat; on the fourth, an eagle faced a peacock; on the fifth, a falcon faced a cock; and on the topmost, a hawk faced a sparrow. All were wrought in pure gold and symbolized that before a judge, the weak need not fear the strong if they have done no wrong.

Above the throne hung a golden seven-branched candelabrum bearing the images and names of the great in the world up to that time. On the left were Adam, Noah and Moses; on the right were Abraham, Isaac and Jacob; and in the center, occupying the place of honor, was the Prophet of the Gentiles, Job.

Around the throne were placed seventy golden chairs for the Seventy Men of the Assembly. And each chair bore the king's insignia, the dove, signifying: *The Mission of Israel is Peace.*

11. *The Great Hippodrome*

Not far from the palace, Solomon erected a great hippodrome and a track for racing. The hippodrome covered an area of three square parasangs. Inside the hippodrome was a race track nearly four square miles around the oval.

Ten thousand trained youths were kept at the palace for the horse races. All the races, which took place every month, were accompanied by great festivities. And on each day a race was held, each of Solomon's thousand wives prepared a sumptuous banquet in the hope that the king would come and dine with her after the races.

12. *The Report of the Mountain Cockerel*

The fame of Solomon's name reached all the four corners of the earth because he was so wise and so learned. Solomon could speak all the languages on earth. He could converse even with ghosts, demons, furies and all the spirits of darkness. He also knew all the languages of the beasts and the birds, and could command them to reveal their secrets.

Once Solomon commanded all the birds, one of each kind, to appear before him. But when they assembled, the mountain cockerel was found missing. The king sent for the missing bird and demanded an explanation for its absence.

"Your Highness," said the cockerel, "it is a long time since I have eaten my food in sorrow and drunk my water in trembling. For I flew over the world to see whether there is any place over which you are not the ruler. Far to the east I found the city of Kitor in the Kingdom of Sheba where the earth is pure gold, and the trees as the trees of the Garden of Eden. There men wear garlands and know not how to wage wars. They worship the sun; and a woman rules over them. She is lovelier than the moon and purer than the sun, and there is not another woman like her. She rules in justice and they all live in peace. But, alas, they worship idols. If you wish, I shall assemble all the birds and we will fly to Kitor, despoil their land, and bring their idolatrous queen to you in chains."

Solomon would not allow the birds to despoil that land. "If they live in peace, yet worship idols, their virtue outweighs their fault," said he.

He instructed his scribes to send a letter to the Queen of Sheba saying:

From me, King Solomon
To you, Queen of Kitor
Greetings!

Let it be known to you and your nobles that God has appointed me king over beasts and birds, over demons and spirits. All the kings of East and West come to my kingdom to honor me. Therefore I invite you to come to my kingdom to salute me, and I, in turn, will show you great honor. But if you fail to come, I will command the beasts in the field, the birds of prey, and the myriads of evil spirits to slay you in the fields, to choke you in your beds, and to despoil your land.

The mountain cockerel placed Solomon's message upon the queen's heart when she was asleep. On waking, she read the letter to her household and councilors. Then she sent back the following reply:

From me, Queen of Sheba
To you, King Solomon
Greetings!

From the city of Kitor to the city of Jerusalem it is a journey of seven years! But so eager am I to greet you that I will reach your palace in less than half that time.

13. *The Queen of Sheba in Solomon's Court*

The Queen of Sheba gathered her ships and filled them with gold and silver, rare woods and precious stones, a crown inlaid with gems, priceless pearls sealed in cases of onyx, and other treasures without end. Then she selected six thousand boys and girls, all born on the same day, and all famed for their grace and beauty, and she dressed them in purple robes of silk and woolen. All these she sent before her as gifts to King Solomon.

And at the end of three years, the queen arrived in Israel. Solomon sent his servant Benaiah to meet her. Benaiah appeared before the queen like the evening star among the stars, like the lily among the flowers of the field. She descended from her chariot to bow to him, thinking he was King Solomon.

"I am not the king," said Benaiah, "but only one of the servants who stand in his presence."

The Queen of Sheba turned to her men and said: "If such is his lair, imagine the lion!"

Then Benaiah brought the queen to King Solomon on his throne.

"I have heard of your wisdom, and wish to test it," said the queen.

"Wisdom is from God," replied the king. "But ask any question, and I shall try to answer."

The queen asked: "A woman said to her son, 'Your father is my father and your grandfather is my husband; you are my son and I am your sister.' Who was she?"

"Lot's daughter talking to her son," said Solomon.

The queen asked: "Three ate and drank on earth yet were not born of male and female. Who were they?"

"The three angels who visited Abraham."

"What is the land upon which the sun shone only once?"

"It is the land of the sea when the waters were divided for one day by Moses."

"What is it that in a storm at sea goes ahead of all; is the cause of praise for the wealthy; of shame to the poor; honors the dead and saddens the living; is a joy to birds and a grief to fish?"

"Flax," said Solomon. "When woven into cloth it makes a sail for the ship, fine clothes for the rich, rags for the poor, shrouds for the dead. The birds delight in its seed; but the fish are caught in the nets made of it."

"Now, tell me, what is the ugliest thing in the world, and what the most beautiful? What the most certain, and what the most uncertain?"

"The ugliest thing in the world is the faithful turning unfaithful; the most beautiful, the repentant sinner. The most certain thing in the world is death; the most uncertain, one's share in the World to Come."

The queen asked other riddles, and Solomon answered them all. Then she asked for his judgment in many difficult cases, and he gave her the correct answers. She inspected the palace he had built and the order of his household. And finally she said: "When the report about your acts and your wisdom reached me in my land, I did not believe it. Now that I have heard with my own ears and seen with my own eyes, I know that they who reported did you an injustice. For you exceed by far the fame that I have heard."

The next day the Queen of Sheba asked King Solomon: "What does your God do and what has He done since Creation?"

"He determines whose daughter shall marry whose son, forty days after they are born," said Solomon.

"That is no occupation for God," said the queen. "Even I can do that. I sent you three thousand boys and three thousand girls. This very evening I shall marry them all."

And so she did.

The next morning they all came to her with eyes blackened, faces scratched, and tears streaming down their faces.

"We are unhappy," they wailed, "because we are unsuited for each other."

The queen then confessed to King Solomon that there was more to matchmaking than she had realized.

Some say that the Queen of Sheba returned to her kingdom and devoted herself to praise of King Solomon. And some say that having met Solomon, the queen could not bear the thought of living far from him, and she remained in the palace as one of his wives.

14. *The Woman of Sidon*

Solomon, like his father David, often traveled in disguise to learn what the people thought of his rule and how they expected him to increase peace in the world and add glory to Israel.

According to an Arabic tale, once, during his travels in disguise, Solomon met in the kingdom of Sidon a woman whose beauty exceeded the beauty of all his other wives. When he returned to his kingdom he sent for her and made her his favorite queen.

One day the king found her weeping bitterly, and he asked: "What makes your heart so heavy, my queen?"

"I long to see my father," said she.

"Why weep then?" asked Solomon. "Visit your father and your homeland until you are consoled, then hasten back to me."

"No," said the queen deceitfully. "For when I am with my father, I shall be just as sorrowful with longing for you. But if you will order an image of my father to be placed in my chamber, I shall look upon it and be consoled."

Solomon ordered a golden image to be made as specified by the woman of Sidon; and she had the craftsmen fashion her favorite idol. This idol she worshiped. And when Solomon came to her chamber, she asked him to bow to it.

For the love of a woman Solomon became an idolater and pawned his soul to Satan. And for his sin, it was decreed in heaven that Solomon should be punished.

15. *The Three Brothers*

The fame of Solomon's wisdom was so great that nobles from distant lands came to serve in his court, in the hope of learning from him.

Among those who came were three brothers. They served the king for seven years, and when they were ready to leave, Solomon offered them the choice of one hundred gold coins or three rules of wisdom. The two older brothers chose the gold, but the youngest chose the rules of wisdom.

The king said to him:

"When you go on a journey, start out at dawn and turn in for the night before darkness falls.

"Do not attempt to cross a swollen river.

"Never confide in a woman."

The brothers started for home. Late in the afternoon the youngest brother stopped at an inn for the night, but the other two went on. A snowstorm arose, and the travelers perished. The youngest brother found them frozen on the road the next day. He buried his two brothers; took the money they had on them; and went on toward home.

The next day he reached a swollen river where several men, leading asses laden with gold, attempted to cross. Heeding Solomon's advice, the young man waited until the river subsided. Then he crossed and found that the men and their animals had been drowned. He took the gold from the dead animals and went on his way.

When he reached home, everyone wondered where he had obtained his fortune, but he would not tell anyone, not even his own wife. One day, in his cups, he revealed to his wife all that had happened. The next time they quarreled, she cried out: "Do you think you can do away with me as you may have done away with your brothers?"

The two sisters-in-law, who had been eavesdropping, brought the man up for murder — all because he did not follow Solomon's advice.

16. *The Doctor and the Merchant*

There was a doctor in the days of King Solomon learned in the art of healing, who spent every free moment studying to increase his knowledge of cures. Yet the more he learned, the fewer became the number of his patients, and he grew poorer with every passing day. He decided to go to King Solomon and ask him what to do.

On his way he met a merchant who was also going to ask advice from the king. The merchant had a large and thriving business, and yet he was losing money all the time.

The king listened carefully to the doctor's story and then he said: "Go home and be kind to your patients." And he would say no more.

To the merchant the king said: "Get up early in the morning!" And he would say no more.

The two men left the king greatly bewildered and wondered why Solomon was considered so wise.

The merchant went home and rose early the next morning, and he discovered that his servants wasted his merchandise when they were not supervised. Now he understood Solomon's advice.

The doctor went home and discovered that he had been so busy studying that he had paid little personal attention to his patients.

When he showed interest in them, they praised him to their friends, and he became sought after and rich.

17. Solomon's Daughter

One of King Solomon's daughters was the fairest maiden in the whole of Israel, and the king loved her above all his other children. One day the king consulted the stars and learned to his dismay that his daughter was destined to marry a beggar, the son of a beggar.

The king was determined to avoid such a marriage for his daughter. He had a tower built on an island in the sea, surrounded with walls so high that no one could scale them. In that castle Solomon placed his daughter, attended by seventy eunuchs, who permitted no stranger to enter.

The eunuchs taught the princess many languages and many arts; and they indulged her in everything her heart desired, excepting the company of young men. And twice each day the sentinel in the tower raised a white flag as a signal to the shore and as a message to the king that all was well with his favorite daughter.

One bitterly cold night a ragged young man on the verge of death from hunger came near the tower. He looked for shelter from the cold and could find none but the hide and skeleton of an ox. The young man climbed into the shelter of the hide and fell asleep. A bird of prey swooped down and carried the skeleton and the hide to the top of the castle.

Early the next morning the princess opened her chamber window and there before her on the roof was the young man.

"Who are you, and how did you get here?" she asked in surprise.

"I am a Jew from Acco. And a bird brought me up here."

The princess gave him food and clean garments. When he had eaten and changed his clothes he seemed more handsome to her than any prince she had ever dreamt of. And he was gentle. And wise. And learned. And witty. So the princess said to him:

"Will you marry me?"

Since there was no ink in the tower, the young man wrote their marriage contract in his own blood. Then he said:

"May God and the angels Michael and Gabriel be our witnesses!"

When the guards found out that there was a young man in the tower, they sent word to King Solomon. The king called his daughter and asked for an explanation.

"An angel of the Lord brought him to me," she explained. "And he is so handsome and so wise!"

When Solomon learned that the young man was the son of the poorest man in Israel, he exclaimed:

"Blessed be the Lord, Who makes all marriages in heaven. And no man can change His plan."

18. *Solomon the Beggar*

When Solomon objected to his daughter marrying a beggar, he little suspected the fate that was to befall him.

Because Solomon maintained race horses, which is forbidden; because he married many woman, which is forbidden; because he slept when it was time for prayer; and because he grew great in his own eyes, God decided to punish him.

One day Solomon asked Asmodeus, "Wherein lies the greatness of demons?"

"Give me your royal ring, and I will show you," said Asmodeus.

The moment Solomon's ring was on his finger, the King of Demons touched the earth with the tip of one wing, and with the other he reached to heaven. He picked up King Solomon and flung him a thousand miles beyond the borders of Israel. Then the demon disguised himself as Solomon and took over his throne.

Solomon wandered from place to place trying to find someone who would believe that he was the King of Israel. The people only laughed and humiliated him. They thought he was a madman and no one would hire him. Solomon had to go begging for his bread.

His grief was greatest when he met people who had known him as king and now failed or refused to recognize him. Often Solomon fed only on the salt of his tears.

For three years he wandered about. Then he reached Ammon, where he found employment as assistant to the royal cook. Solomon proved so skillful that he was appointed royal chef.

One day, as Solomon prepared a fish for the royal meal, he found in it the ring he had given to Asmodeus. He placed the ring on his finger and was at once transported to Jerusalem.

Meanwhile the Council of Seventy had noticed many strange things about their king, who was really the King of Demons. When Solomon returned they were willing to listen to him. They questioned him and he established his claim. Asmodeus was driven from the land and Solomon resumed his reign.

Solomon understood that he had been punished for his sins. He surrounded himself with scholars and, to carry out his promise to God, wrote the book called *The Wisdom of Solomon*.

19. *A King Is Humbled*

One day Solomon said to God: "You have blessed me with riches beyond count, and the increase of my wealth each day is greater than my needs during all the days of my life. I beg to have the privilege of feeding all the creatures of the earth for one year out of my granaries."

"You have asked for what cannot be granted," Solomon was told.

"Then I beg to be permitted to feed them for one month."

"Nor can that be granted."

"Then I pray to be permitted to feed them for a week."

"That also is beyond you."

Then Solomon cried out: "Surely I am not so unworthy that I will not be allowed to feed them for just one day!"

"Try it for one day," he was told.

Solomon joyfully ordered food to be prepared for all the creatures on earth, each according to its needs.

Thousands of cooks baked and stewed and brewed and boiled and broiled and labored for days. Finally everything was in readiness.

The first guest to come was the Leviathan. He gulped down all the food the king's men had prepared and demanded more.

"What you have eaten," Solomon cried, "was intended for all the living things on earth, and it was to last all day!"

"Is that the way to treat a guest?" asked the Leviathan. "I am hungry. What I have eaten is only one third of what God gives me each day."

Meanwhile all the living things on earth, man and beast and birds on wing, came to the king's empty tables and clamored for food.

Solomon sat humbled before all his guests and cried out:

"How beggarly is man's generosity beside the bounty of heaven! The hands of men are empty; but when God's hands are opened all that lives is sustained. I am humbled. And I have learned how far I erred in the knowledge of God!"

20. Solomon's Many Names

King Solomon had many names: He was known as *Jedidioh*, for he was the friend of God; he was known as *Ben*, for he was the builder of the Temple; he was known as *Ithiel*, for God was his witness; he was known as *Yokeh*, because he ruled over all, including the demons. But he is remembered as *Solomon*, because he ruled in peace, and increased peace in the world.

CHAPTER SIXTEEN

The Prophet Elijah

1. *The Reed in the Sea*

King Solomon fell in love with a beautiful Egyptian princess and asked her to marry him.

"What will you give me as a wedding gift?" asked the princess.

"I will close the gates to the city of Jerusalem," said the king, "and all who enter shall pay a toll. And that toll will be your gift."

As the words left King Solomon's lips, the Archangel Gabriel came down and planted a reed in the sea. About this reed the earth gathered. In time it became an island. Upon the island arose the city of Rome, whence came the destruction of the Temple built by Solomon.

When the toll gates to Jerusalem were installed the people began to grumble, even though Solomon had brought them peace, had built the Temple, and magnified the name of Israel among the nations.

Then the Egyptian princess, beautiful daughter of King Shishak, whom Solomon proclaimed his favorite wife, brought a thousand musicians and instructed them to play soft music when the king came to her chamber. And above her bed she hung a canopy studded with diamonds that sparkled like stars in the sky. The sweet music lulled the king to sleep. And when he wakened and saw the sparkling of the jeweled stars, the princess whispered that the night was still young.

While King Solomon slept, with the keys to the Temple under his pillow, the Temple services were delayed, and the reed Gabriel had planted, grew.

The people began to denounce their king, whose pleasure seeking caused neglect of God, and many talked of secession and of establishing a kingdom of their own. And that is how it came to pass that the Kingdom of Israel became divided into two: Judah in the south; and Israel in the north.

2. A Kingdom Divided

When Solomon died, King Shishak of Egypt came to Jerusalem to claim his daughter.

"And while I am here," said he, "I also want to take back all the treasures the Israelites carried off with them when they left Egypt."

"But that was five hundred years ago," the Jews protested.

"That only increases your debt," said Shishak, who was a usurer and a wicked man. "If you will not pay me willingly, I shall have to take it by force."

And he did. He brought an army, conquered Jerusalem, and carried off everything of value that could be transported, including King Solomon's throne and all the king's treasures.

The kingdom of the north and the kingdom of the south made alliances with their idolatrous neighbors, and to please their new allies, the people of Judah and of Israel honored their idols, adopted witchcraft and followed in their ways. And before long the people of Israel even invited Ahab, King of Samaria, to rule over them.

3. Ahab Meets Elijah

King Ahab, who ruled over no less than two hundred and fifty-two kingdoms, was so rich that each of his one hundred and forty children lived in a separate ivory palace. Throughout the world Ahab was renowned for his wealth; but as soon as he became King of Jerusalem he came to be even better known for his wickedness.

One day King Ahab went to Hiel, the commander in chief of his armies, to condole with him on the loss of a son in battle, and in Hiel's home he met a stranger who called himself Elijah, and said he was a Tishbite. The stranger rebuked King Ahab for establishing image worship in Israel.

"Not as you believe do I believe," Ahab told the stranger. "For Moses said that God would let no rain fall if Israel worshiped idols. Yet I, King of Israel, worship many idols and the rain falls nevertheless."

"Be it then as you say!" Elijah replied. "From this day forth, by the God of Israel, there shall be no rain nor dew but according to my word."

Ahab laughed at Elijah's words.

But a week passed and then a month; and the months lengthened to a year; and two years passed; and three. And still there was neither rain nor dew in Israel after Elijah's words. Famine gripped the land, and King Ahab blamed Elijah for causing the drought and vowed to kill him.

Elijah fled to the desert.

4. *Four Signs in the Desert*

Elijah wandered in the desert, wondering how long he could survive without food or water. One day he sat down in the shade of a juniper bush and prayed the Lord to let him die. Then he stretched out and fell asleep. When he awoke an angel stood before him offering food and water.

"Eat and drink," said the angel, "for you have a long journey before you."

"Where am I going?"

And the angel replied: "Wherever the spirit moves you."

After he had eaten, Elijah wandered on through the desert for forty days and forty nights without food or water, yet he felt neither hunger nor thirst. At the end of forty days, Elijah found himself in the cave where God had first revealed Himself to Moses.

An angel appeared at the entrance to the cave and asked: "What are you doing here, Prophet Elijah?"

"Israel is ruled by the High Priests of Baal and the prophets of God are put to death," Elijah answered.

"Why are you not with the people in their time of need?" asked the angel.

"The people, too, are full of sin and their afflictions are the just punishment for their deeds," said Elijah.

Then the angel said to him: "Arise and go up to the top of Mount Horab. When you reach the summit a storm will arise that will uproot mountains and crush the boulders — but the wind will not be God; then an earthquake will shake the earth to its foundations — but the earthquake will not be God; then a fire will come down that will melt the iron from its ore — but the fire will not be God; then you will hear a still small voice. And the Voice will be God."

(When these things came to pass, Elijah understood that he had been shown the four stages of man's destiny: man's life on earth is as fleeting as the wind; the day of his death is like the earthquake that shakes the foundation; like the fire is his trial; and like the still small voice will be his Last Judgment.)

As Elijah stood with his head bowed and his face covered, God said to him:

"I am as a father, and the people as My children. None may speak evil of the children without shaming the father, even though the father may know the children to be full of faults. Therefore, since you have spoken against My children, go and find Elisha, the son of Jehosophat, and anoint him prophet to take your place. Then return to My people."

And Elijah obeyed.

5. Jezebel and the Prophets

King Ahab had a wife who was so wicked that though she died nearly three thousand years ago people still say "as wicked as Jezebel." If she hated a man, though he committed no crime, she decreed his execution. Then she ordered the execution of all his friends so that there would be none to avenge him.

The man Queen Jezebel hated most was the Prophet Elijah. And when he fled to the desert, the queen ordered that two hundred of his friends, each a prophet in his own right, should be arrested and executed.

The person charged to carry out the queen's order was a pious man named Obadiah. He hid the prophets in two caves so that even if one group were discovered, the other group might be saved. Then he informed the queen that the prophets were out of the way. But Obadiah's troubles had just begun. For although he had succeeded in hiding the prophets he did not have enough money to buy food for them and they were in danger of perishing from hunger. Obadiah went to a rich man, named Jehoroam, and borrowed money to buy food for the prophets, but in return he had to promise to pay a high rate of interest and sign away his two sons as security.

6. *The Miracle of the Pitcher*

After Obadiah's death, Jehoroam came to the widow and demanded payment. Since she was very poor and unable to repay the money, he threatened to sell her two sons as slaves. The widow in her distress went to Elijah the Prophet and asked him what she should do.

"What have you of value?" asked Elijah.

"Nothing," said the widow. "My creditors have taken everything, excepting a worthless clay pitcher in which I keep a little olive oil."

"That is enough," said Elijah. "Go home and borrow from all your neighbors casks and tubs and urns and vats and crocks and flasks, and any vessel you can get. Then pour the olive oil into them."

"But I have only a few drops of oil that barely cover the bottom of the pitcher," the widow protested.

"Do as I have advised you," said Elijah.

The widow went home and did as she was told. When her two sons returned from work they found their mother surrounded by a large assortment of vessels and every conceivable container, each filled to the brim with olive oil from her pitcher, out of which the stream still flowed.

The next day the widow sold the oil. She repaid her husband's debts and had enough money left for her and her sons to live without want for the rest of their days.

7. *Elijah and the Informer*

The Prophet Elijah had a friend, named Joshua, who was a very learned man. One day a man eluding the officers of the law sought refuge in Joshua's home. The officers threatened to kill the person who had given refuge to the fugitive, if he did not come forward and reveal the man's whereabouts.

Joshua then informed the officers where the fugitive had been hiding.

After that Elijah stayed away from Joshua's home and shunned him in the street.

One day they met and Joshua asked: "Why do you avoid me, Elijah?"

"I do not wish to associate with an informer," Elijah replied.

"He committed a crime," Joshua protested.

"Is your blood redder than his?" asked Elijah.

Joshua quoted from the Law to justify his conduct. But Elijah replied:

"That is the Law; but more is expected of the learned and the pious. Others might have been right in doing as you did; but you, Joshua, should have preferred death to becoming an informer."

And he never spoke to Joshua again.

8. *The Poor Man's Cow and the Rich Man's Treasure*

One day a fervent disciple asked Elijah for permission to accompany the prophet on one of his many journeys.

"You may come with me," said Elijah, "if you promise not to ask any questions about anything I do. For as soon as you ask for an explanation, we must part company."

The young man promised and they started on their way.

As night fell they came to the house of a poor man whose only possession was a cow. The man and his wife received Elijah and his young friend gladly, gave them food to eat and a comfortable place in which to sleep.

Before they left in the morning, Elijah prayed that the poor man's cow should die. The disciple was surprised at the prophet's prayer, but he kept his promise and did not ask any questions.

The next night they stopped at a mansion. The rich man paid no attention to his guests, offered them nothing to eat or drink, and sent them to sleep in the barn.

As they were leaving the next morning, Elijah noticed a wall, near the house, that had crumbled away. Elijah prayed that the wall repair itself; and the wall rose before them complete and whole. Again they went on their way. And again the disciple refrained from asking questions.

The next day they came to a magnificent temple, with pews of gold and pews of silver. But none of the worshipers invited the wayfarers to their home. They went on their way and Elijah prayed that all the worshipers should become leaders. The disciple's bewilderment grew, but again he refrained from asking questions.

At the next town they reached all the people were friendly and welcomed the strangers, offering them food and drink. When they had rested and were ready to leave, Elijah prayed that God should give them one leader.

The disciple could contain himself no longer and asked: "Where is the justice of your prayers, Elijah?"

And Elijah answered: "The poor man's wife was destined to die the day we left them, and I prayed to God to accept the cow as a vicarious sacrifice. Under the crumbling wall of the rich miser was hidden a treasure of gold which he would have discovered had he rebuilt the wall himself. The grudging worshipers in the temple will all become leaders and be ruined by many disputes. But the inhabitants of this good town, united under one wise leader, will always prosper."

"Now," said the disciple humbly, "I see that there is always justice in God's acts, even when the evildoers seem to prosper."

"Yes," said Elijah. "And now, also, since you have asked for an explanation, we must part company."

9. *Two Wishes That Came True*

One day the Prophet Elijah, in the guise of a beggar, approached a rich man in the market place and asked for alms. The rich man, who was a miser, turned him away.

Elijah then approached the man's brother, who was very poor.

The poor man gave him some coins and invited the stranger home to share his meager meal. Elijah joined in the meal with the poor man and his wife, and before leaving he said to them:

"May God bless you! And may the first act you do be blessed and continue until you cry out: 'Enough!'"

Elijah left and the poor man took out his purse to see if he had enough money to buy a loaf of bread. There were only two copper coins in the purse. He sighed and wished that he had another coin. At once the coins in the purse doubled in number. He took the coins out, and still there was another coin left. All day long and all through the night he kept taking the money out of his purse, and always there was another coin. Finally he shouted: "Enough!" For he now wanted to enjoy his blessing.

When the rich man saw his brother again he was astonished to learn about his newly acquired wealth and where it came from. The miser hurried to the market place in search of the old beggar, and when he found him, brought the old man home to a great feast.

The Prophet Elijah shared the meal with the miser and his wife, and when he was ready to leave he said to them:

"May God bless you! And may the first act you do be blessed and continue until you cry out: 'Enough!'"

"Come," said the avaricious man to his wife as soon as Elijah had gone, "bring out the purse with the gold coins and we shall amass a fortune the like of which no one has ever seen since the beginning of time."

The rich man took the gold coins out of the purse and laid them on the table. Then he looked into the purse. And there was another gold coin. When he took that one out, there was still another. Soon the table was covered with shining gold pieces, and still they kept piling up, one by one. When the table could hold no more coins and they began to gather in heaps on the floor about their feet, the tired wife said:

"I am faint from hunger. Don't you think we have en—"

"Stop!" the husband shouted in anger. And he went on adding gold piece to gold piece all through the hours of the night and all through the hours of the next day. Night came again and still the rich man whispered:

"Only one more! Only one more!"

Several days later the brother came to the house and found the miser and his wife dead, buried in gold pieces.

And that was how the Prophet Elijah taught that a good heart is worthier than gold; and that a greedy person digs his own grave with his greed.

10. *A Share in the World to Come*

One day, when the Prophet Elijah was standing in the market place, a friend of his came up to him and asked:

"Is there anybody in this multitude who will have a share in the World to Come?"

Elijah looked about him and with a sigh he answered: "No."

Then he looked about again and pointed to two men who had just entered the market place and were making their way through the crowds. "Those two will have a share in the World to Come."

"What is their occupation and what have they done to deserve it?" asked Elijah's friend.

"They are clowns," Elijah replied, "and when they see people troubled in mind or heavy with sorrow, they make them laugh; and when they meet people who quarrel, they make peace between them."

11. *Elijah and the Angel of Death*

Elijah's fame as the healer of the sick, the enricher of the poor, and the expounder of God's justice became known throughout the land. He brought about the destruction of the High Priest of Baal; he predicted the violent death of Queen Jezebel; his prayer brought drought as a punishment for his people, and the rain did not fall for three years; and when he finally prayed for rain, rain fell in abundance.

Then the time came for Elijah to depart from the earth. With his disciple, Elisha, he crossed the Jordan into the desert. There, where there was nothing but sand about them, he asked Elisha to pour water on his hands. Elisha held out his hands and a stream of water began to flow from each of his fingers. As Elijah washed his hands, steeds of flame drawing a chariot of fire came down from heaven and stopped before the prophet and his disciple.

Elijah entered the chariot of fire, but Samael, Angel of Death, blocked the way to heaven, saying: "I have been given power over all mankind. And no soul can leave the earth unless it leaves with me."

A Voice came from heaven, saying: "At the creation of heaven and earth it was decreed that the Angel of Death shall have no power over the Prophet Elijah."

"After this," the Angel of Death complained, "other men will ask that what was done for Elijah shall be done for them."

"Elijah is unlike other men. For it is within his power to banish even the Angel of Death from the world."

Samael stooped so that the prophet could pass over his back, and Elijah rose to heaven, where the angels welcomed him.

(Elijah's marvelous deeds on earth did not end with his ascent to heaven. To this day he comes down to earth to perform his deeds disguised as a beggar, as a physician, as a wayfarer, as a court official, or even as a common thief, if the circumstances demand it. And, of course, if he wishes, he can see without being seen, he can hear without being heard. He speaks every language on earth, and knows every law in every land. And though he can be as stern as he was with Ahab and Jezebel, he appears more often to comfort and to heal, to help in time of need and to counsel the perplexed who seek to do what is just and merciful.)

12. *A Good Wife Is a Good Home*

There was a rich man once who lost his fortune, yet he was not downcast.

"I have a good wife," said he, "and she is my fortune."

He went out cheerfully to work as a farmhand to earn his bread. As he was plowing in the field one day, an old beggar came by and asked:

"Is the work hard, my son?"

"Our forefathers in Egypt worked harder, and they were better men than I."

"What makes you think they were better?" asked the stranger.

"They were found worthy to live in the days of Moses and Aaron, and we live in the days when the spy and the thief accumulate riches but the honest man earns only starvation."

"Tell me," said the old man, "if you were offered seven years full of wealth and plenty, would you want them now or at the end of your life?"

"That I cannot decide by myself," said the man.

"Why not?" asked the stranger.

"I am married," the man replied. "Whatever I choose, my good wife will have to share with me. It is therefore her right also to share in my decisions."

That evening, after the children had been put to bed, the man told his wife of the old man in the field and the question he had asked.

"I would want those seven years now," said his wife. "For if they came at the end of our lives, we would know the end was near and that would taint every happy day with sorrow."

"You are a wise woman," said her husband, "and only your good looks exceed your good sense."

The next day the old man appeared in the field and repeated his question.

"If we had the choice, we would want those seven years now," said the man.

"Good," replied the old man, and he disappeared.

On his way home from work that evening, the man was met by his wife, full of joy.

"The children were playing in the courtyard," she told him, "and they found a heap of gold beneath the ashes."

The next seven years were prosperous ones and the man and his wife devoted them to helping the widow and the orphan, to sending children of the poor to school, to visiting the sick and to comforting the bereaved.

One day the man was in the market place and saw again the old man who had appeared to him in the field.

"The seven years have come to an end," said the old man, "and I have come for the wealth which the Lord lent to you."

"I did not accept your offer without first consulting my good wife," said the man. "May I consult her now that you have called for the return of the wealth?"

"Go and ask her, my son, and bring me your answer tomorrow at this very hour and this very place."

That evening the man said to his wife: "Supposing the money found by the children was really money lent to us for seven years by Elijah the Prophet, and supposing he were to call for it now, what would you say to him?"

"I would say to him that if he can find people who will do more good with it, they are certainly welcome to it."

And that was the answer the man gave to the stranger the next day in the market place.

"I will go in search of them without delay," said the old man, "and as soon as I find them, I will return for the money."

He disappeared and the good man never saw him again.

13. *Miracles Are Not for the Wicked*

There was once a poor shoemaker who was so good that his neighbors believed he was one of the Thirty-Six for whose sake the world is preserved.

One bitterly cold day a young boy came to him with his only pair of shoes that were completely worn out. The boy explained that he must take his sick mother's place at the market, to earn food for the family. The shoemaker took the shoe for resoling. He had no leather, nor money with which to buy any. So he took off his own shoes, tore off the soles and placed them on the poor boy's shoes.

The following day a stranger came in to the shoemaker and ordered a pair of sandals.

"I will pay you two shekels now," said the stranger, "and the rest when the sandals are ready."

The shoemaker put one shekel aside for leather and with the other he went out to buy food for the Sabbath.

"Here is a silver shekel," he said to the fish dealer, "and give me half a shekel's worth of carp."

The fish dealer took the coin and laughed. "I am growing old, but I can still tell the difference between a silver shekel and a gold daric."

The shoemaker looked at the coin; it was a gold daric. He bought a shekel's worth of fish and took nine silver shekels in change.

At the baker's, where he went to buy Sabbath loaves, the same thing happened. Then he bought wine, and meat, and fruit. And each time he took out a silver shekel from his pocket it turned into a gold daric in his hand.

The shoemaker went home laden with food and his pockets bulging with money. He and his wife prepared a great feast for the poor and gave a silver shekel to each of their guests. But for every shekel they gave away, a gold daric took its place in their purse. Soon they had so many gold darics that it required a large chest to keep them in.

The news of the gold darics reached the king and he sent the Royal Treasurer with a hundred soldiers to confiscate the shoemaker's gold. But when the treasurer opened the chest he could see no gold. The chest was full of silver shekels.

"Gold or silver," said the treasurer, "I was sent to bring it to the king and that I will do."

On the way to the palace, the treasurer said to his men: "I wonder why the king wants to bother with silver coins!" He opened the chest again, but he could see no silver in it. The chest was full of copper gerahs. He would have abandoned the chest right there, but he feared he might arouse the king's suspicion.

He brought the chest before the king, and opened it at the royal command. Not a copper coin was to be seen. The chest was full of lead.

"Return this to the shoemaker," the king commanded, "and tell him the king never covets anything that belongs to a subject."

The chest was taken back with the king's message. But when the shoemaker opened it, there again were all the gold darics.

When the stranger came for his sandals the shoemaker told him all that had happened.

"That only goes to prove," said the stranger, "that miracles do happen, but not for the benefit of the wicked."

Then he disappeared.

14. *Who Is Elijah?*

When Elijah first appeared on earth, people asked: "Who is this prophet?" When he ascended to heaven in a chariot of fire, people wondered again. And when he began to reappear on earth on his varied missions, there was speculation once more about Elijah.

It is believed that Elijah is an angel who implored God for permission to make himself useful on earth to the sons of men. His request was granted with the provision that half of his time would be spent in heaven, recording the deeds of men and the chronicles of the world.

Besides his missions of mercy on earth and his duties as chronicler in heaven, Elijah weaves the prayers of the worthy into garlands to be placed on the Throne of Glory.

For Elijah's name in heaven is Metatron. And Metatron is the only angel so honored in the eyes of God that he is permitted to remain seated while recording the merits of the righteous. And he is the only angel who assists God in teaching the young wisdom.

In the entire range of Biblical folklore, there is not another character who stimulated the folk imagination more than Elijah. Myriads of wonders and miracles are attributed to him; and when misfortune overtakes a good man, he says: "If the Prophet Elijah were only here he would interpret the meaning of my woes, for he taught us to understand the justice of His ways."

CHAPTER SEVENTEEN

The Age of Prophets

1. *Elisha Heals a Spring*

Elisha was found worthy to witness the appearance of the chariot of flame and the horses of fire that carried the Prophet Elijah to heaven. As Elisha bowed in grief and in prayer, Elijah's mantle slowly floated down from the skies and fell upon his shoulders.

Elisha arose from his prayers and went toward the Jordan. As he neared, the waters piled up on each side to the height of the highest mountain, and Elisha crossed over on dry land.

He went up to Jericho, where the people were perishing from thirst because their wells had become polluted. A handful of wicked merchants were selling good water in bottles, at prices only the rich could afford. And the poor suffered pains of thirst greater than the pangs of hunger.

Elisha commanded the springs to become clean again, and he turned in wrath upon the wicked merchants, whose very names exuded an evil odor. The prophet cursed them with a bitter curse, and as the words passed his lips a forest suddenly appeared where no forest had been before, and hungry bears rushed upon the evil merchants to devour them.

The prophet prepared to go on his way, but he was stricken with an illness, and lay helpless upon his bed. And as he lay ill, he learned that he was being punished for the curse he had issued in wrath. And he received a warning:

"Only because of your great pity for the poor are you spared, and the spirit of prophecy will not forsake you. But the spirit of prophecy cannot for long reside in an angry man."

2. *Shonamith of Shonem*

Elisha, like most prophets of his time, traveled over Israel and Judah to urge the people to turn from evil and to instruct them in the ways of righteousness. Elisha also moved from place to place because his face was so radiant that when a woman beheld him she would die from longing. The prophet concealed himself in caves and on mountaintops, and never appeared before a woman unless his face was partly covered.

One day Elisha came to the city of Shonem. Here lived Shonamith, sister of Abishag, who had comforted King David in his old age. Shonamith and her husband, Iddo, invited the prophet to rest at their home. And each time Elisha and his servant, Gehazi, came to Shonem, they stayed there.

One day the good woman said to her husband: "The holy man, Elisha, comes often to our city. Let us build him a room on top of our house, so that when he comes to Shonem he will have a place of his own to live in."

The next time Elisha came to Shonem and saw the place which had been built for him, he said to Iddo and Shonamith:

"I should like to repay you for your kindness."

"What we did for you, we did not do for recompense."

"Shall I speak for you to King Jehoash or his councilors?"

"We live among our own and need no favors from the king," they answered.

When they had left, Elisha turned to his servant and said: "I wish I could think of something that Iddo and Shonamith would like to have."

"I know what that would be," said Gehazi. "They would like to have a son. But then Iddo is old and only three paces from the grave."

"Call Shonamith," said Elisha.

Shonamith came and stood in the doorway. Without turning or looking up, Elisha said:

"One year from today you will hold a son in your arms, and he will put his arms about your neck."

"You are a holy man and should not ridicule me."

"What I foretell will come to pass," said Elisha.

"All my life I have wanted a son. And yet I would rather not have one, if he should be destined to die young."

"I will pray for a son for you and I will pray that he may be given many days."

A year later Shonamith gave birth to a son. But when the boy was seven years old he went out one morning to his father in the field at the time of the gathering of the harvest. And he said to his father:

"My head, father! My head hurts so much!"

Iddo asked a worker in the field to carry the boy back to his mother. Shonamith took the boy upon her lap and held him there until noon. And then the boy died.

She carried the dead child to Elisha's room. Then she sent word to Iddo and told him that she was going to Mount Carmel to find the holy man. But she did not tell her husband that their son was dead.

When Elisha saw her coming, he went to greet her and asked: "Is all well with you?"

Shonamith fell at his feet in tears and answered: "I would rather not have had a son than see him dead so young!"

Elisha held out his rod to Gehazi and said: "Take up my rod and hasten to Shonem. And place it upon the child."

Gehazi took the rod and said: "I will go as you command me. But since when can a rod resurrect the dead?"

Elisha, hearing Gehazi's doubts, took the rod away from him and went himself to Shonem. When he reached the room where the dead child lay upon the bed, he locked the door, sat down beside the boy, and prayed for a long time. Then he stretched himself out on the cold body of the boy, his mouth on the boy's mouth, his eyes on the boy's eyes, his warm hands on the boy's cold hands. And soon warmth returned to the child. But there was no breath in his nostrils.

Elisha paced the room, back and forth, praying. His prayer was interrupted by the sound of a sneeze. Seven times the child sneezed, then opened his eyes.

Elisha sent for Shonamith and said to her: "Take your son, and may his days be many."

3. *Jonah ben Amittai*

In the days of King Jehoash of Israel, Jonah ben Amittai, a disciple of Elisha's, prophesied the destruction of Jerusalem and all its inhabitants for their wickedness, unless they repented. The people listened to the voice of the prophet and the city and its people were spared. But Jonah was nicknamed "the false prophet," because what he foretold had not come to pass.

Some time later God commanded Jonah to go to the city of Nineveh and warn its inhabitants that unless they reformed their ways, they and their city would be destroyed.

Jonah gathered his family and his Nazarene disciples and started out on the journey to the land of Syria. Within sight of Nineveh, Jonah pitched his tent and ordered his wife and his followers to remain behind while he went alone to warn the inhabitants of the city.

"If forty days pass and I do not return," Jonah told his wife, "you will know that I have met the fate of many other prophets enlisted in the service of the One God."

Jonah wrapped himself in a coarse hair-mantle, took his staff in hand, and walked barefoot toward Nineveh. On reaching the city he called out in a loud voice, so loud that all could hear him:

"Banish your idols and turn from your evil ways, or God will destroy you and your city!"

The citizens of Nineveh mocked him, threw stones at him, and tried to drive him out of their city. But Jonah suffered all the insults and the blows, yet would not leave, and he continued to preach repentance as he had been commanded to do by God.

The King of Nineveh heard of the stranger and ordered him placed in a dark and filthy prison for forty days and nights, without food or water, for disturbing the people's peace.

At the end of forty days, when the king's men came to the prison, they found Jonah praying by the light of a lamp brighter than the sun, and his cell was fragrant with the aroma of fruit.

"This man is nothing but a sorcerer and a magician," said the king. "Drive him out of our kingdom and, if he ever returns, imprison him forever."

Jonah was told of the king's warning and taken outside the city gates.

4. *The Curse of the Forty Colors*

As Jonah rested outside Nineveh he fell asleep. God came to him in a dream and said:

"Jonah, return to Nineveh and command the people to listen to your words. If they refuse, the first day their skins shall turn as yellow as the crocus; and if their ears are still deaf to your words the second day, their faces and their skins shall turn as scarlet as the cochineal; and the next day they will turn black as pitch; and I will make the color of their skin change every day for forty days, until they repent."

And so it happened.

When the citizens of Nineveh saw their skins turn yellow and red and black and purple and green, day after day, each day a different color, they ran to the king and begged him to save them. Then they repented, and prayed to God, and asked to be forgiven.

Meanwhile Jonah had left Nineveh to join his wife and his disciples, and on the way he met Satan disguised as a shepherd tending his flocks.

"Where are you from?" asked Jonah.

"I am from Nineveh," said the shepherd.

"And how does it go with your people in Nineveh?"

"It goes well with them," said Satan. "Of late a madman arrived in our midst and prophesied evil for forty days, and for forty days he worked magic with colors. But his words were as the wind, and no evil befell the people."

"And what do the people say of this prophet?" asked Jonah.

"They say he is a false prophet and he is the laughingstock of Nineveh."

Jonah returned home grieved and downcast.

5. *Jonah Flees*

Some time later the men of Nineveh forgot their repentance and again indulged in sin and wickedness. God ordered Jonah to return to the Syrian city and once again warn the people.

And Jonah thought: "I know what will happen. I will go there. I will warn the heathen. They will repent again. And I will be in disgrace and called a 'false prophet.' Since God dwells in Israel, I will run away to Tarshish. The Lord will not follow me with His commands, and I shall know peace."

Jonah fled to the seaport of Joppa and boarded a ship leaving for Tarshish. When the boat was far out at sea a storm arose, and it seemed as if the ship would break in two.

There were passengers on the boat from seventy different nations, and they began to pray in seventy languages to seventy different gods. Only Jonah did not pray. He slept a sound sleep in the midst of the storm.

When the captain of the ship found Jonah fast asleep he woke him in anger: "We toss between life and death, and you sleep! Pray to your God or we will throw you overboard."

All the people on the ship prayed, but the fury of the storm did not diminish.

"There is one among us whom his God wishes to destroy," said the passengers. "Let us cast lots to find the culprit and throw him overboard."

"I am the culprit," said Jonah. "Throw me into the sea and you will all be saved."

The passengers would not believe him.

"Lower me into the water," said Jonah, "and you will be convinced."

They lowered Jonah until the water rose to his waist, and the storm ceased. They raised him out of the water and the storm redoubled its fury. They lowered him several times, and each time the same thing happened.

The passengers then said to God: "He is Your prophet and You must know why You want him thrown into the sea." And they cast Jonah overboard.

6. Jonah and the Whale

But that was not the end of Jonah. When the passengers let go of him he fell, not into the waters, but into the mouth of a mammoth whale. This was the whale especially created on the Fifth Day of Creation to serve the Prophet Jonah. Its mouth was like a gate, its tongue like a carpet; a precious stone lit up every part inside the fish; and walks led from part to part. If he wished, Jonah could walk into its eye and look out into the ocean.

"Today is the day," said the whale sadly, "when the Leviathan will devour me."

"Take me to him," said Jonah, "and I will rescue you."

When they came near the Leviathan, Jonah said: "I have come to see you, King of the Fish, for when the Messiah comes you will be served at the great feast."

The Leviathan turned and raced away.

"I have saved your life," said Jonah to the whale. "Now take me to see all the wonders of the deep."

7. *The Wonders of the Deep*

The whale took Jonah to see everything in the Great Okeanus that surrounds the earth. He showed him where Korah and his followers sank; where the Jews crossed the Red Sea; the underwater entrance to *Gehinnom*; the mouth of the river from which all the oceans flow; and the River of Youth at the gates of the Garden of Eden.

For three days Jonah traveled in the whale to see the wonders of the sea and they so engrossed him that he forgot his daily prayers.

"He is too comfortable where he is," said God.

Instantly another and even larger whale appeared and called: "In the name of God, give up the prophet you harbor. If you fail to obey, I shall devour you."

The whale spat Jonah out and the female whale swallowed him. Here Jonah was crowded. It was dark inside. And he could not see through the whale's eyes.

Jonah prayed: "Creator of the World, how foolish was I to think that I could escape You. Heaven is Your seat and the earth is Your footstool. Not a deed nor a thought escapes You. Your abode is not Israel but the Universe. Help me, O Lord, and deliver me from my prison in the deep. You who can mete out death to the living and life to the dead, help me!"

God commanded the whale to spit Jonah out. This she did with such force that he landed nine hundred and fifty-six miles inland from the nearest shore.

"Now," said God, "go to Nineveh and warn the people to repent."

8. *The Power of Repentance*

When the passengers of Jonah's ship saw him in Nineveh and heard how he had been saved, they renounced idolatry and took their families to Jerusalem to worship the One God.

And the rest of the people of Nineveh listened to Jonah and repented. Jonah marveled at the power of repentance. And he learned that repentance was created before the Beginning.

(There are seven days in the week; and seven things were created ages and ages before the Universe:

(*Wisdom, Paradise, Gehinnom, the Two Thrones of Glory, the Sanctuary, the Name of the Messiah, and Repentance.*

(*Wisdom* was incorporated in the Five Books of Moses as a road and destination; as a guiding light by which men could live;

(*Paradise* was created for the righteous; and its ruby gates are guarded by sixty myriads of angels whose faces glow with the splendor of the firmament;

(*Gehinnom* was created for the wicked who, when given the choice to do good or evil, choose evil; and when given the choice of peace or war, choose war;

(*Two Thrones of Glory* were created: The Throne of Justice and the Throne of Mercy. Three hours each day God sits in judgment of the world. When the people are so wicked as to deserve destruction, God rises from the Throne of Justice and sits on the Throne of Mercy;

(*The Sanctuary* was created as the holiest place in the Holy of Holies in the Temple;

(*The Name of the Messiah* is the promise of the Millennium and the World to Come, when death and sorrow will be banished forever;

(And *Repentance* was created so that the human soul might find redemption.

(So great is the power of repentance that, though the wickedness of Nineveh rivaled the wickedness of the generation of Noah, when the people repented they were forgiven and their city spared.)

9. *Jonah in the Desert*

Jonah still feared the people would call him a false prophet and try to kill him. He left Nineveh and went far into the desert. When he sat down to rest, a tree rose out of the sand bearing one large leaf which shaded the prophet from the rays of the sun.

Jonah remained there, but the next day a worm ate up the leaf. Jonah began to complain. Then God said to him:

"Jonah! You are grieved because a single leaf, which grew without your effort, was destroyed. Yet you fret because I pitied a great city which contains three hundred and twenty thousand young mothers, and as many infants, who have not sinned yet would have perished if the city were destroyed."

Jonah confessed his shortcomings and asked to be forgiven, as God had forgiven the idolatrous citizens of Nineveh.

10. *The Prophet of Consolation*

The Prophet Hosea died in Babylon; the Prophet Amos was killed with a red-hot iron by the evil King Uzziah; but when their voices were stilled, a member of the royal family began to exhort the people and to console them in their trials. His name was Isaiah, son of Amos, brother of King Amoziah, and this is how he came to be known as *The Prophet of Consolation.*

One day when Isaiah reproached himself for his failure to influence the impious and evil King Uzziah, he heard angels singing. Isaiah listened in silent joy, and when the song ended, he said:

"Would that I had joined the angels in their praise of God, for that would have made me immortal."

But upon reflection he concluded: "Perhaps it was better that I remained silent. For I am a man of unclean lips and dwell among a people of unclean lips."

And a Voice rebuked him, saying: "Of yourself you may speak as you please; but who has given you the right to slander the Children of Israel?"

Then an angel took a coal so hot that he needed tongs with which to hold the tongs which held the coal, and touched Isaiah's lips which had slandered Israel. The prophet was not hurt, for even before the angel could fetch the coal Isaiah had repented his words and realized that it was not his mission to slander his people but to defend them and to console them in their trials.

The rest of his life he devoted to writing a book, which has ever since been known as the Book of Consolations, and its author is sometimes called Isaiah, but more often the Prophet of Consolation.

11. *The Eye of the Mind*

In the days when Shalmaneser took the Ten Tribes of Israel captive to Media and replaced them with Cutheans, a rich Cuthean merchant bought a Hebrew slave in the markets of Ecbatana. When he reached home he discovered that the slave was blind in one eye.

"Why did you deceive me?" shouted the Cuthean in anger.

"I was neither the buyer nor the seller," said the slave. "Therefore I could not have deceived you."

"But you are half blind," said the merchant.

"Seeing is with the mind as well as with the eye," said the Hebrew slave. "And the eye of the mind is the more important."

The next day the merchant went on a journey and took the slave with him. When they reached the desert the slave said:

"If we hasten our pace we will be able to catch up with some travelers who are not more than ten leagues ahead of us."

"Can you see them?" asked the Cuthean sarcastically.

"No," said the slave. "But I know that there are at least two people just ahead of us belonging to different nationalities. The camel they lead is blind in one eye and loaded with two gourds, one full of oil and the other full of wine."

"How can you know all that?" asked the unbelieving master.

"The sand tells me all that," replied the slave. "The sand shows where a camel rested a short while ago. The brush to the right of the road is plucked in places, as a camel plucks it while passing. But it is not plucked on the left side of the road, so the camel must be blind in the left eye. If you look carefully, you will see drops on both sides of the camel's tracks. On the right the drops sank into the sand — they are drops of wine; but on the left the drops remain on the surface — they are drops of oil. As for the nationality of the travelers: one of them, you can see, spat in front of him in the middle of the road; whereas the other, of a more refined race, walked a little aside for the same act."

"But how do you know how far they are, since you cannot see them?"

"A camel's footprints do not last very long. The breeze covers them with sand before the beast has gone ten leagues. Therefore, if we hurry, we will catch up with them."

They hurried and soon caught up with the travelers ahead, and the amazed Cuthean found that everything his slave had told him was true.

"Where did you learn this wisdom?" the Cuthean asked the slave in admiration.

"Before my people were taken captive I sat at the feet of our prophets. And they taught us that the sight of the mind and of reason is greater than the sight of the eye."

"As a reward for your wisdom," said the Cuthean merchant, "I shall set you free, and henceforth you shall be my councilor."

12. *The Battle of the Gnats*

There was an Assyrian king once whose name struck fear into the hearts of men. His name was Sennacherib and he went out to conquer the entire world. His father, Shalmaneser, had already conquered many lands, including the kingdom of Israel. And Sennacherib followed in his father's footsteps. He conquered nation after nation and in the end decided to add the kingdom of Judah to his other conquests.

Sennacherib gathered together an army of three million horsemen, led by forty-five thousand generals. With this mighty army Sennacherib marched upon Jerusalem. Before attacking the city, a spy was sent to find out what manner of defense Judah planned. The spy returned with a strange report:

"Hezekiah, King of Judah, neither drinks wine nor eats meat. Instead of gathering an army, he gathers books; instead of soldiers, he trains scholars; instead of generals he consults prophets. And the words of Isaiah he never disobeys."

"In that case," said Sennacherib, "we can save ourselves the trouble of fighting. We will send a message to King Hezekiah to open the gates and turn over Jerusalem to us."

But to their surprise Hezekiah sent back the reply: "Your armies are great and powerful. But He who is All-Powerful can put a ring in your nose and a bridle in your mouth. Come and take our city if you can — if the God who emancipated us from Egypt with a powerful arm will permit it."

King Sennacherib fumed. The insult of the reply was as fire in his mouth. He ordered three heralds to approach Jerusalem and announce in the gates that on the morrow he would advance with an army so vast that when each man had picked up a handful of dust, where there had been a proud city on three mountains, only three desolate valleys would remain.

The heralds found the gates of Jerusalem locked. From inside the city they heard men singing joyfully:

> *Fear you not the reproach of men,*
> *Nor be afraid of their reviling;*
> *For the moth shall eat them up like a garment;*
> *And the worm shall eat them up like wool.*

The next morning the heralds started back for their camp. But they could not find it. They raised their hands to shield their eyes from the sun, and there before them lay the field covered with dead soldiers, stretching for miles and miles. They saw a lone figure standing upright in the distance and they raced toward him. It was Sennacherib, their king.

And Sennacherib told them how the night before a cloud of

insects fell upon the camp. They filled the ears, they blinded the eyes, they entered the nostrils, they drove the men mad. The men fought each other when they could do nothing against the insect pests. And all night long they struggled with the plague.

"What happened by morning, you can see for yourselves," the king ended. "I alone survived the battle of the gnats."

The heralds remembered the words of the song inside the walls of Jerusalem, and they now understood their meaning.

13. *Whiter Than Milk*

In the days of many sinners, there are many prophets; in the days of many prophets, there are many disciples.

When the wicked King Menasseh ruled there were many prophets: Micah, Nahum, Zephaniah, Jeremiah, and many more. The prophets wrote their prophecies in books, and the disciples of the prophets memorized their books and pondered about them at their work.

There lived in those days a famous herb dealer in Jerusalem who collected the works of the prophets just as he collected all the different healing herbs. One day the herb dealer called his only son, Asa, and said:

"I am growing old. But before I die I would like you to go to the kingdom on the Island of Rohoh, for I am told they grow herbs of great healing power."

"I shall go wherever you send me, Father."

"The people of Rohoh, I am told, are rich and learned. But they have no prophets. Take the works of our prophets with you to keep you from straying into the ways of evil."

"I shall do whatever you wish," said the son.

Asa gathered together all that he needed for the great journey and sailed off to the far-away island in the Great Sea. And upon arriving in the new land, Asa distributed alms to the poor, remembering that the prophets said: "Charity saves from death." To his great surprise he was promptly arrested and told that he was encouraging laziness among the poor and that this was a major crime in Rohoh. Asa promised not to do it again.

"If I cannot follow the prophets and distribute charity," thought Asa, "I will follow their advice and cast my bread upon the waters." And every day he threw a loaf of bread to the fish in the Great Sea.

The people of Rohoh saw Asa throw good bread into the sea and they threw him in after the bread in anger.

But Asa did not drown. For the fish had recognized the man who fed them, and they took him to their king, the Leviathan, to honor him. The King of All the Fish showed Asa the Wonders of the Deep. Then he took him to a great treasure of ambergris and jewels and said:

"Which would you rather have: this great treasure, or the knowledge of the languages of all the birds, the beasts and the fish?"

"He who does not prefer knowledge to pearls is no follower of the prophets," said Asa.

Asa was taught all the languages; and he was then returned safely to the shore. On the way back to the city, Asa lay down under a tree to rest. Two crows arrived and alighted side by side on a branch above his head.

"I wish I could pick this man's eyes out," Asa heard one crow say.

"He's not asleep and will catch you," replied the other.

"Even if he did he would have to let me go soon," said the first crow. "For this path leads to a crossroad. If he turns left, wild beasts will attack him, and in his fear he will let me go. If he turns right, robbers will fall upon him, and in his panic he will let me go. If he follows the straight road he will discover a fortune, and in his great joy he will release me."

Asa jumped up and followed the straight road until he found the fortune. Then he carried it back with him to the city.

The people who had thrown him into the sea were surprised to see him, and wanted to know how he had saved himself from drowning and how he had gained his fortune. And when Asa told them all that had happened to him, they took him before the king to test his knowledge and wisdom.

"What is whiter than milk?" asked the king.

"Daylight is whiter than milk," replied Asa.

"What does not grow with time?" asked the king.

"Grief does not grow with time," said Asa.

"What is stronger than knowledge?"

"Instinct is stronger than knowledge."

The people admitted that Asa was very wise. They permitted him to gather all the healing herbs he wanted, and sent their blessings with him when he went home to his father in Jerusalem, saying:

"Blessed is the nation whose prophets have such wise disciples."

PART V

The Unconquered

The people of Judah, taken into the Babylonian captivity in 586 B.C., returned to Palestine and, with the aid of Prince Zerubbabel, Governor Nehemiah, Queen Esther and her uncle Mordecai, and the many wise and learned scribes and teachers, rebuilt the Holy City and the Temple. Their deeds have been recorded jubilantly in the lore.

But what happened to the Ten Tribes of the Kingdom of Israel, taken captive by Shalmaneser, Emperor of Assyria, in 722 B.C.? Were they dispersed in Halah, Hebor and Gazan? Did they travel to Iernes to establish ten kingdoms under ten separate kings? Are the Kashmiris, the Tartars and the Tadjiks the descendants of the Ten Lost Tribes, as has been claimed? Could it be, as related in *The Book of the Mormon*, that the Ten Tribes migrated to America and multiplied throughout the north, central and southern part of the continent? Did the Ten Tribes migrate to the islands of Japan and there establish a kingdom, as given by N. McLeod in his *Epitome of the Ancient History of Japan*? Or should we rather incline our ears to that vastly popular author of the 19th century, Edward Hines, who in the best seller of his day identified the British nation with the Ten Tribes?

Where the fact seems blurred and uncertain, the fancy is sharp and decisive. In the lore, as we shall see, there remain no doubts about the fate of the Ten Tribes of Israel, who crossed the Sea Okeanus to inhabit a land so vast that all of mankind could find refuge in one of its forests.

CHAPTER EIGHTEEN

The Ten Lost Tribes

1. *Beyond the Mountains of Darkness*

For a long time the people of Judah did not know what had happened to their brothers of Israel. But when the Levites on their way into captivity refused to play their harps and were condemned to die the next day, angels came at dawn and transported all the condemned men far beyond the Mountains of Darkness, beyond the restless River Sambatyon, beyond the peaceful River of Youth, into the land of the Ten Lost Tribes of Israel, known as the Land of the Red Jews.

Unlike any other land is that land of eternal spring. Poisonous snakes or insect pests are unknown there. As are unknown envy or greed. The soil is rich and the crops abundant. They eat no meat there, and they share their food as they share their labor. They spend little time on physical comforts, and much of their time upon things of the spirit. There are no enemies from without to disturb them, and no rivalries from within to disgrace them. And all their days are filled with laughter and joy.

The Levites of Judah revealed themselves to their brothers of Israel, and have lived among them ever since.

2. *The Great Alexander*

We would never have known with certainty what became of the Ten Lost Tribes had no one ever returned from the Land Beyond the Mountains of Darkness. But one man did reach that land and returned to tell of its existence and its greatness. That man was Alexander the Great, King of Macedonia. And this is how it happened:

After King Alexander had conquered all the nations on earth, he went to Jerusalem to find out from the wise and learned men whether there remained a land anywhere outside his rule.

Alexander walked along a street in Jerusalem wondering how he could find out which was the wisest man, when he noticed a young boy carrying a covered jar.

"What have you there?" asked the king.

"If my mother had wanted people to know what was in the jar she would not have covered it," the boy answered.

Alexander liked the reply and decided to test the boy further. He said: "I will give you a talent in gold if you will do three things for me."

"I will do them, if I can," said the boy, "and if they can be done without shame."

"First," said the king, "I want you to get me a bottle of wine."

The boy asked for money with which to buy the wine. But the king said: "Anyone can get wine with money. But a wise boy like you should be able to get it without money."

The boy left and soon returned with a bottle which he handed to the king.

"But this bottle is empty!" the king protested.

"Anyone can drink from a full bottle. But a man as wise as you are should be able to drink from an empty one."

Then the king said: "I have another errand for you. Here is some money. Buy me two kinds of food, both white: one that will last a very long time; and the other, good for one meal."

The boy returned with a sack of salt and a measure of cheese.

"Good," said the king. "Now, here is a broken brass vessel. Take it to a tailor and have him sew it up."

"I will do that, if you can give me thread made of sand," said the boy.

When Alexander gave the boy his reward he told the king that he would gladly return the gold, if the king could answer these three questions.

"What is the lightest thing in the world?

"What is the hardest thing in the world?

"Where will you be a year from now?"

"That is easy," replied the king. "The lightest thing in the world is a feather; the hardest, is iron; and a year from now I will be home in my palace in Macedonia."

"You are wrong," said the boy. "The lightest thing in the world is an infant in its mother's arms. The hardest is for a mother to see her son go off to war. And no man can foretell where he will be a year hence."

"Wisely spoken," said the king. "Now, can you tell me whether there is any kingdom left on earth that has not yet come under my rule?"

"Only the angels guarding the gates of the Garden of Eden can answer that question," said the boy.

3. Alexander and the Eagle

Alexander decided to go to the gates of the Garden of Eden. He went high up into the mountains and hid himself near the nest of an eagle. When the youngest and strongest eagle had settled down on its nest, the king jumped upon the bird's back. The frightened eagle soared up into the sky, carrying the king along with him.

The king held out in front of the bird a long fork, on the end of which he had fastened a large piece of meat. The bird tried to snatch the meat, but the king held it just out of reach, and in that way Alexander steered the eagle all the way to the gates of the Garden of Eden.

The angel at the gates asked Alexander what he wanted, and the king replied that he had come to find out whether there was a land or kingdom over which he did not rule.

"There is one," said the angel. "It is the Land of the Ten Lost Tribes of Israel beyond the Mountains of Darkness." The angel then told the king how to find those mountains and the River Sambatyon.

"Since I have come as far as the gates, may I enter and see the Garden of Eden?" asked Alexander.

The angel gave the king a polished stone that looked like a human eye, and without saying a word he locked the gates to the Garden of Eden, and disappeared.

Alexander started back on his way home. Whenever the eagle

tired he fed him some of the meat he had brought along. But on the third day there was no meat left. And the eagle turned about to fly in the direction of his nest in the mountains. The king took his sword, cut off a piece of his own flesh, and steered the eagle on until he reached the palace and home.

4. *Water from Paradise*

When the king recovered from his journey to the gates of the Garden of Eden, he gathered together an army and marched toward the Mountains of Darkness. After many months Alexander and his men reached a river whose rippling was like thunder and whose sparkling was like distant lightning. The air over the river was as fragrant as if it were above a river of perfume. The king feared that the water might be unfit to drink and forbade his soldiers to bathe in it or to touch it. They dug a well for their needs, but kept at a distance from the banks of the river.

One day Alexander's armor-bearer shot several birds and they fell into the river. But as soon as the dead birds touched the water they came to life again and flew away. The armor-bearer rushed to tell the king what he had seen.

"This must be the river flowing from the Garden of Eden," thought Alexander, "and they who drink of its waters will live forever."

He sent his men to bring him a large vessel full of water from the river, wishing to drink of it himself and to take some home to his family so that he and his son would live and rule the world forever."

The men returned with an empty vessel. The river, they reported, had disappeared, and no trace of it could be found anywhere.

Alexander understood that he had been tried; and he resumed his journey into the Mountains of Darkness.

5. *The Restless Sambatyon*

One day Alexander came to a range of mountains so high that the light of day never penetrated into the narrow valleys. The king and his men followed a path through the mountains in complete darkness, until at last, one Sabbath afternoon, they came out upon a river more beautiful and more peaceful than any they had ever seen.

By the time the king and his men were ready to cross the river, the first star of evening had appeared. The Sabbath was over, and the peaceful river had suddenly turned into a seething cauldron, which hurled hot rocks into the air. Alexander and his men waited. For six days the river could not be neared. On the seventh day it became calm once more. But one day was not sufficient time for the king and his men to cross the river in safety. And the River Sambatyon rested only on the Sabbath.

Alexander, who had won so many battles, realized that there could be no victory for him in a battle with the Sambatyon. He led his men back home and decided to go to Jerusalem once again for guidance.

6. *Alexander and Simon*

In Jerusalem Alexander sought out Simon, the wisest member of the Great Assembly, and told him of his experiences in trying to reach the Land Beyond the River Sambatyon.

Then the king held out his hand in which he held what looked like an eye made of polished stone. "This was given to me by the angel at the gates of the Garden of Eden," he said. "But what it means I cannot understand."

"Have you tried to weigh it?" asked Simon.

"I have," said the king. "But no matter what we put on the other side of the scale, the eye always outweighs it."

Simon took the eye from the king and placed it on one side of a balance scale. On the other side of the scale he placed much gold and silver. The scale swung down on the side of the eye. Then Simon bent down, gathered up a handful of dust, and sprinkled the dust over the eye. At once the balance swung to the opposite side. All the gold and silver was removed, and Simon replaced it with a feather. But even the feather now outweighed the eye.

"That is what the angel meant," said Simon to the king. "The human eye is full of desire and not all the treasures on earth suffice to satisfy it. But when a man dies and a little dust covers him, the eye needs nothing more, not even to the weight of a feather."

Then Simon told Alexander how to cross the Sambatyon: "Take three white asses accustomed to walk in the dark. Load them with seven knolls of twine, each seven thousand times seven thousand ells in length. When you enter the Mountains of Darkness, tie the end of the twine to a rock and unroll the knoll as you travel. Should you get lost, you will be able to return to your starting point by following the white twine. When you reach the Sambatyon, wait until the first star appears on Friday. Then enter a boat and utter the words I will write down for you. And you will reach the other side in safety."

The king did exactly as he was told and arrived safely in the Land of the Red Jews.

7. Alexander and the Ten Tribes

King Alexander found that the countryside in the Land of the Red Jews looked not much different from the beautiful sunny lands of the Islands in the Sea. The pepper tree, with its clusters of ruby berries, the pomegranate in bloom, the long rows of eucalyptus trees, the many fruit trees that grow only in warm climes, the limes, the orange and guava, the varied kinds of palm trees, all these reminded the king of places he had seen.

Then he came to a town, and it seemed like many other towns he had known. Nor were the people in the streets much different from the people of Jerusalem or Shushan.

A boy came walking down the street who looked very much like the boy he had talked with in Jerusalem, and the king said:

"Where is the palace of your king?"

"King?" asked the boy. "The only kings we have are in our stories for little children."

"Then where is the garrison of your soldiers?"

"What does the word 'soldier' mean?" asked the boy.

"If you have no soldiers, who fights your wars?"

"There is no word like 'wars' in our language," the boy assured the king.

"Then where is your Court of Justice?"

"We haven't any," said the boy.

"Who judges the thieves, the slanderers and the men who commit murder?"

"No one," said the boy. "Such people are unknown here, just as snakes and insect pests are unknown."

"What do people do who have disputes?"

"They take their disagreements to the learned men and do whatever they are advised," said the boy.

Alexander then decided to test the boy's wisdom.

"Which is farther," he asked, "from east to west, or from earth to heaven?"

"From east to west is farther," the boy replied. "For when the sun rises and sets we can look at it, but when it is at the zenith at midday it is nearer, and we cannot look at it."

"Is it better to live on land or on sea?" he asked.

"On land," said the boy, "for all who go to sea must return to land."

"If all the water comes from the ocean," asked the king, "why is the water of the sea salty and the water of the rain sweet?"

"The water of the sea goes up in vapor," was the boy's answer, "and it leaves the salt behind."

King Alexander then asked the boy to direct him to the home of one of the town's leaders. The boy sent him to Aaron the Scholar.

8. *Gold for Dinner*

As King Alexander and Aaron the Scholar were talking, two men came to Aaron for advice.

One man said: "I bought a field from my neighbor and in it I found a great treasure. Since I bought the field and not the treasure, the treasure clearly belongs to him."

But the neighbor argued: "I sold him the field with everything in it, therefore the treasure is his."

Aaron thought for a while, then asked one of the men: "Do you have a son?"

"Yes," was the reply.

"Do you have a daughter?" Aaron asked the second man.

"Yes," said he.

"Then let them marry, and give the treasure to your children," Aaron advised.

When the men left, Alexander said: "That was the strangest judgment I have ever heard."

"How would you have ruled in such a case in your country?"

"We would have put both men in prison and confiscated the treasure."

Alexander was invited to have dinner at Aaron's home, and he observed with surprise that the great scholars and the leaders waited upon the guests.

"Why do you allow your great men to serve you?" the king asked.

"That is what leaders should do," he was told. "They should always remember that the Creator of the World serves even the animals in the field, growing food for the cattle to eat and providing water for the beasts to drink."

Just then Aaron came up and offered the king a large platter laden with fruit and bread — all made of pure gold.

"I cannot eat these," said Alexander.

"What do you eat?"

"Whatever you eat," said the hungry king.

"If you cannot eat gold, why do you love it so much?" asked Aaron.

"We need gold to live by," replied the king. "Gold is money. With it we can buy honey and meat and all the things we want and need. And without it we would perish."

"Does the sun shine in your country? Do the trees grow? Does the rain fall? Do the crops ripen? For if they do, you need no gold; you have the food God has given all men."

Upon Alexander's return from the Land Beyond the Mountains of Darkness, he went to Simon of the Great Assembly in Jerusalem, and told him all he had seen and heard. His words were recorded, and that is how we know about that wonderful land.

CHAPTER NINETEEN

Babylon Is Taken

1. *Prophet of Lamentation*

In the days of King Zedekiah, there lived a prophet named Jeremiah, and his life was so bitter that he was called the Prophet of Lamentation.

At the moment of his birth Jeremiah called out: "*The walls of my heart tremble, for I will bring the cup of wrath to Jerusalem, and I will make the people of Judah drink the waters of bitterness.*"

And when he was still a very small boy he pleaded with God not to bestow the spirit of prophecy upon him: "I cannot mete out judgment to one suspected of adultery, knowing that woman is my own mother; and I cannot foretell the destruction of a great but sinful city, knowing that city is Jerusalem."

God answered: "You shall go on whatever errand I send you."

And just as Jeremiah had feared, he was given the terrible task of warning King Zedekiah and his people that they would be turned over into the hands of their enemies if they did not give up their wickedness.

Jeremiah incurred the wrath of the court and the people. He was jeered at, imprisoned and tortured. And once the king came to him, mocking:

"Have you had another revelation from God?"

The prophet replied sorrowfully: "Mine has been the unhappy revelation that the King of Babylonia is on his way to carry you off into exile."

2. *Capture of Jerusalem*

Nebuchadnezzar, son of King Solomon and the Queen of Sheba, was the dreaded King of Babylonia. He was determined to con-

quer the Holy City. By the strength of his armies and the weakness
of Jerusalem, Nebuchadnezzar counted on an easy victory.

He was mistaken. Although Judah was weak and the Chaldean
armies very strong, each day Jeremiah's prayers rose like a mighty
wall, and for three long years the Babylonians remained thwarted
outside the gates of Jerusalem. So long as Jeremiah prayed within
the city no breach appeared in the walls.

God then sent the prophet on a mission far from Jerusalem.
When Jeremiah left, an angel opened the gates to the enemy. And
Nebuchadnezzar and his hordes flooded the Holy City.

3. *David's Tomb*

Like so many other kings of old, Nebuchadnezzar loved gold.
And when he entered Jerusalem he went directly to David's tomb
to rob it of the treasure he knew was buried there.

King David, before his death, had asked that a thousand talents
in gold be buried with him for a day in the future when it would
be needed for the glory of Israel. Nebuchadnezzar wanted that
gold.

The soldiers, under the eyes of their king, marched to the gates
of the tomb to open them. But as they touched the gates, the soldiers fell to the ground dead. Others tried to force the gates, and
they met the same fate.

Nebuchadnezzar then gathered together all the priests of Judah
and threatened to slay them if they did not open the tomb for
him. The priests prayed, and the gates to the tomb opened without the touch of any hand.

The king's men took the gold from its hiding place and put it on
a cart drawn by two horses. But when the cart was loaded, the
horses could not budge it. Two more horses were added, and still
no matter how hard they tugged and pulled, no matter how hard
the whips were snapped, the cart did not move. The horses were
taken away and in their place sixteen mules were hitched to the
cart. Yet the sixteen mules could not budge the cart even the distance of the breadth of the king's smallest finger.

"Replace the mules with camels," the king commanded.

Thirty-two camels took the place of the mules. But the cart remained rooted in the same spot. Then sixty-four elephants replaced the camels. Still the cart could not be moved.

At this the King of Babylonia became frightened. He ordered the gold replaced in the tomb and a guard stationed at the gates so that no thief could ever enter.

4. *Blood of the Prophet*

King Nebuchadnezzar and his soldiers went to Jerusalem to pillage the Temple and there the king saw blood seething upon one of the stones of the floor.

"Why has this blood not been washed away?" he asked.

"The stone has been scoured many times, but the blood always remains," he was told.

"Remove the stone and replace it with another," the king commanded.

The stone was removed and replaced with another, but the blood reappeared.

"Whose blood is this?" the king asked.

"It is the blood of a prophet," the people confessed. "His name was Zachariah and he foretold our doom. In their anger the people stoned him in the Temple on a Sabbath day, before the Day of Atonement. And his seething blood has never been stilled."

The king ordered his captain, Nebuzardan, to still the blood.

The captain spilled the blood of seventy priests of Judah upon the stone. But the blood of the prophet would not be stilled.

He killed seventy school children on the same spot. But the blood would not be stilled. The captain killed more and more innocent people. But all their blood could not still the blood of the prophet.

At last Nebuzardan covered his face and cried out: "Zachariah! Zachariah! If God avenges a single prophet so harshly, how great is my sin, who have killed so many?"

Immediately the blood sank into the ground and was stilled.

Nebuzardan fled from the Chaldeans, changed his name, and repented.

5. *The Road into Captivity*

Nebuchadnezzar put all the princes and the priests and the people of Judah in chains, and led them into captivity. The king rode ahead of his victorious armies, carrying the trophies of gold and silver taken from the Temple of Solomon. Behind him walked the captives, prodded by guards who had been told not to let any of the people rest until they reached the Euphrates.

All through the long and bitter journey, each time a group of Jews paused to pray, the Chaldeans, fearing God would come to the aid of the captives, disrupted the worshipers and killed their leaders.

The captives wept and knew repentance. Their Prophet Jeremiah had been taken from them. Their Holy City had been laid in ashes and their Temple desecrated. And they were set upon the road into captivity and were not even allowed to pray.

Nebuchadnezzar came riding down one day to look over the prisoners of war and noticed a group of men who did not carry any burden.

"Who are these captives? And why have they no burdens on their backs?" asked the king.

"These are the princes of Judah. And we had nothing for them to carry," he was told.

"Then make sacks out of their Holy Scrolls and fill the sacks with desert sand. And let the princes of Judah carry them."

The captives wept so bitterly when they saw the Holy Scrolls torn that the river of their tears reached up to heaven. Whereupon angels descended and carried the burdens of the captives to the end of their journey.

Near Babylon many of the Chaldeans came to greet their victorious king. And at the feast in his tents they asked to hear the music of the Levites, whose fame had reached them.

When the messengers of the king commanded the Levites to play before Nebuchadnezzar and his guests, they hung their harps upon the willows, slashed their hands with knives and came before the king saying:

"We cannot play — for our fingers are cut and bleeding."

The angry king condemned the musicians to death. And he

vowed that as soon as the Jews reached Babylonia he would turn
their hearts from God and convert them to the worship of idols.

6. *The Three Pillars*

Babylon had grown great and rich on the plunder of war. And
wealth had filled the Babylonians with arrogance. They justified
whatever they did, no matter how wicked their deeds. And no
matter how wicked their deeds, they demanded that everyone in
their domain do just as they did.

The king built an idol in the city of Babylon with the gold he
had plundered in many wars. The idol was a hundred feet high,
and ten feet at the base, and cast in solid gold, ornamented with
precious jewels. This idol was placed on a stone pedestal so high
that it could be seen a thousand miles away. Then Nebuchadnezzar
sent out an edict that everyone under his rule must worship this
idol or suffer death by fire.

Some time later the king's spies reported that they had found
three men, brought into captivity from Jerusalem, who despised the
king's order.

"Bring them to me," the king shouted.

When the three appeared, the king asked: "What are your
names?"

"Hannaniah," said one.

"Mishael," said the second.

"Azariah," said the third.

"Is it true that you disobeyed my command to worship my god?"

"It is true," they replied. "For our knees have not been given the
power to bend to idols."

"Did not your Prophet Jeremiah say that it was your duty to obey
the king of the land?"

"We are willing to obey you," the three replied. "We will not
walk in the middle of the street. We will be discreet in public
places. We will pay your taxes and your tolls. But in matters of
faith we obey the King of Kings."

"There are no kings beside me," Nebuchadnezzar shouted in
rage. And he ordered the three men thrown into a furnace.

A fire was built in a furnace so huge that when its doors were opened to throw in the three condemned men, hundreds of Babylonian soldiers standing nearby died of the heat. The king ordered the fires increased each day for seven days. The terrible heat from the enormous furnace burned the crops and consumed the people for miles around. Yet the king would not permit the fires in the furnace to be banked until the seven days were over.

At last the furnace was opened. And the king saw the three men strolling about in the flames unharmed, discussing the first commandment with a fourth man, a stranger.

"Come out of there!" the king shouted.

"Only He who protected these three can order them to leave," said the stranger in the furnace.

"And who are you?" asked the king.

"I am Gabriel," said the stranger, "who caused the destruction of Sennacherib's armies."

The king trembled and said: "If you will let them come out, I will make them the collectors of my taxes."

"They will not leave until you promise that you will never force the Children of Israel to worship idols," said the Angel Gabriel.

"I promise," said the king.

"And you promise never to force any man to give up his faith for yours."

The king promised.

"And you must promise never to try any man for what in his heart he believes to be the truth."

The king promised again.

The three Jews came out of the furnace singing in praise of the Lord, and the king returned to his palace confused and humbled.

(Ever since that time, it is said: "God supports the world on three pillars, and their names are: *Hannaniah, Mishael* and *Azariah.*")

7. The Miracle in the Valley of Dura

After his encounter with the Angel Gabriel, King Nebuchadnezzar feared that he would be punished for destroying Jerusalem and the Temple. His High Priests consoled him, saying:

"Not by your strength was Judah conquered but by their wickedness. Therefore avenge yourself for your humiliation. Gather together all their young men and slay them. Then they will not boast that their God humbled you."

Sixty thousand young men, taken captive in Judah, were brought to the Valley of Dura and slain by the king's command. The Prophet Ezekiel then appeared and said to the wicked and vain king:

"Look upon the bodies of the men you have slain and the bones of the others who fell by your sword! By the God of Israel, they shall be revived. And I shall revive many who did not believe in the resurrection of the dead. And I shall revive many who polluted the Temple with idolatrous rites. And I shall revive the young men of Judah, whose radiance when they appeared in the streets of Babylon seemed to darken the sun in comparison, and whom you slew in your jealousy."

Then four winds came into the valley from the four corners of the earth, and all the dead arose and came to life as Ezekiel had prophesied.

Only one man among all the dead did not arise and live again, for he was a usurer. As it is written that a usurer shall be considered more sinful than a murderer and, when he dies, he shall remain dead forever.

8. *Susanna and the Elders*

This folk tale of Susanna and the Elders, set down over two thousand years ago, is so fresh in the writing that the fingers which held the pen still seem to be moving. For this reason, the story is set down here, as nearly as possible, in the language of the original, and as found in the Authorized Version.

There dwelt a man in Babylon, called Joachim, and he took a wife, whose name was Susanna, a very fair woman and one that feared the Lord. Joachim was a rich man and in his house the elders assembled, and all who had any disputes came to them.

When the people departed, Susanna went into her husband's

garden to walk. And the two elders who were appointed judges saw her there every day and their lust was inflamed toward her, yet each dared not show the other his grief.

Yet they watched diligently from day to day to see her.

And one said to the other, "Let us go home now, for it is dinner time."

They parted, and turning back again they came to the same place; and after they had asked one another the cause, they acknowledged their lust, then plotted to find her alone.

One hot day Susanna and her two maids came into the garden, and there was none there save the elders, who had hid themselves and watched her.

Then Susanna said to her maids: "Bring me oil and washing balls and shut the garden doors."

When the maids were gone, the two elders ran to Susanna and said: "Behold, the garden doors are shut. No man can see us and we are in love with you. Therefore consent to lie with us. If you will not, we will bear witness against you that a young man was with you and that is why you sent your maids away."

But Susanna cried out in a loud voice. And when the servants of the house heard the cry in the garden they rushed in to her.

The next day, when the people were assembled, the two elders came full of mischievous imagination, and said:

"As we walked in the garden alone, this woman came in with two maids, and shut the garden doors and sent the maids away. Then a young man came and lay with her. Seeing this wickedness, we ran to them and saw them together. The man we could not hold for he was stronger than we and opened the door and leaped out. We asked who the young man was but she would not tell us."

The assembly believed them and Susanna was condemned to death for committing adultery.

Then a youth, whose name was Daniel, cried out in a loud voice: "I am clear from the blood of this woman!"

"What mean these words?" the people asked.

Daniel answered: "Return again to the place of judgment, for they have borne false witness against her."

"Seeing that God has given you the honor of an elder, come and sit with the judges."

Then Daniel advised that the two witnesses against Susanna be examined separately. And in his separate examination of them they contradicted each other. When the assembly was convinced that the two elders had by their own words admitted their guilt, they did to them as the elders had maliciously intended to do to their neighbor. And they put them to death.

Joachim and all his kindred then praised God for Susanna, because there was no dishonesty found in her.

And from that day forth Daniel was held in great repute in the sight of the people.

9. Nebuchadnezzar's Dream

When the king returned from the Valley of Dura, strange dreams troubled his sleep.

"I have dreamt a dream and wish you could tell me what it means," said the king to his wise men.

"What was the dream?" they asked.

"That I do not remember."

"We cannot interpret a dream you do not remember," said the wise men.

Rabsaris, the king's councilor, spoke up and said that he had heard of a man in Babylon, a young Jew named Daniel, who might be able to recall the king's dream and tell him what it meant.

When Daniel was brought before the king and told of the dream, he said: "You saw in your dream a great image that frightened you. It was a giant with a head of gold, hands of silver, a body of brass and feet of clay. Then you saw a stone thrown at the giant that shattered him into fragments."

"That is the dream!" said the king. "What does it mean?"

"You dreamt of yourself," said Daniel. "That is all that anyone can dream of."

"But what does the dream mean?" the king demanded.

Daniel could see in his mind's eye that Nebuchadnezzar was doomed to a horrible punishment for his wickedness, and he remained silent.

"If you fail to interpret my dream," said the king, "I will order your execution."

"Do not kill me," said Daniel, "for you may soon need me."

And as he spoke, before the eyes of all those assembled, Nebuchadnezzar turned into a beast, half ox and half lion. He ran out of the palace and fled to the forest. There he lived the life of a hunted animal. He was to live the life of a beast for seven years, but Daniel's prayers reduced the king's punishment to seven months.

When the king returned to the throne, he appointed Daniel his Royal Advisor and consulted him in all matters until the day he died.

10. *Daniel Becomes Governor*

Belshazzar, son of Nebuchadnezzar, was not as wicked as his father, nor was he as clever. He was not avaricious — nor very ambitious — that is, for a king in those days. But he was a drunkard.

One day at the feasting table Belshazzar saw a hand appear in mid-air, and as it reached the wall it wrote, in letters so clear that they could be seen across the hall:

Mene, Mene, Tekel, Upharsin

The king and all his guests could read what the hand had written upon the wall. But what the words meant no one in the court knew. Belshazzar sent for Daniel and promised him many gifts and great honors if he would interpret the writing on the wall.

And Daniel told Belshazzar that before another sunrise the king would be dead and his kingdom, which Nebuchadnezzar thought he had established to last forever, would fall into the hands of King Cyrus of Persia and his father-in-law, Darius of Media.

That night Belshazzar was murdered by his own servants, who took his head to Cyrus and Darius. When the kings were told of Daniel's prophecy, they bestowed great honors upon Daniel, and Darius appointed him Governor of his kingdom.

11. *Daniel and the Lions*

The Babylonians had an idol, called Bel, whom everybody worshiped, including the king. But Daniel refused to bow to Bel.

"I will not bend my knee to an idol made of brass or clay," said he.

"Bel is not an ordinary idol," the king argued. "He is a living god. Every day I place before him twelve measures of fine flour, forty sheep, and six vessels of wine. And these he consumes every night. A clay idol could not do that!"

"Do not be deceived, my king," said Daniel. "Bel never eats or drinks anything."

"Then who devours my daily sacrifices?"

"Ask your priests and let them answer."

The king called together his threescore and ten priests and said to them:

"Daniel claims that Bel neither eats nor drinks my sacrifices. If that be proven true, you shall die. But if you can prove to me beyond a doubt that Bel really consumes them, then Daniel shall die."

"Well spoken," said the priests. "Let us go to the Temple of Bel and place the meat and the flour and the wine upon the altar. Then we will leave. Lock the doors and seal them with the Royal Seal. Tomorrow we will break the seal, unlock the doors, and see whether your sacrifices remain uneaten. If they are there, you shall kill us, but if they are gone, you shall kill Daniel."

The king agreed to the test. And when he returned the next day with Daniel, the food and wine were gone. The king prostrated himself before the idol, but Daniel only laughed.

"Look!" he said to the king, pointing to the floor, "Can you see those footprints, as of many people?"

"Yes," said the king, "I see footprints of men, women and children."

"Those are the footprints of your priests, their wives and their children! They enter the temple each night through an underground passage, and grow fat on your sacrifices."

The king searched the place, and when he found that Daniel had spoken the truth, he ordered the priests slain, and turned Bel over to Daniel for destruction.

Bel was no sooner destroyed than the foolish King Darius established a dragon in the idol's place. The dragon was fearful to behold and his hunger for sacrifices was without bottom and without end. The king ordered the people to worship the dragon and to appease its hunger.

But Daniel refused to worship the dragon and said: "A creature that can be slain by man is no god. Give me leave, my king, and I shall slay this dragon without sword or staff."

"I give you leave," said the king.

Daniel then brought a sacrifice of molten pitch and boiling fat and poured them down the dragon's throat. And the dragon dropped dead.

The priests were frightened and whispered amongst themselves: "If Daniel is not destroyed he will surely turn the king to the God of Israel."

Secretly they went to the king and accused Daniel of many terrible crimes.

"Throw him into the lions' den," they insisted, "and if he is innocent he will come out alive."

Daniel was thrown into a pit full of hungry lions and left there for six days. On the morning of the seventh day the king came to the pit, sorrowful about the fate of his friend. But when he looked down into the pit, his sorrow turned to joy. For there was Daniel, unhurt, with the lions lying at his feet and looking up at him like dogs adoring their master.

The king drew Daniel out and cast the accusers into the den, and they were devoured before his eyes.

"You can have three wishes," said the king to Daniel. "Up to half of my kingdom you may ask, and it shall be yours."

Daniel bowed and said: "These are my three wishes:

"My first wish is that you will believe in the One True God;

"My second wish is that you will allow all the children of Israel, taken captive by Nebuchadnezzar, to return home if they so desire;

"And my third wish is that you help us rebuild the city of Jerusalem and the Holy Temple."

And the king granted Daniel's three wishes.

CHAPTER TWENTY

In the Days of Ahasuerus

1. *The Feast in Shushan*

Solomon was the wisest of kings; and Ahasuerus, the richest. So rich was Ahasuerus that in the third year of his reign he gave a feast the like of which had never been known before nor has ever been known since.

Three thousand three hundred and thirty-three messengers, speaking the seventy languages of the world, were sent out to the one hundred and twenty-seven nations of the earth. They invited the kings, princes and nobles to the feast in Shushan, which was to last one hundred and eighty days.

When the guests arrived with their families, the men were assigned quarters in the king's palace, and the women and the children were assigned quarters in the queen's palace. So immense were the palaces of the king and queen that though the guests numbered in the tens of thousands, there was ample room for them all, and their attendants, and their menservants and their maidservants.

The king entertained his guests in the royal gardens, which covered many parasangs. From the fragrant trees hung silken bands in bright colors, embroidered with rubies and sapphires. And curtains of fine linen stretched from tree to tree, with cords of gold which would form a tent between any four trees for the guests who desired privacy. The couches in the garden were made of rare woods, covered with purple draperies; and the marble walks were inlaid with crystal and outlined with precious stones that illuminated the walks at night.

Beverages were served to the guests in golden goblets, each different in shape and design, and no guest ever drank twice from the same vessel. The wine served was in each case older by a year than the guest who drank it, and in each case it came from the country of the drinker. No guest was asked to drink much or little. And whatever a guest desired in food or other pleasures, the wish was fulfilled as soon as the thought was translated into words.

Each month of the feast the king displayed different treasures, collections of sacred scrolls, and the gifts brought by the many royal guests.

One day the king and his guests were discussing the beauty of women. The Persians claimed that their women were the most beautiful in the world, and the Medians made the same claim.

The king, who was in his cups, boasted: "My wife, Queen Vashti, is neither Persian nor Median, but Chaldean. Yet she is the most beautiful woman in all my kingdoms."

Ahasuerus then sent a message commanding Queen Vashti to appear before his guests. When she refused to heed him, in his drunkenness, he ordered her driven from the palace.

2. Contest for a Queen

When the king sobered and his anger subsided, he was sorry Vashti had been banished. He sent a decree throughout the kingdom that the most beautiful maidens of every region should come to the queen's palace, and the one finding favor in his eyes would be crowned queen.

Ahasuerus told Hagai, the Chief Eunuch, to give all the maidens who came to the palace fine garments, perfumes, and any adornments they asked for, and to serve them with royal food as long as they remained in the palace.

Thousands of contestants began to arrive on camels, on horseback, in golden carriages and in shamianahs on the backs of elephants. Those who were admitted to the palace were allotted seven servants each, and it was their duty to wait upon and beautify their mistress.

One day the king was informed that a man in Shushan named Mordecai had not brought to the palace his beautiful orphaned niece. The king sent out a proclamation that anyone hiding a beautiful maiden would be hanged.

Mordecai brought his niece out of her hiding place and left her in Hagai's care at the palace.

3. *Esther's Beauty*

Mordecai had come to Shushan from Babylon where his parents were brought captive from Jerusalem. From Babylon he had brought with him his orphaned niece. Her name was Hadassah, meaning "myrtle"; but when Mordecai hid her in Shushan, he re-named her Esther, meaning "the concealed one."

When Esther was brought to the palace her behavior distressed Hagai. She asked for nothing and, unlike the other maidens, she used no paints, no perfumes, no dazzling gowns or jewels. And she would not touch meat. Hagai feared that if the king discovered that Esther did nothing to enhance her beauty he would blame the Keeper of the Harem and hang him on the royal gallows.

Esther consoled him, saying: "Fear not, for among so many beautiful young women the king will never notice me."

After four years of preparation, the day arrived for the selection of the queen. Perfumed and painted, resplendent in their gowns and jewels, the maidens from many lands took their places. They were dazzling to behold; each as beautiful as the others.

Between the maidens of Media and Persia, who looked all alike, stood Esther, neither tall nor short, her shoulders straight and her head held high. She wore no jewels or any ornament. Her long soft hair had its natural color. And the color of her cheeks, like the color of her lips, was her own. She looked young but not immature. And when the gentle maiden blushed, she did not blush in shame. For the king had left his throne and was coming directly toward her. He placed a crown upon her head and pronounced her queen of all the one hundred and twenty-seven kingdoms over which he reigned.

4. *How Esther Remembered the Sabbath*

Esther liked being the queen of so many kingdoms, but one thing troubled her. In the palace, each day was a holiday; and all the days were alike. She found it hard to remember the Sabbath, so that she could observe it as a Holy Day.

Esther finally discovered a way of knowing exactly when the Sabbath arrived.

She renamed seven of her maids, each for a day in the week, and told them to serve her in rotation. When *Firmament* came to serve her, the queen knew it must be Sunday, *Workaday* came Monday; *Garden* came Tuesday; *Luminous* came Wednesday; *Quick* came Thursday; *Lamb* came Friday. And when *Rest* came, the queen knew that it was the Sabbath.

This was only one of many clever devices Esther used to keep her from straying from the path of righteousness, though queen in the palace of idolaters.

5. *Why Haman Hated Jews*

All might have gone well for Queen Esther, if it had not been for the king's chamberlain, Haman. The chamberlain, she learned, was plotting to kill her uncle Mordecai and then kill all the Jews in the kingdom.

And this is how Haman came to hate Mordecai and the Jews:

When Haman was a young man serving in the army, one day he and a number of his companions were cut off by the enemy from the rest of their battalion. Haman felt worse than the others for his bag was empty of food and his gourd dry. He went from soldier to soldier begging for food and water and vowing that he would offer himself as a slave for life, in return. None of his companions would listen to him, each saying that they needed food and water more than they needed a slave. But one soldier, a Jew, said:

"If we are not saved soon, we will all die of hunger. Come then and share my food and water."

That same day Haman and the others were rescued and the incident was forgotten. When the war was over Haman went back to Tarshish, his birthplace, married a girl named Zerish and raised a family of ten sons and one daughter. His growing family gave Haman pride without evil. But his growing wealth corrupted his heart.

Haman soon became so rich that he began to crave power and honors. He moved to Shushan and did everything that would bring him favor in the eyes of the king. At last Haman was appointed Chief of Princes and the king's chamberlain, and when he came to the palace the people all bowed down before him.

One day, as the king's chamberlain came to the palace gates, he noticed one man who did not bow and who looked aside to avoid seeing him.

Haman approached the man and said: "I am Chief of Princes and chamberlain to the king. Why do you not bow before me when I approach?"

"I do not bow to one who vowed to be my slave."

Haman grew pale, for he recognized the Jewish soldier, Mordecai, who had shared his food.

That evening Haman told his wife about the man at the palace gates. Zerish advised him to have Mordecai killed and clear away forever the shameful memory of his vow.

"It is more difficult than you think," said Haman, "for I have found out that this Mordecai is protected by Queen Esther."

"Then," said Zerish, "you must find a way to kill not only Mordecai but every Jew in all the one hundred and twenty-seven kingdoms."

From that day forth Haman could not sleep. Every night he would weave a new plot in which to destroy the Jews whom he now hated blindly and increasingly, because one of them had helped him in time of distress.

6. *Haman Complains to the King*

Being the king's chamberlain, Haman observed, had the great advantage that he could always talk to the king when they were alone. And the first chance he had, Haman said to the king:

"We have in our midst a people that do us no good. They are proud and they are exclusive. They will not marry our daughters, nor let their daughters marry us. Their religion is unlike any other religion. When they are hired in the king's service, it is impossible to get any work out of them. They will do no work on the Sabbath, nor on their New Year, nor on the Day of Atonement, nor on the Passover, nor on the Ninth of Ab, nor on the Holiday of the Greens, nor on the Holiday of the Tents. Even if it is none of these days, their labor amounts to little. The first hour of the day they say the Waking Prayers. The next hour is devoted to Morning Prayers. Then they say grace. Then they eat. Then they say the long after-meal benedictions. Then they must take time to instruct their children in their Holy Law. By that time they are tired and their wives come and say: 'Come and rest and do not exhaust yourselves in the king's service.' That's the kind of people they are."

"What do you advise me to do?" asked the king.

"I want you to remember," Haman went on, "that those Jews caused the death of Pharaoh and his armies; they slew Amalek, your ancestor, when Joshua unfairly kept the sun from setting; they caused a great general like Sisera to die at the hand of a woman. There is but one thing to do: destroy them."

"I will ask my Council of Wise Men," said the king. "If they accept your plan I will send out the decree to destroy the Jews."

Haman went out and bribed the princes, satraps, grandees and councilors with silver and gold. And at the assembly with the king they all advised the destruction of the Jews.

The king sent out a decree in seventy languages, setting the date for the murder of all Jews. Then he and his chamberlain celebrated until they were both drunk as owls.

7. *The Queen's Prayer*

The next day Mordecai heard of the king's edict, but he did not despair. He walked down the street and met three Jewish children returning from school.

"What have you learned today?" Mordecai asked.

"Be not afraid of sudden danger," said one.

"Let them speak the word, but it shall be brought to naught," said the second.

And the youngest one said: *"I have made and I will bear; I will carry and I will deliver."*

Mordecai thanked the boys and smiled. And when he met

Haman near the palace he called out: "I rejoice in the good tidings I have heard today from the mouths of school children."

When Queen Esther heard of the edict, she withdrew to her chamber in tears and prayed:

"O Creator of the World, I am unworthy. But my prayer is not for myself; it is for Israel. Their help must come from You. As You helped Hannaniah, Mishael and Azariah, the Three Pillars of the World, during their trial by fire; as You helped Daniel in the lions' den; help me to save my people. All-Merciful One, do not forsake us! And you, O Angels, weep for us, and intercede for us! And you, our forefathers, Abraham, Isaac and Jacob, observe our sorrow, and pray for us before the Throne of Glory so that the words of the wicked shall be brought to naught. Amen!"

Then the queen arose and put on her finest garments and her rarest jewels, and on her head she placed the crown wrought for her by the craftsmen of Africa. And she went unannounced to the king's chamber.

The king's heart gladdened when he saw her, and he said: "What does my queen wish? Ask, and it shall be given you, even to half of my kingdom."

The queen bowed and said: "It is not your kingdom, but your company I crave. I beg that you and your chamberlain join me in a feast tomorrow."

The king accepted and Esther left rejoicing.

When Haman told his wife of the invitation she asked at once: "Was I also invited?"

"Only the king and myself," said Haman.

The reply made Zerish angry. She had hated Queen Vashti because the queen had never invited Zerish to the palace feasts; and she hated Queen Esther because Zerish had hoped her own daughter would be chosen by the king. Now Zerish hated the queen even more for not inviting her to the feast with Haman.

"I saw Mordecai again at the gates of the palace," said Haman, "and I am glad I shall not have to see him much longer."

Zerish sighed and said: "You cannot burn him, remembering how Abraham was saved in Nimrod's furnace; you cannot cut his throat, remembering how Isaac was rescued; you cannot drown him, remembering how Moses was drawn out of the Nile; you cannot throw him to the lions, remembering how Daniel came forth unharmed; and you cannot stone him, remembering how Goliath met his end. Therefore you must hang him. Go at once and build a gallows. And tomorrow ask the king to let you hang Mordecai."

8. *Whom the King Wishes to Honor*

That night the king could not fall asleep. He called his secretary Oducan to read to him from the Book of Chronicles. Oducan read to him the incident of the two royal guards who had plotted to murder King Ahasuerus and how the Jew named Mordecai learned of the plot and informed the queen, and how she informed the king, and how the plotters were punished.

"Read to me what was done to reward this man who saved my life," said the king.

"Of that there is no record," said Oducan.

"No record means there was nothing to record," said the king. "Remind me to consult Haman on how to reward this man who saved my life."

The next morning, when Haman came to the palace, the king said to him: "Tell me, my chamberlain, what should be done for a man whom I wish to honor?"

Haman was certain the king wanted to honor his chamberlain, and he said: "Place the royal cloak about him and your crown upon his head; and have him led on a royal steed through the streets of Shushan by the highest man in your court. And let the heralds run before him and shout: 'Thus is it done to the man whom the king wishes to honor!'"

"Good," said the king. "Go and do thus to Mordecai."

"Which Mordecai?" Haman stammered.

"Mordecai the Jew, who saved my life."

"That man is my enemy. I would rather give him ten thousand talents of silver than lead him through the streets."

"You shall give him the silver and do him the honor besides," said the king.

"Honor him by making him ruler of a city instead," Haman pleaded.

"I will make him ruler of a province, and you shall do him the honor you advised."

Finally Haman pleaded: "You have sent out an edict to have all the Jews murdered two days from tomorrow. Recall the edict rather than that I should lead Mordecai in honor through the streets of Shushan."

"I will recall the edict," said the king, "and you will do as I command you. For I wish to honor the man who saved my life."

Haman knew he was defeated and he went and did as the king commanded.

9. *The Fate of the Wicked*

That evening Haman returned in time to attend Esther's feast. At the table, the queen said:

"When I came to you, my king, I told you that my parents died when I was an infant and I did not know them. That is true. But I know my nation. Mordecai, who saved your life, is my uncle. If you had listened to Haman all my people would have been murdered. Mordecai would have been killed. And I would have died also."

The king left the table in great distress and walked out into the garden. Haman realized his plight. He fell upon his knees and asked the queen for mercy. When the king returned into the room he found Haman beside Esther, kissing her hands and the queen struggling to get away from him.

"Wicked fool!" shouted the king. "You dare to force your attentions on the queen?" And the king summoned the guard, Harbonoh, and asked him: "What should be done to a man whom the king wishes to punish?"

Harbonoh was a friend of Haman's and knew of the plot to destroy Mordecai. He was certain Mordecai must be the man the king wished to punish. The guard tried to help the chamberlain and said: "Your Majesty, last night the Prince of Princes, Haman, and his sons built a gallows. The man the king wishes to punish should be hanged upon it."

"Then take Haman," the king commanded, "and hang him on the gallows he has built!"

Mordecai was called to the palace. The king took off his ring and placed it on Mordecai's finger, and thereby appointed him Prince of Princes and governor of his kingdom.

A great feast was prepared for the princes, nobles and satraps. And at this feast the new Prince of Princes proclaimed a holiday to be celebrated every year by all the Jews in all the kingdoms to commemorate the victory over the evil designs of Haman.

The Walls of Jerusalem

1. *Mightier Than the King*

A hundred years after the Jews had been taken into the Babylonian captivity, they returned to Jerusalem to rebuild the Temple and the Holy City.

And it all happened in this way:

When Daniel died, his place was taken at the court of Emperor Darius by the Jewish Prince Zerubbabel, who acted as the king's adviser and councilor.

On the tenth anniversary of his reign the emperor decided to give a hundred-day feast in the city of Shushan, and he sent invitations to all the princes, tetrarchs, governors and nobles of the earth.

At the appointed time the royal and honored guests arrived, bringing gifts of spices and perfumes, fine cloth and rare tapestries, gold and silver goblets, priceless jewels and old wines. The king sat upon his throne and the guests were seated, each according to his rank and age.

On the seventy-fifth day of the festivity, Darius said to his guests:

"There are three councilors in my court who are the wisest of men on earth. One is old, and he is a Persian prince; one is in his middle age, and he is a Hindu prince; and the third is very young, and he is a Jewish prince. But which of these is the wisest, I do not know. Help me judge which of the three is the wisest, that I may reward him as he deserves."

One of the guests, the Prince of Nebo, was a very clever man. He suggested that the three princes should be brought to the feast and tested. "Let each declare what is the strongest thing in the world," said the prince, "and by their answers we will judge them."

The Persian prince, who was the oldest, gave his answer first. He declared that *wine* was the strongest thing in the world, because wine has the power to make the sad feel happy; the slave, free; the foolish, wise; the poor, rich; the coward, brave; the shy, talkative. *Wine*, he concluded, was clearly the strongest thing in the world.

The Hindu prince gave his answer next. He declared that the *king* was strongest, because the king had the power to send men to war; to free the enslaved; to tear down walls and cause cities to be built; to command men to turn mountains into plains, and plains into valleys. The *king*, he concluded, was clearly the greatest power in the world.

Then the Jewish prince gave his answer. He said that *women* had greater power than either wine or king, for all men, even rulers, are the children of women. Nor could anyone be happy without them. For the sake of a woman kings have given up their kingdoms; the drinker his drink; the miser, his gold. Yet there is a power beside which the combined strength of wine, king and women is as a drop of water compared with the sea. And that power is *truth*. For the strength of truth abides forever.

All the guests at the feast agreed that the youngest was the wisest of the king's advisers.

The king arose and kissed the young prince on the forehead and said: "Great is Truth and mighty above all things; Blessed is the God of Truth! And because you have been judged the wisest of my councilors you shall sit beside me, and I will call you cousin. And you shall have as a reward anything you may ask, unto half of my kingdom."

And Zerubbabel answered: "Your kindness is my shield, Great King. I need nothing you have not already given me. But your illustrious father decreed that the Jews should be allowed to return to Judah, and you have vowed to rebuild the city and the Temple made desolate by the Chaldeans. Now, my Lord and my King, my wish would be that your father's decree and your vow be fulfilled."

"It shall be as you desire," said Darius.

First the king asked that each of the thousands of guests at his feast send gifts to help rebuild Jerusalem and the Temple. Then he wrote letters to all his governors, officers and treasurers, to offer protection to the returning captives and to help them settle in their land.

At the end of seven days of feasting, Emperor Darius allowed Zerubbabel to return as the leader of his people in the Holy City.

2. *Builder of the Walls*

King Cyrus befriended Daniel. His son, Darius, befriended Prince Zerubbabel. And his grandson, King Artaxerxes, befriended Nehemiah, grandson of the Jewish High Priest. Daniel had acted as adviser and interpreter of dreams; Zerubbabel was the king's chief steward and councilor; and Nehemiah was the royal cupbearer.

One day, when Nehemiah waited upon the king and the queen, they noticed that their cupbearer looked sad.

"What makes you so sorrowful?" asked the queen.

"An uncle of mine has come to visit me."

"If your uncle is troubling you," said the king, "I shall have him beheaded."

"I love my uncle," Nehemiah hastened to assure the king. "But he has brought me sad news from the city of Jerusalem."

"My grandfather permitted the Jews to return to Jerusalem. My father allowed Zerubbabel to rebuild the Temple. Why then is the news so sad?" asked the king.

"What you say is true," said Nehemiah. "But as long as the walls of the city are in ruins, the city and the Temple are in constant danger."

"Then you have my permission to join Zerubbabel and rebuild the walls of Jerusalem," said the king.

Nehemiah shook his head. "To rebuild the walls I would need authority, or the people would not obey me. Only if I were Governor of Judea would the people obey me."

Artaxerxes then and there appointed Nehemiah Governor of Judea. But the new governor remained depressed.

"What makes you sad now?" asked the king.

"Don't ask him any more questions," said the queen, "or Nehemiah will walk out of here with your crown upon his head."

Nehemiah's sadness left him and he laughed, and the king and queen laughed with him.

A banquet was given by the king for the newly appointed Governor of Judea; and then Nehemiah left Shushan in Persia for Jerusalem to rebuild the walls that had lain in ruins for over a century.

3. *Seed of the Olive*

In the days of Governor Nehemiah there lived a wealthy Jewish merchant in Persia who had an only son named Rahman. When the merchant grew old, he called in his son and said to him:

"You have studied much and you are now very learned in books. But you must also go into the world and learn the ways of men from experience, so that when I die you can carry on my affairs."

He gave the son one thousand shekels in gold and Rahman left home. Some time later, as he wandered about in a strange countryside, he sought shelter in a cave from the cold and wild beasts.

Late that night he heard two men come to the cave, saying to each other that they ought to bury the money they had stolen from the king's treasury; if they were caught without the loot they could not be found guilty; and later they would come back to the cave and get the money. Then he heard them digging.

When morning came Rahman found the spot where the money had been buried. He dug it up and started on his way to return it to the king. The king's men, who had been searching for the thieves all night, met Rahman and found the stolen money on him. They brought him before the king, and he was promptly found guilty as a thief and condemned to hang.

As he was led to the gallows, Rahman said to his guard: "I know a wonderful secret, and it is regrettable that it should die with me. I know how to plant the seed of an olive so that the next morning it becomes a full-grown olive tree bearing fruit."

The guard sent word to the palace about the wonderful secret, and Rahman was again brought before the king.

"Here is an olive seed," said the king. "Let us see how you plant it so that it becomes a tree by morning."

"There is one difficulty," said Rahman. "The planting must be done by one who has never told a lie and never stolen anything. Since I'm condemned as a thief and you think that I lie when I say I'm innocent, I cannot plant it. Let the treasurer of your kingdom do the planting. But if the tree fails to grow, it will only prove that he has lied at one time or another, or has stolen from the treasury."

The treasurer refused to plant the seed. "I'm a treasurer," said he. "You know how it is when you handle money — "

The seed was offered next to the collector of taxes. He, too, refused to plant the seed. The seed was offered in turn to each of the men in the king's court, and each found an excuse for refusing. At last Rahman said to the king:

"Why don't you plant it yourself?"

The king shifted upon his throne and said: "I am a king. When a king wants something — well, as all kings do, so do I — "

Rahman turned to the king and his men: "You have condemned me to death for theft and lying. Yet you all admit guilt of these crimes. Besides, if you would send messengers to my birthplace, you would find that I am neither a thief nor a liar."

The king sent messengers to Rahman's birthplace and they returned confirming Rahman's claims. To show his regret for the unjust charge, and as a reward for the return of the treasury money, the king gave Rahman five thousand shekels in gold and sent him home.

Rahman related to his old and worried father all that had happened to him on his journey.

"What are you going to do with the reward of your wisdom?" asked the proud father.

"The reward is not mine," said Rahman, "for the wisdom was not mine. I learned it from my teachers who are now busy rebuilding the walls of Jerusalem. And to them I shall send it, to help in their task, for the reward truly belongs to them."

4. The Three Precepts

In those days there lived an Idumean who was very rich, but he wanted to be also very wise. He went to Menasseh, a Jew famed for his learning and wisdom, and said: "Teach me three great precepts, and I will give you a fortune."

"My son," said Menasseh, "I will teach them to you through a story:

"There was a foolish man once who owned a beautiful garden. And this garden was as dear to him as the apple of his eye. One day when he came into the garden he found the flower beds trampled and the fruit of the trees despoiled. As he stood there in grief wondering who the culprit could be he saw a hummingbird dip its long beak into a flower.

"The man flung his cap over the bird and caught it. Then he accused the tiny creature of ruining his garden.

" 'How could a little creature like me do that much damage?' protested the bird.

"But the foolish man would not listen to reason and threatened to kill the hummingbird.

" 'If you will let me go,' said the hummingbird, 'I will teach you three precepts. If you follow them, they will bring you great fortune.'

"The man promised to let the bird go, and the hummingbird said: 'These are the three precepts:

Do not regret the irretrievable;
Do not believe the unbelievable;
Do not try to obtain the unattainable.'

"The man released the bird as he had promised. The hummingbird fluttered out of reach and began to taunt the foolish man, saying:

" 'If you had killed me as you threatened, you would have found in my body a diamond the size of a walnut.'

"The man tried to tempt the bird to come within reach by flattering it on its wisdom. But the bird would not be tempted and alighted on the topmost bough of a huge tree in the center of the garden. The man climbed after the hummingbird and finally reached the topmost branch. When he crawled out toward the end of the limb, it broke and the man crashed to the ground.

"The hummingbird fluttered above the man's head and said: 'Wisdom is only for the wise. I told you not to regret the irretrievable, yet as soon as you let me go, you regretted it; I told you not to believe the unbelievable, yet you believed that a tiny bird like myself could hold a diamond the size of a walnut; and I told you not to try to attain the unattainable, yet you tried to catch a bird in a tree.'"

When the learned man finished the story, he said: "Those are the three precepts."

The Idumean thanked Menasseh for the precepts and gave him a fortune as he had promised. And Menasseh sent it to Nehemiah for the walls of Jerusalem.

5. *Heaven Is Not "Up"*

When the Jews returned from captivity to rebuild their land, their Holy City and their Temple, there lived a Jew in Egypt named Nittai, who was a gatherer of books.

He prepared to go for a trip one day and sent his servant to buy a camel and a saddle. The servant returned and when the saddle was removed from the camel, a fortune in rare diamonds was discovered hidden in a pouch. Nittai sent the diamonds back to the camel dealer with the message:

"I bought a camel and a saddle, but not these jewels."

The grateful merchant came to thank Nittai. "Had you kept them," he said, "I could not have brought you to court."

"That is true. But had I kept them, I would have lost my integrity. One can enter the Heavenly Kingdom without diamonds, but not without honesty."

"I have heard about this Heavenly Kingdom," said the camel dealer. "How does one get up there?"

"First, my son, heaven is neither 'up' nor 'down,' but in our hearts," said Nittai. "The way to reach it is through good deeds; and the best road of all is through charity. These are the eight stations along the road to the Heavenly Kingdom:

"The first is reached by him who gives charity with his hand but not with his heart;

"The second station is reached by him who gives with his hand and his heart but not generously;

"The third station is reached by him who gives generously with hand and heart, but not until he is asked;

"The fourth station is reached by him who gives generously without being asked, but gives directly to those in need and thereby causes them humiliation and shame;

"The fifth station is reached by him who gives generously, without being asked, and in a manner that the giver does not know the receiver, but the receiver knows the giver;

"The sixth station is reached by him who gives generously, and knows the receiver, but the receiver does not know the giver;

"The seventh station is reached by him who gives generously, and both receiver and giver do not know each other;

"And the eighth station is reached by him who gives charity to keep people from ever needing charity.

"And that is the road to the Heavenly Kingdom."

"What you have taught me," said the camel dealer, "is of greater worth than those jewels. And I want to give them to you to show my gratitude."

"I have already been rewarded in seeing the seed of my words take root so quickly. Therefore, if you wish to give the jewels away, give them to Governor Nehemiah in Jerusalem and he will use them in a worthy cause."

6. Judith and Holofernes

There was a king in Assur in those days who wished to rule the whole world and vowed to destroy those who would stand in the way of his ambition. He called in Holofernes, the commander of his armies, and ordered him to gather his trained soldiers and go out and cover the earth with the feet of his marching men, and to slay all those who refused to place their necks in his yoke. Holofernes was a mighty and cruel soldier, and he delighted in carrying out the king's command.

Holofernes gathered a great army and he destroyed Phud and Lud, Rasses and Ismael; he killed all who resisted him in Cilicia; and he burned the Tabernacles of Madian. He reached Damascus in the season of the crops and set the fields afire and drove the flocks and herds into the pyres. The young men were destroyed by the edge of the sword; and the women, by all that is evil in the eyes of God.

The fear of Holofernes traveled before him to Sidon and Tyre, and it reached the dwellers of Azotus and Ascalon. When the Children of Israel, who were newly returned to Judea from captivity, heard of the evil deeds of Holofernes, they were exceedingly grieved. They gathered their armies at the mouth of a narrow gorge in the mountains near the city of Bethulia. So narrow was the gorge that an army could pass only in single file and could easily be destroyed. Holofernes was forced to camp outside the boundaries of Judea or face defeat.

A spy came to Holofernes and informed him that there were neither wells nor springs in the city of Bethulia, and its inhabitants depended on the water coming through the gorge.

"Cut off their water supply," said the spy, "and the gates of Bethulia will soon be opened to you by the thirsty people."

Holofernes camped near the gorge for thirty-four days, waiting for the people of Bethulia to surrender. By that time all the cisterns of Bethulia had run dry and the citizens fainted from thirst. The people began to demand that their leader Ozias open the city gates to the enemy.

And Ozias said: "Let us gather and pray and hold out just five more days. If our prayers are not answered by then, I will do according to your words."

There lived at that time in Bethulia a beautiful woman named Judith. Her husband had died during the harvest in the heat of the sun, and he had left his wife great wealth in gold and silver, cattle and lands, and servants many in number. Though rich and beautiful, Judith mourned her husband, devoted herself to charity, and there was none in Bethulia who gave her an ill word.

When Judith heard that Ozias had promised to open the gates to the enemy at the end of five days, she called him and asked:

"Who are you to set a time to the Lord in which to show His mercy? He knows the limits of our endurance; and if He wishes to destroy us, let Him guide the enemy through our gates. But what you have done may provoke the Lord our God to anger."

"The people are thirsty beyond reason," said Ozias. "If you know of a way to fill our cisterns, we shall not yield to the enemy."

"I know a way," said Judith. "Tonight, at midnight, you shall open the gates of the city to me and my maid. Then lock the gates and pray for me. But do not inquire what I plan to do, for I shall not declare it to any man."

That evening Judith took off her widow's garments and anointed herself with precious ointments; she braided her hair and put a band upon it; she clothed herself in a dress of purple and gold; she put sandals on her feet and bracelets on her hands; and she adorned herself with jewels to allure the eye of any man who would look upon her.

Then Judith and her maid left Bethulia at midnight. They walked through the valley all night and at sunrise reached the enemy camp. Judith approached the first guard of the army of Assur and said:

"Take me to Holofernes, the chief captain of your army, for I have information whereby he can conquer Judea without losing a single soldier."

Holofernes was resting under a canopy woven with gold, emeralds and precious stones, when Judith was brought before him.

"I am a Jewess and a prophetess," said Judith, "who fled from Bethulia because the Lord our God has decreed that none of your men shall die in battle for Judea. Permit me to remain here and go out into the hills each midnight to pray until God's will is fulfilled."

Holofernes looked upon her beauty with lust, and said: "God has done well to send you to me. For after my victory you shall dwell in my house and be renowned throughout the world."

A tent was set up for Judith and her maid and there they remained for three days, leaving each midnight to pray in the hills. On the fourth evening Holofernes arranged a great feast. And when Judith appeared, Holofernes was ravished with desire and waited impatiently for the banquet to end and his guests to leave that he might be alone with her. He offered Judith drink, and he drank more strong wine than he had drunk at any time in one evening since the day he was born.

When they were alone, Holofernes unsheathed his sword and offered it to Judith, saying drunkenly: "Before you I am defenseless."

Judith took the sword and whispered: "Strengthen my hand, O

Lord, God of Israel!" And she smote Holofernes twice upon the neck with all her might, and the head tumbled from his body.

Then she and her maid left the camp at midnight, as they had done all the nights before, and went back to Bethulia. There they displayed the head of the enemy, Holofernes, chief captain of the army of Assur, smitten by the hand of a woman.

The next morning the people hung the head of Holofernes upon the wall of their city, and went out to fight the enemy. The men of Assur waited for their captain to send them into battle, and when he failed to come, they went into his tent. There they found him, slain and headless. Then confusion reigned, and the great army of Assur fled in every direction and into the hills.

When the war was over, the people of Judea gathered to praise the Lord their God and to bless Judith. And they placed a garland of olive on her head and on the head of the maid that was with her in the camp of Holofernes, and Judith led all the people in a dance.

And there was none that made the Children of Israel any more afraid in the days of Judith, nor a long time after her death.

7. *The Bride at the Wedding*

There lived a righteous man in Babylon who enjoyed a great reputation among the people for his skill in the laws of Moses, and he was called Ezra the Learned. One day Ezra appeared before King Xerxes and pleaded:

"I wish to go up to Jerusalem, the Holy City, to help rebuild it; and I want to take with me those Jews in Babylon who are my followers and who wish to join me."

"What do you want of me?" asked the king.

"I want an epistle to the governors of Syria so that they will know who I and my followers are and will not molest us in our mission in the city of Jerusalem."

"Tell me, Ezra, why do you and your people wish to leave the glorious Babylon and return to devasted Jerusalem? And why do you always talk of Jerusalem the city, and not of Judea your country?" asked Xerxes.

"What the heart is to the body, what Moses is to the prophets, the Holy City is to the places on earth," said Ezra.

"What makes it so holy?" the king asked.

"When God created the earth, He began with the center where He placed a stone upon which the Holy Temple was later to be built. When the earth was completed, Judea was in the center of the earth, like an honored guest at a banquet table; the city of Jerusalem was in the center of Judea; the site of the Holy Temple was in the center of Jerusalem; the Holy of Holies was in the center of the Temple; and the Ark in the Holy of Holies was placed right over the foundation stone of the earth."

"Did God create this holy place just for your people?" asked the king.

"He created it for all who obey the Ten Commandments and fulfill the Six Hundred and Thirteen Articles of Faith. He therefore created the Holy City for all the righteous of mankind."

"Then why," asked the king, "do you consider yourselves the guardians and trustees of Jerusalem?"

"The Creator has seventy names; Israel has seventy names; and Jerusalem has seventy names. And the three are inseparable. Each of the seventy names of the Holy City represents one of our Holy Days: fifty-two for the Sabbaths; seven for the Passover; eight for Tabernacles; one for Pentecost; one for the New Year's Day; and one for the Day of Atonement. One may forget sixty-nine of the names of the Holy City and still be forgiven. But he who forgets Jerusalem — God may forget his right hand."

"If God, Israel and Jerusalem are so inseparable," asked the king, "why did God allow the city to be destroyed and the people taken captive?"

"When the iniquities of Israel were great, God wanted to mete out a punishment to equal the transgressions; and there is no punishment greater than the separation of the Jews from their Holy City. But after the Children of Israel had been punished, and they repented, God wanted them to return to Jerusalem and rebuild it."

King Xerxes was convinced, and he wrote a letter to all the governors of Syria, saying:

"Let it be known that I, Xerxes, King of Kings, hereby grant Ezra the Learned, reader in the Divine Law, the right to assemble his followers wherever they may be in my kingdom, and return from Babylon to Judea to help rebuild the City of Jerusalem, which they regard as the bride at the wedding; and I command you to help Ezra and not hinder him."

On the twelfth day of the first month of the seventh year of the reign of Xerxes, Ezra and his many followers left the Valley of Euphrates and returned to Jerusalem with prayer in their hearts and with songs upon their lips.

8. *Builder of Imperishable Walls*

The learned Ezra, who was also known as Malachi, after he returned from Babylon gathered the prophets Haggai and Zachariah about him, and together they surrounded themselves with a great assembly of learned men. And to them Ezra said:

"It is well that the walls of Jerusalem are being restored. Yet walls of stone do not make a fastness; nor walls of brick, a safe retreat. Men like Holofernes may rise again when there is no Judith to destroy them. Therefore, let us build walls of learning and faith that will be as walls of fire about us. Let us gather together all our knowledge and out of that raise up new walls of Jerusalem that shall remain standing forever; and that no tyrant will be able to destroy."

Ezra selected from the assembly five scribes who could write as fast as he could speak, and with them he withdrew for forty days. In their retreat an angel brought a chalice filled with liquid fire and offered it to Ezra. He took the chalice from the angel and drank from it. Then he dictated without a pause for forty days. When one of the scribes tired, another took his place. Only Ezra neither tired nor stopped until he had finished.

And when Ezra had finished at the end of forty days, ninety-four books had been dictated and written down. Of these, twenty-four comprised the Twenty-Four Books of the Holy Scriptures, intended for all the people; and the other seventy books, interpretations of the Law, intended for the scholars and the leaders.

And the books gathered by Ezra became the lasting foundation upon which were to be built walls for Jerusalem that could never be destroyed.

And the name of Ezra the Scribe will be remembered, along with the name of Moses, as long as the Law endures.

The Prophets of the Old Testament

The prophet appears in almost every religious lore. But nowhere does he assume the significance and stature of the Hebrew prophet of the Old Testament. The reason is not hard to find. The prophets of other nations constitute a number of individuals who, as Professor F. W. Robertson states it, "had the power of expounding the will and the word of God." They neither augmented nor supplemented each other in a system of prophecy. Whereas the Hebrew prophets, collectively, evolved a concrete ethic and a practical way of life, the core of which might be summed up by paraphrasing Micah's words: What the Lord requires of each man is that he should deal in justice, love mercy, and live humbly in the world that belongs to God.

All the Hebrew prophets, according to the lore, were healthy in body, sound in mind, had divine imagination, and, above all, understood clearly the yearnings in man's heart and the conflict of his desires. And they prophesied the resolution of man's conflicts. What they prophesied is recorded in the Books of the Prophets — from Moses to Malachi — and constitute the major part of the Old Testament.

True and False Prophets: *There are many prophets in the folklore of the Bible, some good and some bad, or rather, some true and some false. The difference between the true and the false prophet is a matter of definition.*

Anyone inspired of God, or who had "seen" God, or through whom God had "spoken," or through whom God had communicated His truth to the rulers and the people, was called a prophet. Where the names of the prophets' parents are given in the Bible, the parents are also counted among the prophets in folklore. And in the lore the birthplace of all the prophets was assumed to be Jerusalem, the Holy City, unless otherwise specifically given.

The false prophet was he who, seeing with his hidden eye, and hearing with his hidden ear, allowed fear of the king and the people to make his prophecy a lying spirit in his mouth. Worst of all, he sold his prophecy for a price and sank to the level of the fortune-teller and the stargazer.

The true prophet always spoke as the Lord had "spoken." He warned. He condemned. And he comforted. Above all, he prophesied for peace. "The prophet who prophesieth of peace," said Jeremiah, "when the word of the prophet shall come to pass, then shall the prophet be known that the Lord hath truly sent him." (Jer. 28:9) Peace, wherewith the world was created and without which the world cannot survive, is the test and touchstone of the Hebrew prophet.

According to folklore, prophecies for peace or any blessing will always be fulfilled — if prophesied by a true prophet, but prophecies of war or any other misfortune may or may not be fulfilled, since God might withhold punishment if the forewarned repent. But whether his prophecy is fulfilled or not, the true prophet always interprets the will of God.

The Number of Prophets: *According to some folklore sources, the number of prophets before the Babylonian Captivity was indeed very great. All the ancients, before the Patriarchs, had the power of prophecy and each could name his children by the events that were to happen to them later in their lives. All the Patriarchs, of course, had the power of prophecy. Later we find all the Judges credited with the power of prophecy.*

Samuel established "guilds of prophets" whose number was considerable. In the days of the Kings, the Old Testament mentions hundreds of prophets. Ahab, King of Israel, and Jehosophat, King of Judah, "gathered the prophets together, about four hundred men," and consulted them about going to war against Gilead. The wicked Queen Jezebel executed hundreds of prophets. Obadiah, according to the Bible, saved a hundred prophets from execution by Jezebel and "hid them by fifty in a cave." In Elijah's times there were many schools of prophets and a great number of disciples of Elijah and Elisha.

In the days of the Kings, most of the prophets were related to the royal families and were financially independent. They kept apart from political or military matters, and acted as mentors and critics of the court and as spiritual guides to the people.

So gifted was Israel in prophecy, that in one part of the Babylonian Talmud (devoted to the Book of Esther) it is claimed that there were twice as many prophets in Israel as the total number of Jews who left Egypt under the leadership of Moses — six hundred thousand prophets according to that reckoning. But the same source, a little later, reduces the number considerably, stating that after Moses, the Prophet of Prophets, "Forty-eight prophets and seven prophetesses spoke prophecies for Israel, and they neither deducted from nor added to what was written in the Five Books of Moses."

The seven prophetesses were: Sarah, Miriam, Deborah, Hannah, Abigail, Huldah and Esther.

The forty-eight prophets included the Patriarchs, the pre-Mosaic saints, and the prophets given in the Bible. The names of these forty-eight prophets are not enumerated, and various lists have been drawn up by later commentators on this passage.

Traditional Division: *One widely accepted division of the prophets designates them as:* Moses, *who is placed in a category by himself as the Prophet of Prophets;* Joshua and the Prophet Judges; *the* Early Prophets, *which include* Samuel, Nathan and Gad; *Elijah, Elisha and Ahijah; the* Latter or Great Prophets: *Isaiah, Jeremiah and Ezekiel (and some add Daniel as the fourth of the Great Prophets); then come the* Three Pillars of the World: *Hannaniah, Mishael and Azariah; followed by the* Twelve Minor Prophets: *Hosea, Joel, Amos, Obadiah, Jonah, Micah, Nahum, Haggai, Zechariah, Sephaniah, Habakkuk and Malachi. And finally there is* Job, *the Prophet of the Gentiles, who is also in a category by himself.*

1. MOSES, the Prophet of Prophets

Born in Egyptian slavery as the younger son of Amram and Jocheved. Since the names of both his parents are given, they, too, had the power of prophecy. In folklore the birth of Moses was attended by many miracles, as were all the days of his life. Moses emancipated the Jews from slavery, and is credited with being the author of the Five Books of Moses (the Pentateuch), which he wrote by divine inspiration.

2. JOSHUA, the Successor to Moses

The story of Joshua the son of Nun, and a member of the Tribe of Ephraim, is given in the Sixth Book of the Old Testament, which bears his name. Some Biblical scholars consider the Book of Joshua as a continuation of Deuteronomy, and add it to the Pentateuch, thus forming the Hexateuch. Joshua is regarded very highly in both Jewish tradition and in Jewish lore, and is considered one of the few men in the entire history of mankind who "died without sin."

3. THE PROPHET JUDGES

In the Seventh Book of the Old Testament, which the Talmud ascribes to the Prophet Samuel, we are given a record of fourteen Judges, and all had the power of prophecy. These Judges were: Othniel, son of Kenaz; Ehud, son of Greah; Shagmar, son of Anot; Deborah, wife of Lapidoth; Barak, son of Abinoam; Gideon, son of Joash; Abimelech, son of Gideon; Toalh, son of Push; Jair, the Gileadite; Jephtah, son of Gilead and a harlot; Izban of Bethlehem; Elon, the Zebulenite; Abdon, son of Hillel; and the far-famed Samson, son of Manoah.

The traditional period of the Judges is four hundred and ten years; but critically it has been estimated to have lasted less than three hundred years. Whatever the length, it was a fierce period in which the guidance of prophecy was more important to the people than the service of the magistrates. And it was in this period that some of the greatest folklore stories of the Bible were created.

4. SAMUEL, the Kingmaker

The Eighth Book of the Old Testament, in the original Hebrew, is devoted to the Prophet Samuel, considered the first of the Early Prophets, who inspired many legends covering his long and eventful life. Samuel was dedicated to the priesthood before his birth, and received the call to become a prophet of God when still a child serving in the Temple of Shiloh under the High Priest Eli. Later, when his own unworthy sons were grown, Samuel warned the people against the tyranny of kings before he yielded to their demands and anointed Saul the first king in Israel. In his old age, when Samuel became displeased with Saul, he secretly anointed David as Saul's successor. The best-known legends about Samuel are those that tell of his childhood; and the weird tale of the Witch of Endor who conjured up his soul to foretell King Saul's end.

5. NATHAN, Successor to Samuel

We know little about this prophet, excepting that he was a friend of King David until David caused the death of one of his generals in order to appropriate his wife, Bath-sheba. Nathan's rebuke to King David resulted in one of the most beautiful parables in Biblical folklore, "The Parable of the Poor Man's Lamb." Nathan took part in securing the throne for Bath-sheba's son, Solomon. He is also credited with the authorship of the fifty-first Psalm.

6. GAD

Gad, like Nathan, is known mainly through Samuel. He appears to have been an adviser to King David for a long time. Whereas Nathan rebuked the king for breaking the com-

mandment against coveting a neighbor's wife, Gad rebuked him for having taken a census, which was prohibited in the command to Moses. In the choice King David made of three punishments offered by Gad, a great folk lesson was taught.

7. ELIJAH, the Tishbite

Elijah, the Tishbite, lived in the days of King Ahab and the wicked Queen Jezebel, in the 9th century B.C. Though not counted among the major prophets, he is the most beloved in folklore. He is the favorite of the Chassidic sect, whose pious members "recognize" the Prophet Elijah in every man who does a kindly deed — particularly to those in need. And as Prince Elijah the Green, he is often on the lips of the Moslems.

8. ELISHA

Elisha, inheritor of Elijah's mantle, was the son of a wealthy landowner. He left his father's home and heritage to follow in Elijah's footsteps. Elisha lived most of his long life in Samaria and prophesied for over sixty years. There are many legends about Elisha and his miracles, but he is best remembered for a sermon of only three words: "God is Salvation."

9. AHIJAH, the Shilomite

Ahijah, the Shilomite, we know only as the prophet who foretold the breaking up of the Jewish Kingdom, the Ten Tribes coming under the rule of Jeroboam the Ephraimite. Only two tribes, according to legend, remained in the Kingdom of Judah under the rule of Solomon's descendants — one tribe for the sake of King David and another for the sake of the city of Jerusalem.

10. ISAIAH, the Incomparable

Isaiah, the Incomparable, was born in 760 B.C. and was probably of royal descent. He prophesied for forty years, from 740 to 700 B.C., until he was executed by King Menasseh. Isaiah lived through the sorrowful years of the downfall of the Kingdom of Israel. He is the first of the Great Prophets and esteemed only second to Moses. His profound mind and deep understanding of human sorrow was equaled by his poetic imagery and gift of expression. There are many legends about the martyrdom of Isaiah; and one great legend about the Ascension of Isaiah to heaven is found in a pseudepigraphic work by that name.

11. JEREMIAH

Jeremiah, known both as The Tragic and The Gentle, was born in 650 B.C. in Anathoth, a small town near Jerusalem. It is claimed that he was a direct descendant of Joshua. Isaiah lived through the downfall of the Kingdom of Israel; Jeremiah witnessed the destruction of the Kingdom of Judah. When the Temple was destroyed and the people taken captive into Babylonia, Jeremiah escaped to Egypt where he died as sorrowfully as he lived. Jeremiah is often described as shy, sensitive, peace-loving, and gentle. According to apocryphal and other sources, the prophecies of Jeremiah and the Lamentations ascribed to him were dictated to his disciple and secretary, Baruch ben Neriah, who edited and revised them.

12. EZEKIEL, the Fearless

Ezekiel, the Fearless, first prophet in Exile, began to prophesy in 592 B.C., when he was already in exile himself, and he foretold the fall of Jerusalem and the Babylonian Captivity.

Five years later, when his people were led into captivity, Ezekiel strengthened their faith by prophesying their ultimate restoration to their homeland. Ezekiel was a fierce prophet, a harsh believer in absolute justice, the deed always determining the reward. He was also an esoteric and symbolical prophet who gave the rational Talmudists the greatest concern; and to the Cabbalists, the greatest comfort. In folklore he is best remembered for his exploits in the Valley of Dry Bones.

13. DANIEL

Daniel, whom the Christians include (and the Jews exclude from) among the Great Prophets, lived in the days of Ezekiel. Daniel was brought as a captive to Babylon when very young and he received his education in Babylonia. He reminds one of Joseph in his visions and wisdom; his interpretation of dreams; his escapes from danger; and the adventurous life he led. In folklore Daniel's wisdom is extolled in the judgment of Susanna; his courage, in the lions' den; and his imagination, in the description of the marvelous contents of dreams and visions.

14. HANNANIAH, MISHAEL and AZARIAH

Hannaniah, Mishael and Azariah have left us no prophecies of their own, and we know about them, scripturally, through Daniel. Yet they occupy seats of honor among the prophets in the lore. They have been named The Three Pillars of the World. *So important are these three regarded that, according to one Midrashic source, "at the Creation God made a condition . . . with fire not to injure" them when thrust into a furnace in Babylon. And when God becomes despondent over the wickedness of mankind He remembers the goodness of Hannaniah, Mishael and Azariah, and for their sake He allows the world to continue to exist.*

15. THE TWELVE or THE MINOR PROPHETS

The Twelve or The Minor Prophets, lived between the 8th and 5th centuries B.C. We know little about most of them and their total contribution is not very great. All twelve, combined, are lesser in volume than the Book of Isaiah; and considerably lesser in their content. Hosea, Micah, Amos, and Jonah lived in the 6th century B.C.; Nahum, Habakkuk and Zephaniah lived a century later; Haggai and Zechariah lived in the 6th century; Joel, Obadiah and Malachi belong to the 5th century. Malachi has the distinction of being the last of the Hebrew prophets and the lesser distinction of being the least inspired of them all. But in folklore he assumes importance because of the speculation about his identity. Some Talmudic commentators definitely identify him as Ezra the Scribe.

The order of the Twelve varies in different versions of the Old Testament. The King James version follows the Hebrew order. The Septuagint arranges them by length of Book, the longest Book coming first.

16. JOB, the Prophet of the Gentiles

Job, the Prophet of the Gentiles, is identified in the Septuagint with King Jobab of Edom, which would make him an Edomite. But in Biblical lore, Job's identity is the subject of many contradictory legends, some even claiming that he never existed. Although regarded very highly by the Jews (in the Hebrew Bible the Book of Job is placed after the Psalms and the Proverbs and before the Song of Songs, thereby indicating the high place it holds in the Sacred Writings), Job is nowhere treated as a prophet nor included among them. But in the folklore his prophetic powers are extolled and his saintliness praised above his patience, for he is recognized as the one whom God considered "a perfect and upright man."

Basic Sources

A *selected list is given in the* Reading List with Notes *of specific editions of the Bible, biblical interpretations, Apocrypha and pseudepigrapha, the Midrashim and other haggadic sources, collections of biblical folklore, and miscellaneous works bearing on this topic. But there are several generic sources which everyone interested in the lore will want to know about, particularly their structural relationship. They are:*

(a) The Bible: *Biblical lore quite naturally begins with* The Bible. *Not only is it the topic and the prompter of all this folklore, but is itself a great treasury of legends, parables, proverbs and precepts.*

In Hebrew the Old Testament is divided into three parts: the Pentateuch; *the* Prophets *and the* Hagiographa. *The Books of the Old Testament are the same in both Hebrew and English versions, although the order in which they appear differs. (In Hebrew, the Thirty Nine Books are enumerated under twenty-four titles, and invariably so listed in the Talmud. Josephus mentions only twenty-two books* (Apion I:8), *which was apparently another arrangement to correspond to the twenty-two letters of the Hebrew alphabet.)*

(b) The Apocrypha: *The fourteen books excluded from the Hebrew and Protestant versions of the Old Testament are included in the Greek Orthodox and Roman Catholic versions.*

(c) Pseudepigrapha: *These rejected books are not as fixed as the Apocrypha, and the inclusion varies in different editions. An outstanding collection will be found in the second volume of* The Apocrypha and the Pseudepigrapha of the Old Testament, *edited by R. H. Charles.*

(d) The Mishnah: *Next only to the Scriptures is the collection of books known as* Mishnah, *meaning* Repetition.

The Mishnah existed for generations and was transmitted orally before it was set down in writing during the 3rd Century B.C. The Mishnah is divided into six Orders: Torts, Women, Seasons, Purities, Seeds *and* Sanctities. *These Six Books are divided into sixty-three tractates, or treatises; each treatise is divided into chapters; and each chapter into paragraphs. Curiously enough, each paragraph in the Mishnah is called a Mishnah.*

(e) The Talmud: *Around the Mishnah two great schools of study developed, one in Babylonia and the other in Jerusalem. Their various expositions, explanations, interpretations and anecdotal examples fill many large volumes, and are known as* Gemara, *meaning* Completion. *The Mishnah together with Gemara is called* Talmud, *meaning simply* Study *and commonly accepted to mean* Study of the Law.

There are two encyclopedic works of the Talmud:

The Babylonian Talmud, *finished about 500 A.D., which contains the unequal contributions of nearly 2200 scholars, is written principally in Aramaic and covers thirty-six of the sixty-three Mishnaic treatises. Whether the Gemara of the remaining twenty-seven treatises were similarly covered and lost in manuscript is unknown. The entire of the Babylonian Talmud was compiled and edited by two men, known to us only as Rab and Samuel.*

The Palestinian Talmud, *or more correctly, the* Talmud of Jerusalem, *is generally held in lesser esteem by theologians and students. Though it covers thirty-nine treatises of the Mishnah, it is less than one third the size of the Babylonian Talmud.*

The Talmud is divided into the rules and regulations whereby a Jew must live, known as Halachah, *which means* The Path; *and the explanatory material and narratives known as* Haggadah, *meaning* The Legends. *Whereas Halachah is the law inflexible, the Haggadah is merely the opinion of the expositor. About one third of the Babylonian Talmud is devoted to Haggadah, a source of so much of the folklore of the Old Testament.*

(f) The Midrash *(plural* Midrashim), *meaning* Definition: *Midrashim, the richest source of Biblical folklore, began to appear very early, long before either Talmud was compiled, and continued to be written down to the Middle Ages. The most important Midrashim*

deal with Haggadah, often an entire book being devoted to one Biblical character or one important Biblical event, such as the Creation, the Deluge, the Exodus; and there are Midrashim devoted to Esther, the Psalms, Ecclesiastes and other Books.

(g) Talmudic Commentaries: The Talmud exerted a great influence on Jews the world over and great importance was attached to its study. From time to time a teacher or scholar would write a commentary on the Talmud. The best of these, and generally so recognized, is the commentary of Rabbi Solomon ben Isaac, who lived toward the end of the 11th Century A.D. and is known as Rashi. Wherever the Talmud was studied after his time, Rashi's commentaries were also studied.

(h) Zohar, meaning The Splendor: This is a mystical commentary on the Pentateuch, and was regarded by its followers, the Cabbalists (and, later, by the religious sect known as Chassidim), the equal of the Mishnah and the superior of the Gemara. Its influence on Biblical folklore is inestimable, particularly in its symbolic and mystic ways of buttressing joy as an instrument of faith.

(i) The Tzenoh-u-Renoh: The Women's Bible in Yiddish is neither a translation of the Bible nor a commentary upon it, but a partial paraphrase of some of the Scriptures, interwoven with many folk tales drawn from various sources and retold to suit the circumstances of the people for whom these books were produced. Though scorned by Biblical scholars as lacking in originality and, in parts, spurious, these books are basic as sources of lore adapted for and accepted by the common and uneducated people.

Beyond these basic sources, the literature on the topic is extensive and the range as wide as one's inclinations. Practically all the encyclopedias contain Biblical lore by topics, from Adam and Creation to Nehemiah and Zerubbabel. There are a number of valuable treasuries of Talmudic and Midrashic lore. And there are comparatively recent collections of the legends of the Old Testament, mostly in Hebrew. The most important of these sources are given in the Reading List.

Notes on Sources

The sources of Biblical folklore are numerous and often confusing because the same legend frequently appears in different forms in diverse versions, or is attributed to different Biblical characters. To indicate all the variations and the reasons for selecting one and rejecting others would require considerably more space than has been given to the legends themselves; and for the same reason it is equally impossible to key every allusion in every legend.

The reader will find that, wherever possible, the *English translation of an original source* is given — assuming that most readers may not have access to the Midrashim, the Talmudim, the Yalkutim, the Otzarim and similar works. Also, many of the original source books contain neither index nor table of contents and, if a different edition were consulted than the one given in this book, it would be difficult to trace a legend; whereas all the English sources contain tables of contents, and most of them contain indices.

Specific editions for each source are given, because many of them have appeared in a number of editions, differing widely in pagination, in order of chapters, and even in contents. The reader who cannot obtain the edition cited in this book, and who finds a discrepancy in either material or page numbers, is advised to look up the legend or belief topically, in the index of any obtainable edition. The reader who is eager to track down a legend or belief in its many variations, and encounters difficulties, is advised to consult, topically, *The Jewish Encyclopedia,* which is the best reference work in English on the folklore of the Old Testament; he may also wish to consult the *Otzar Yisroel* (*The Hebrew Encyclopedia*), and the detailed Index (Volume VII) to *The Legends of the Jews* by Louis Ginzberg.

For Mohammedan legends, the reader is referred to *The Encyclopedia of Islam.*

To obviate confusion, the number of titles included in these sources has been limited, and arranged alphabetically; and to avoid repetition of frequently referred-to titles and all their necessary vital statistics (author, publisher, edition, date) symbols are used for the titles. If the work is in more than one volume, the volume number is given; and where the text on the page is printed in more than one column, the letters *a*, *b* and *c* are used after the page number to designate the column.

(For brief estimates of each of the sources given here, see *Reading List with Notes*.)

SYMBOLS USED:

AOT   *The Old Testament Apocrypha* as they appear in the Authorized King James Version, in the edition of C. Ewer and T. Bedlington, Boston, 1827

ARN   *Aboth d'Rabbi Nathan* (The Sayings of the Fathers according to Rabbi Nathan), in Hebrew, edited by S. Z. Schechter; Shulsinger Press, New York, 1945

BB   *The Burning Bush*, in English, by Joseph Gaer; The Sinai Press (Union of American Hebrew Congregations), Cincinnati, 1929

BT   *The Babylonian Talmud*, in English, edited by Isidore Epstein; in 34 volumes; Soncino Press, London, 1935–1950

BTA   *Bible Tales in Arab Folk-lore*, in English, by Joseph Meyouhas; translated from the Hebrew by Victor N. Levi; Alfred A. Knopf, London, 1928

ET   *Everyman's Talmud*, in English, by A. Cohen; new American edition, E. P. Dutton & Co., New York, 1949

FJ   *The Folklore of the Jews*, in English, by Angelo S. Rappoport; Soncino Press, London, 1937

GP   *The Guide for the Perplexed*, by Moses Maimonides, translated from the Arabic by M. Friedländer; new American edition, Pardes Publishing House, New York, 1946

ICP   *And It Came to Pass*, by C. N. Bialik, translated from the Hebrew by Herbert Danby; Hebrew Publishing Company, New York, 1935

KHY   *Kol Haggodoth Yisroel* (All the Legends of the Jews), in Hebrew, edited by J. B. Levner; in 4 volumes (often bound in one volume); Toshia Press, Warsaw, 1902

LI   *The Legends of Israel*, edited by J. B. Levner; Book I (From Creation to the Death of Joseph) translated into English by Joel Snowman; James Clarke & Company, London, 1946

LJ *The Legends of the Jews*, in English, by Louis Ginzberg; translated from the German manuscript by Henrietta Szold; in 7 volumes (three volumes devoted to notes on sources and an index); Jewish Publication Society of America, Philadelphia, 1909–1938

M *The Mishnah* (The Oral Torah), in Hebrew;[1] compiled by Rabbi Judah ben Simeon about 1st century B.C.; consists of 63 Tractates, divided into 6 books, called Orders; Romm Edition cited in this book is bound in 5 volumes, with introductions to the Orders *Zeraim* (Seeds) and *Toharoth* (Purities) by Moses Maimonides; Romm Press, Vilna, 1908

MF *The Magic Flight*, in English, by Joseph Gaer; Frank-Maurice, New York, 1926

MH *M'Otzar Ha'Haggadah* by Micah J. Berdyczewski (known also as Bin Gurion); 8 parts in 2 volumes; Achisepher Press, Berlin, 1913

MR *Midrash Rabah* (The Great Midrashim on the Pentateuch ınd the Five Megiloth: Song of Songs; Ruth; Lamentations; Ecclesiastes; and Esther), in Hebrew; 3 volumes, Grossman Press, Stettin, 1860

OM *Otzar Midrashim* (The Treasury of the Midrashim), edited by J. D. Eisenstein; in 2 volumes, arranged alphabetically, and includes, in addition to the Great Midrash, all the minor Midrashim; Eisenstein Publishers, New York, 1915

PA *Pirke Aboth* (Sayings of the Fathers), in Hebrew; the Ninth Tractate in the Order *Nezikin* (Torts) of the Mishnah; appears in numerous editions with profuse comments; edition cited in this book is the one edited by Joseph H. Hertz; Behrman House, New York, 1945 (see SF)

PRE *Pirke d'Rabbi Eliezer* (Comments of Rabbi Eliezer), in Hebrew, by Rabbi Eliezer ben Hurkenos; P. Levinson Press, Warsaw, 1879

S *Sifre debe Rab* (The Books of Rab) in Hebrew, a commentary

---

[1] When citing the Mishnah, first the Order and then the Tractate is given, the page number coming last, as follows: *M: Moed-Shabbath, 54b* which stands for: *The Mishnah*, Order *Moed* (The Season), Tractate *Shabbath* (The Sabbath), page 54, second column.

on Numbers and Deuteronomy by one of the editors of the Babylonian Talmud; edited by M. Friedman; J. Holtzworth Press, Vienna, 1864

SF   *Sayings of the Fathers* (see PA), English translation, with parallel text in Hebrew, by Joseph H. Hertz, Behrman House, New York, 1945

SH   *Sepher Ha'Haggadah* (The Book of Narratives) by J. D. Ravnitzki and C. N. Bialik; in 6 books (bound in 3 volumes); Moriah Press, Jerusalem and Berlin, 1922

SK   *The Short Koran,* in English, edited by George M. Lamsa; Ziff-Davis Publishing Company, Chicago, 1949

ST   *Midrash Shocher Tov: Tehillim* (Midrash to the Psalms by Shocher Tov), in Hebrew; in all likelihood a collective work in spite of the title; edited by Solomon Buber; Romm Press, Vilna, 1891

T   *The Talmud* (The Study of the Mishnah), in Hebrew and Aramaic (See The Talmud, *Reading List*);[2] only the Talmud Bavli (Babylonian Talmud) is cited in this book; edition used: Talmud Bavli, in 18 volumes, edited by Aggudath Horabonim d'Artzuth Hebrith ve Canada; the Eagle Publishing Company, Montreal, 1919

TAN   *Midrash Tanchuma* (Commentary on the Pentateuch), in Hebrew, by Rabbi Tanchuma ben Rabbi Abba; edited by Solomon Buber; Romm Press, Vilna, 1885

TZ   *Tzenoh-u-Renoh* (Let Us Go Out and See), in Yiddish, by Jacob ben Isaac Ashkenazi; first published in 1620; edition cited in 2 volumes; Matza Press, Vilna, 1906

UN   *The Unconquered,* in English, by Joseph Gaer; The Sinai Press (Union of American Hebrew Congregations), Cincinnati, 1932

UO   *Fon Unser Otzar* (From Our Treasury), in Yiddish; in 2 volumes — Volume I edited by Chaim Shauss, Volume II edited by B. J. Bialostovsky; Central Yiddish Culture Organization (Cyco Publishers), New York, 1945–1949

---

[2] As in the case of the Mishnah, the Order and Tractate precede the page number.

Yalkut Shimoni (Collection of Comments on the Old Testament), in Hebrew, by Rabbi Shimon of Frankfurt; Chorov Press, Berlin, 1925

Sepher Ha'Zohar al Ha'Torah, in Hebrew and Aramaic, issued by Moses ben Shem Tov de Leon and attributed to Rabbi Shimon ben Yohai; in 3 volumes; Goldman Press, Warsaw, 1867

PART I: *In the Beginning*

CHAPTER ONE: THE WEEK OF CREATION

1. *The First Day of Creation* (T: Moed-Chagigah, 12a, 12b; Moed-Yoma 21b; Moed-Taanith 10a; Nezikin-Baba Bathra 25a. MR: Gen. I–XII; Exod. XV, 22; Num. II, 10; Deut. 306, 132a; Esther I, 12. TZ: Supplications I, 2; Gen. I, 3a. LJ: I, 8–13. ET: 29–38. FJ: 23.)

2. *The Second Day of Creation* (TZ: I, 2-3. LJ: I, 15.)

3. *The Third Day of Creation* (PRE: 51. LJ: I, 19. GP: Part III, XXIX, 318 gives the quarrel between the althea and the mandragora as to which plant is more effective in witchcraft. See also LJ: I, 31–32, and V, Notes 147–148, which give further references to "plant-men" and women who grew on trees." GP: Part III, XXIX, 318 tells of wonderful and terrible plants, attributed to the Book of Adam in a book, *On the Nabatean Agriculture*.)

4. *The Fourth Day of Creation* (T: Kodashin-Chullin, 60. TZ: I, 4b, 5a. LJ: I, 23–24. MH: I, 5.) . . . *The Sun Sets Sadly* (T: Nezikin-Baba Bathra, 84a. ET: 380.) . . . *How Many Stars Are There?* (T: Zeraim-Berachoth, 32a. ET: 380. Z: II, 176 advances the idea that every plant and animal is represented by a star in heaven. Not only the birds and bees but the herbs and trees have stars. Even each variety of stone has a star, which appears at nightfall and shines three hours past midnight. A similar idea is expounded in GP: Part II, V, 159, and X, 164.)

5. *The Fifth Day of Creation* (T: Zeraim-Berachoth, 40a. TZ: I, 5b. LJ: I, 26–27. GP: Part III, XXIII, 303 describes the Leviathan.) . . . *After the Fish the Birds* (TZ: I, 6b.) . . . *Then Came the Angels* (MR: Gen. VIII, 11, XLIII, 14; Exod. XVIII, 5, XXI, 4. T: Nezikin-Sanhedrin, 38b; Zeraim-Berachoth, 19a, 46a; Nezikin-Baba Kamma, 60b. ET: 47–58. GP: Part II, VI, 160-162)

6. *The Last Day of Creation* (TZ: I, 8.) ... *The Creation of M*
(MR: Gen. V, 5–8; VIII, 11. KHY: 11, 69. PRE: 11. TZ: I, 7. LI: 2
SK: 61. ET: 68. MH: I, 9.) ... *The Ten Wonders of the World* (1
Nezikin-Aboth V, 9. PA: 86–88. SF: 87–89. ET: 11. SH: I, 14.)

7. *The Perfect Creation* (T: Moed-Shabbath, 77b; MR: Gen. VII
4; IX, 5–9; XII, 1. ET: 17, 38–39.)

8. *The Sabbath* (T: Moed-Taanith, 27b. ET: 78. GP: Part II, XXX
218–219. TZ: I: Sabbath Prayers, 11b.)

CHAPTER TWO: THE GARDEN OF EDEN

1. *God's Dilemma* (OM: 164b. TZ: I, 12.)

2. *The First Hour of Man's Creation* (TZ: I, 11. In the *Sibylline Or*
cles III, 24–26, and the *Slavonic Book of Enoch* another version is give
on the selection of the dust from which Adam was fashioned.)

3. *The Second Hour of Man's Creation* (T: Teharoth-Oaloth, I,
MR: Gen. LXVII, 3; Num. XVII, 22. TZ: I, Sabbath Prayers, 12. Ge
11. ET: 70–71.) ... *The Importance of the Tongue* (ET: 99. TZ: I
487–489. ICP: 117–127.) ... *The Image of the Universe* (ARN: XXX
ET: 70. T: Nezikin-Sanhedrin, 38a. LJ: I, 49–50. GP: Part I, LXXI
113–119.)

4. *The Third and Fourth Hours of Man's Creation* (ET: 67, 76. MI
Gen. XXIV, 7. T: Nezikin-Sanhedrin, 38a. TZ: I, 12. MH: I, 13. GI
Part I, I, 14.)

5. *The Fifth Hour of Man's Creation* (KHY: I, 20. LI: 28–29. 1
XX. UO: I, 34.)

6. *The Sixth Hour of Man's Creation* (LJ: I, 61–62; V, 86. MH: I, 1
SK: 61–63. TZ: I, 13–14.)

7. *The Seventh Hour of Man's Creation* (LJ: I, 64–65. TZ: I, 14
... *The Creation of Woman* (KHY: I, 19. LI: 27–28. SH: I, 15–1
TZ: I, 14–15. UO: I, 35–36. T: Moed-Erubin, 18a, where the idea
expressed that Adam and Eve were at first one being.)

8. *The Eighth Hour of Man's Creation* (MR: Gen. XVIII. LJ: I, 68
... *The Story of Quarina* (BTA: 15–16. [This Arabic legend is obvious
based on the story of Lilith, which is of Babylonian origin and adopte

in many Jewish sources.] See GP: Part III, XXXVII, 333 on women and witchcraft; see also UO: I, 34–35.)

9. *The Ninth Hour of Man's Creation* (LJ: I, 62–64. In the Second Book of the Secrets of Enoch: 29, 4–5 Satan is called Satanael. See GP: Part II, XXX, 217 on Tree of Life.) . . . *Why Cherries are Red* (KHY: I, 27. MF: 83–91.)

CHAPTER THREE: THE FALL OF MAN

1. *The Plot of the Serpent* (KHY: I, 20. LI: 29. LJ: I, 74–75, and 95–96; V, Note on Adam, 70. GP: II, XXX, 213. FJ: 29. TZ: I, 15–16. UO: I, 33 and 37–38.)

2. *The Deathless Hoyl* (KHY: I, 21–22. LI: 29–30. LJ: I, 32. TZ: I, 16–18. MH: I, 16.)

3. *The Judgment* (ET: 192. TZ: I, 13 on Adam's gift to David, and 18–21. UO: I, 55–56.)

4. *The Expulsion* (ST: XCII. PRE: XI. OM: 10a, b gives the ten punishments each of Adam, Eve and the serpent. *See also:* TZ: I, 22–23. FJ: 64. . . . In *The Nabatean Agriculture,* according to Maimonides, Adam took with him into exile trees of gold and of stone, trees with leaves that could not be burned, and one tree, the height of a man, that could provide shelter for ten thousand men. GP: Part III, XXIX, 316.)

5. *The First Tears* (KHY: I, 23–24. LI: 30–31. OM: 401b. LJ: I, 90–94. Z: I, 55b.)

6. *The Light of Fire* (MR: Gen. II, 12. ST: 92. KHY: I, 22–24. LI: 31–32. UO: I, 40–41.)

7. *The First Family* (TZ: I, 23.)

8. *The Child in the Mother's Womb* (ET: 70. T: Teharoth-Niddah, 30b.)

9. *The First Winter* (The Book of Adam and Eve, as translated by S. C. Malan, for this entire chapter.)

10. *Why the Swallow Has a Forked Tail* (MF: 39–45.)

11. *The Quarrel of the Brothers* (KHY: I, 24–26. LI: 32–33. TZ: I, 22–28. MH: I, 24–25. SH: I, 18–19. SK: 64. UO: I, 47–50.)

12. *Cain's Punishment* (LJ: I, 109–113. MR: Gen. XXII. TZ: I, 23–25; this variation on the "marking" of Cain maintains that as soon as Cain killed his brother he began to grow a horn in the middle of his forehead.)

13. *The Heart of a Fox* (LJ: 153–157. MH: I, 17–20. UO: II, 188–191.)

14. *Lemech's Family* (TZ: I, 25–26. TAN: Gen. II gives an interesting account of the end of Cain at the hands of Lemech.)

CHAPTER FOUR: THE GREAT DELUGE

1. *The Fallen Angels* (MR: Noah, 34. KHY: I, 33–34. LI: 40. LJ: I, 124–125. MH: I, 31–32. Book of Enoch I, IX, X. TZ: I, 26. UO: I, 64.)

2. *From Wickedness to Idolatry* (SH: I, 20.)

3. *The Man Who Walked with God* (KHY: I, 36–39. LI: 36–39. TZ: I, 28–29. LJ: I, 127–140. Book of Jubilees. MH: I, 27–28. OM: 183a, b. UO: I, 56–58.)

4. *Enoch the Writer* (BTA: 19. Book of Jubilees 4:15–25.)

5. *The Little Deluge* (LJ: I, 123, 127. MR. Gen. XXIII.)

6. *The Good Noah* (LJ: I, 145–147 on the miracles at the birth of Noah. See also: SK: 66. TZ: I, 33.)

7. *Noah Preaches Repentance* (TZ: I, 32–34. SKY: I, 40–41. MR: Gen. 30. UO: I, 68.)

8. *Noah Builds an Ark* (LJ: I, 153–154. TZ: I, 33–34.)

9. *How Big Is God?* (LJ: I, 29. MF: 115–120.)

10. *Invitation to the Ark* (TZ: I, 34–35.)

11. *Falsehood and Misfortune* (KHY: I, 41–42. LI: 45–46. ST: 7. UO: I, 69.)

12. *The Decree of Continence* (TZ: I, 39.)

13. *The Deluge Begins* (MR: Noah, 32. LJ: I, 158. KHY: I, 44–45. LI: 48. UO: I, 75–76.)

14. *Tragedy in the Ark* (T: Nezikin-Sanhedrin, 108b. PRE: 23. KHY: I, 47–48.)

15. *The Covenant of the Rainbow* (MR: Gen. XXXIII. LJ: I, 166; V, Noah, Note 55.)

16. *Noah's Vineyard* (TAN: Gen. 13. LJ: I, 167–168. KHY: I, 47. LI: 50. UO: I, 82.)

17. *Noah's Story* (TZ: I, 43.)

CHAPTER FIVE: THE AGE OF CONFUSION

1. *Nimrod the Hunter* (LJ: I, 177–178. KHY: I, 48. LI: 51. UO: I, 84.)

2. *Nimrod the King* (PRE: 24. KHY: I, 49. LI: 51.)

3. *Nimrod Wants to Be God* (LJ: I, 178; V, Noah, Note 87.)

4. *The Tower of Babel* (LJ: I, 179–181. ET: 260–261. MH: I, 41–42. TZ: I, 43–44. UO: I, 85–86.)

5. *The Confusion of Tongues* (LJ: I, 180. ET: 99. ARN: XII.)

6. *The Fate of the Tower and Its Builders* (MR: Gen. XXXVIII. T: Nezikin-Sanhedrin, 109a. TZ: I, 44.)

PART II: *The Patriarchs*

CHAPTER SIX: FATHER ABRAHAM

1. *Miracles at Birth* (TAN: Lech Lechah, 3. TZ: 61. OM: I, 2b, 6b, 7b. LI: 52–54. KHY: I, 50–53. BTA: 35–39. UO: I, 90.)

2. *Abraham in the Cave* (ET: 2. OM: 3a. BTA: 35–39. Apocalypse of Abraham.)

3. *Abraham the Idol Breaker* (MR: Noah, 38. KHY: I, 53–54. LI: 54–56. OM: 5a. TZ: I, 45. BTA: 35–39. SK: 71–72. UO: I, 91–92.)

4. *Trial by Fire* (SH: I, 27. OM: 5b–6a. LI: 56–58. MR: Gen. XXXIII. GP: Part III, XXIX, 315. TZ: I, 45. SK: 72. UO: I, 95–96.)

5. *Haran's Error* (LJ: I, 202, 216; V, Abraham, Note 40. TZ: I, 45–46. UO: I, 97.)

6. *Abraham Leaves Home* (LI: 58–61. TZ: I, 46, 48–50. LJ: I, 203–206.)

7. *Abraham in Egypt* (TZ: I, Sepher Hayosher, 49–52, 53–54. KHY: I, 61–62. LI: 61. TAN: Lech Lechah, 8. UO: I, 108, 109.)

8. *The Wickedness of Sodom* (PRE: 28. KHY: I, 72. LI: 70–75. TZ: I, 56–58, 76. UO: I, 123–126.)

9. *The Voice That Reached to Heaven* (MH: I, 49–50. KHY: I, 79. LI: 75–76. TZ: I, 58. UO: I, 126.)

10. *The Destruction of Sodom and Gomorrah* (PRE: 25. KHY: I, 72–82. LI: 77–78. TZ: I, 78–80. SK: 79–80. UO: I, 128–129.)

11. *Isaac Means "Joy"* (ET: 11, 275–276. T: Moed-Shabbath, 156a. KHY: I, 83. LI: 79–80. TZ: I, 64, 84–85.)

12. *Abraham's First-born Leaves Home* (KHY: I, 85–86. LI: 81. TZ: Sepher Hayosher, 73. TZ: I, 85–86. UO: I, 143.)

13. *Abraham's Visit to Ishmael* (MH: I, 47–48. KHY: I, 91–93. LI: 85–86. TZ: I, Sepher Hayosher, 74–75. UO: I, 145–146.)

14. *Abraham's Tenth Trial* (MH: I, 52–54. SH: I, 33–36. MR: Gen. LV. TZ: I, 46, 49, 87. KHY: I, 93–96. LI: 86–89. UO: I, 146–151. PRE: XXIV gives a different list of the Ten Trials of Abraham.)

15. *The Meeting with Satan* (ET: 56. MR: Gen. LVI. KHY: I, 96–98. LI: 89–90. TZ: I, 87, 89. GP: Part II, XXX, 217 identifies Satan as Samael.)

16. *The Promise* (PRE: 31. KHY: I, 99. LI: 91–92. TZ: I, 91.)

17. *Sarah's Death* (MH: I, 59. KHY: I, 102. LI: 94–96. TZ: I, 63, 95. UO: I, 152–153.)

18. *Abraham Prays for Death* (MR: Gen. 64. KHY: I, 114. LI: 110. TZ: I, 62–64. BTA: 51–56.)

CHAPTER SEVEN: ISAAC AND JACOB

1. *Rebekah of Nahor* (MR: Gen. XII–XVII. LJ: I, 294–296. TZ: I, Sepher Hayosher, 97–100. KHY: I, 106–111. LI: 97.)

2. *Marriages Are Made in Heaven* (KHY: I, 111–113. LI: 101. TZ: I, 103–105, 107.)

3. *The Twins* (PRE: 32. KHY: I, 115. LI: 104–105. TZ: I, Sepher Hayosher, 112–113.)

4. *Esau and King Nimrod* (KHY: I, 123. LI: 110. BB: 67–73.)

5. *Because of a Pot of Lentils* (MH: I, 61–62. MR: Gen. 63–64. KHY: I, 124. UO: I, 171–172. TZ: I, 119–121.)

6. *Esau and Satan* (LJ: I, 330, 337. TZ: I, Ohel Yaccob, 122–123.)

7. *Jacob's Dream* (KHY I, 136–139. LI: 120–123. MR: Gen. 68. TZ: I, 126–128.)

8. *Jacob Falls in Love* (MR: Gen. LXX. ET: 45. LJ: I, 355–358. TZ: I, 125–128, 130–132. UO: I, 190–192.)

9. *She-Leilah* (MR: Gen. 70. TZ: I, Sepher Hayosher, 131–133. KHY: I, 144. LI: 125–127. Z: Gen. 22lb. UO: I, 192–193.)

10. *Jacob Marries Rachel* (LJ: I, 361. MR: Gen. LXX. Josephus, *Antiquities:* I, XIX gives a different version of Jacob's wait after marrying Leah, before marrying Rachel. The Midrash Rabah states seven days; and Josephus, seven years.)

11. *Jacob Goes Home* (MR: Gen. 74. TZ: I, 140–142. ET: 193. KHY: I, 148. LI: 129.)

12. *Jacob and the Angel* (PRE: 37. KHY: I, 156. LI: 135. TZ: I, 150–152. UO: I, 206–207.)

13. *The Wages of Curiosity* (PRE: 28. Josephus, *Antiquities:* I, XXI. LJ: I, 395–396. TZ: I, 153–155. MR: Gen. LXXX.)

14. *Rachel's Death* (KHY: I, 167–168. LI: 144. TZ: I, 157.)

15. *Pearls in the Sand* (Ruth Rabah, 27.)

CHAPTER EIGHT: THE GREAT FAMINE

1. *Joseph the Dreamer* (KHY: I, 187–188. LI: 159. BTA: 68–70. SK: 82. UO: I, 229.)

2. *Joseph Is Sold as a Slave* (KHY: I, 192. LI: 163. SK: 85. TZ: I, 168. UO: I, 230–232.)

3. *Reuben's Grief* (KHY: I, 193. LI: 168. MH: I, 66–67. SK: 83–84. GP: Part II, XXXVI, 227 explains why Jacob received no revelation during his days of mourning for Joseph.)

4. *Joseph in Potiphar's House* (KHY: I, 202. LI: 171–174. SK: 85. BTA: 75–77. Joseph's demonstration to show the impossibility of a human being to look upon God is attributed in Sepher Hayosher to a discussion between Joseph and Potiphar, and later attributed to Joseph and Zuleika. See also: KHY: I, 206–208. LI: 175. TZ: I, Sepher Hayosher, 160–164, 175–176. SK: 85–86. UO: I, 246–249.)

5. *Dreams of the Butler and the Baker* (KHY: I, 209. LI: 176. SK: 86–87. UO: I, 252–255.)

6. *Two Dreams and One Meaning* (KHY: I, 220. LI: 184. SK: 87–88. TZ: I, Sepher Hayosher, 180–181. UO: I, 261–263.)

7. *Joseph and Asinath* (PRE: 38. LI: 157. TZ: I, 186. UO: I, 268.)

8. *The Famine Begins* (LI: 190. MR: Gen. 91. TAN: Gen. XLI, 7.)

9. *Joseph and the "Spies"* (MR: Gen. 91. KHY: I, 228. LI: 190–193. TAN: Gen. XLI, 8.)

10. *The Brothers Return* (KHY: I, 231–237. LI: 194–197. SK: 91.)

11. *The Governor's Banquet* (KHY: I, 237–238. LI: 197–198.)

12. *Joseph Reveals Himself* (KHY: I, 246–247. LI: 204–205. TZ: I, 197–198.)

13. *Jacob's Reception in Egypt* (KHY: I, 251–252. LI: 208–209. TZ. I, 205.)

PART III: *In the Days of Moses*

CHAPTER NINE: EGYPTIAN BONDAGE

1. *The Wicked Pharaoh* (KHY: I, 276–277. TZ: I, 209–210. Ohel Yaccob, 240. SH: I, 49. OM: 257a.)

2. *Almaqube the King* (BTA: 86–87.)

3. *Pithom and Raamses* (KHY: I, 277–278. LJ: II, 247–248.)

4. *Jethro, Job and Balaam* (LJ: II, 296. Midrash Hagodol, II, XX. KHY: I, 279–280. TZ: I, 227.)

5. *Young Rider on a Lion* (BTA: 88–89. OM: 257 gives a different version of the contents of the dream, although giving the same interpretation of the warning.)

6. *Thermutis, "Daughter of God"* (KHY: II, 4–5. TZ: I, Sepher Hayosher, 225. BTA: 113 gives an interesting story about the reward of all those who believed in Moses as God's Messenger.)

7. *When Moses Burned His Tongue* (KHY: II, 6–7. OM: 358a. TZ: I, 235.)

8. *Moses Destroys a Wicked Man* (OM: 258b. TZ: I, 231. KHY: II, 9–10. BTA: 96. SK: 98.)

9. *Moses in Midian* (KHY: II, 17–18.)

10. *The Rod in Jethro's Garden* (KHY: II, 21–22. FJ: 126. OM: 360a.)

11. *The Dream Moses Dreamt* (LJ: II, 304–316. MH: I, 71 gives another version of Moses's dream. Other versions of the seven heavens are given in the apocalyptic Book of the Secrets of Enoch and in the story of the Ascension of Moses.)

12. *The Burning Bush* (LJ: II, 303–304. BTA: 100. KHY: II, 22–23. TZ: I, 235.)

13. *Moses Before Pharaoh* (KHY: II, 29–34. MR: Ex. V. BTA: 107–111. SK: 101–105. TZ: I, 236. BTA: 104–107 gives a remarkable account of Aaron's being commanded, in a dream, to prepare himself to become his brother's spokesman before Pharaoh.)

14. *The Penitence of Jannes and Mambres* (*The Lost Apocrypha of the Old Testament*, by M. R. James, 32–38; *Legends of Old Testament Characters*, by S. Baring-Gould, II, 68ff.)

15. *The Plague of Blood* (KHY: II, 35–42. SH: I, 59–60. TZ: I, 242–244.)

CHAPTER TEN: THE LONG MIGRATION

1. *The Parable of Father and Son* (ET: 21.)

2. *The Crossing of the Red Sea* (LJ: III, 18–25. KHY: II, 46–49. TZ: I, 261–264.)

3. *The Miracle That Happened to a Fish* (See GP: Part II, XXXV, 224 on Wonders. BB: 138–144.)

4. *Pharaoh and His Hosts* (LJ: III, 25–31. TZ: I, 267. ET: 19–20. Book of Jubilees: XLVIII gives the number of the Egyptian army drowned as one million and one thousand charioteers, horsemen and foot soldiers.)

5. *Bread from Heaven* (SH: I, 65–66. KHY: II, 54–55. TZ: I, 272–273; II, 470–471, 573.)

6. *The War with Amalek* (SH: I, 66. KHY:II, 58–59. TZ: I, 275. GP: Part III, XLI, 349.)

7. *The Ten Commandments* (OM: 450a–461a. ET: 53. KHY: II, 66–67. TZ: I, 72, 290.)

8. *The Meaning of the Ordinal* (Y: 3. TZ: I, 293, 294.)

9. *Not for Israel Alone* (ET: 61–62, 97. MR: Gen. XLIX. MR: Num. XIV. T: Moed-Megillah, 13a.)

10. *The Six Hundred and Thirteen Articles of Faith* (ET: 43. MR: Ex. XXXIV. See also GP: Part III, XXXV–VLIX on the division of the precepts of the Law into fourteen classes.)

11. *The Golden Calf* (SH: I, 72–74. ET: 56–57. T: Moed-Shabbath, 89. KHY: II, 74–79. TZ: I, 339, 343.)

12. *Moses and Elijah* (BTA: 117–121.)

13. *The Spies Are Cowards* (KHY: II, 89–95. TZ: II, 481–485.)

14. *Korah's Revolt* (MR: Num. V. ET: 57. KHY: II, 98–107. TZ: II, 492–498.)

15. *Aaron the Peacemaker* (ET: 204–205. PA: I, 12. ARN: XII.)

16. *Aaron's Death* (SH: I, 80–82 gives another version of Aaron's death. See also: GP: Part III, LI, 390. BTA: 122–124. KHY, II, 116–120.)

17. *Balak, Son of the Birds* (KHY: II, 125. TZ: II, 517–519.)

18. *Balaam's Ass* (KHY: II, 126–132. SH: I, 83–84. GP: Part II, XLV, 242. TZ: II, 518–526.)

19. *Moses Departs* (OM: 362a–382b. MH: I, 83–86. KHY: II, 151. TZ: II, 634–636. BB: 158–164.)

CHAPTER ELEVEN: JOB, THE AFFLICTED

1. *The Servant of God* (ARN: XLIII. MR: Num. XIV. KHY: IV, 39–40. ET: 145. T: Nezikin-Baba Bathra, 15a describes the Book of Job as a parable and not as an historical record.)

2. *The Inn at the Crossroads* (ET: 225. ARN: III. LJ: II, 229. Apochryphal *Testament of Job*. MR: Gen. XXX.)

3. *Satan's Challenge* (KHY: IV, 43–44. LJ: II, 231–232. *Testament of Job*. T: Nezikin-Baba Bathra, 16.)

4. *Job's Trials* (GP: Part III, XXII and XXIII, 296–303. ARN: 164. KHY: IV, 44–45.)

5. *The Humbled Queen* (MR: Gen. XIX. *Testament of Job*.)

6. *The Three Friends* (T: Nezikin-Baba Bathra, 16a, b. ARN: XXXVII. KHY: IV, 46–47.)

7. *The Heavenly Gift* (*Testament of Job*.)

8. *Job's Bequest* (*Testament of Job*, a Greek apochryphal work, originally called *Testament of Job the Blameless, the Conqueror in Many Contests, the Sainted*, gives the fullest story of Job, or Johab, his wife, his friends, and his children. On the antiquity of Job, see "The Historical Background of the Book of Job" by B. Maisler, in *Zion: Quarterly for Research in Jewish History* [Hebrew], September 1945.)

9. *Lukeman Al-Hakim* (BTA: 29–34.)

10. *The Reward of Wisdom* (*The Story of Ahikar. Pseudepigrapha*, by R.H. Charles, pp. 715–784, for the entire story of Ahiyakar.)

11. *Ahiyakar Adopts a Son* (MH: II, 133–134. *The Story of Ahikar*.)

12. *The Wheel of Fortune* (*The Story of Ahikar*.)

13. *Ahiyakar in Egypt* (*The Story of Ahikar*.)

PART IV: *The Promised Land*

CHAPTER TWELVE: THE CONQUEST OF CANAAN

1. *The Miracle That Happened to a Hangman* (LJ: IV, 3–4. MR: Esther.)

2. *God Speaks to Joshua* (LJ: IV, 4. TZ: II, Haftorah Berochoh, 653; Haftorah L'yom Rishon L'Pesach, 672.)

3. *The Good Rahab* (MR: Num. VIII. LJ: IV, 5. TZ: II, Haftorah Sholach, 491–492.)

4. *The Longest Day in History* (T: Nezikin-Sanhedrin, 10, Zeraim-Berachoth, 54. LJ: VI, 174. PRE: 52. GP: Part II, XXXV, 224.)

5. *The Deathless City of Luz* (MH: II, 91. LJ: IV, 29–30. MR: Gen. XXIII mentions Luz as the indestructible spinal bone from which human beings will grow in the Hereafter.)

6. *The Judge Who Liked to Sing* (MH: II, 96. Y: Judges 43. TZ: I, 276–280.)

7. *The Man Who Refused to Be King* (LJ: IV, 39–41; VI, 200. Josephus, *Antiquities:* V, VI, 3.)

8. *The Bramble That Would Be King* (LJ: IV, 42. Parable, Judges: IX, 7–15.)

9. *The Chief Freebooter of Ledja* (LJ: IV, 43–47; VI, 203–204. MH: II, 98–99. T: Moed-Taanith, 4. TZ: II, 516–517.)

10. *The Faithful Ruth* (OM: 515a–519b. LJ: IV, 30–34. MR: Ruth. TZ: II, Ruth, 759–774. MH: II, 95–96. Y: Judges, 42. ICP: 11–15.)

11. *Nathan the Rich* (TZ: II, Megilloth Ruth, 764–765.)

12. *The Weakness of a Strong Man* (MH: II, 101–102. T: Nashim-Sotah, 81. Y: Judges, 69. TZ: II, 461. KHY: II, 194–196.)

CHAPTER THIRTEEN: KING SAUL

1. *Hannah's Vow* (LJ: IV, 57–59. KHY: II, 197–198.)

2. *Samuel in Shiloh* (LJ: VI, 217. KHY: II, 198–199.)

3. *Samuel and the Stargazer* (TZ: I, 67–68, Haftorath Lech Lechah.)

4. *"We Want a King"* (Josephus, *Antiquities:* IV, III, 5. KHY: II, 208–209.)

5. *King by Accident* (T: Zeraim-Berachoth, 48. KHY: II, 209–211.)

6. *Taluth the Water Carrier* (BTA: 140–143. SK: 117.)

7. *David Meets Saul* (MH: II, 119–120. KHY:II, 225–228. ICP: 17–21.)

8. *David and Goliath* (LJ: IV, 83–89. ET: 271–272. MR: Lev. XXVI. KHY: II, 222–223, 229–235. ICP: 15, 22–24.)

9. *Reason for Madness* (LJ: IV, 89–91. KHY: II, 237. ICP: 25–28.)

10. *Because of Agag a Crown Is Lost* (LJ: IV, 68. T: Moed-Joma, 22.)

11. *And So Died the First King* (TZ: II, Haftorath Korah, 501–502. KHY: II, 249–250.)

CHAPTER FOURTEEN: KING DAVID

1. *David Acquires Jerusalem* (TZ: II, Haftorah Shemini, 391. KHY: III, 11.)

2. *How David Saved the World* (TZ: I, Sabbath Prayers, 13a, b.)

3. *The King Spearmaker* (BTA: 157–158.)

4. *David's Councilor* (LJ: IV, 94–97; VI, 256–257. ST: 55.)

5. *General Joab* (LJ: IV, 97–101; VI, 259.)

6. *David and Satan* (MH: II, 108. T: Zeraim-Berachoth. LJ: IV, 101. Z: III, 222b. Y: II, 889. BTA 160–161. KHY: III, 22.)

7. *The Poor Man's Lamb* (Parable, II Samuel, 2–7.)

8. *David in the Desert* (BTA: 162ff. KHY: III, 23.)

9. *Gad's Offer* (LJ: IV, 112. KHY: III, 46–48.)

10. *David's Death* (MH: II, 108–109. BTA: 164–166. SH: I, 102. LJ: IV, 113–114. ICP: 38–39.)

11. *King David in Heaven* (LJ: IV, 115–116; VI, 272–273.)

CHAPTER FIFTEEN: KING SOLOMON

1. *Solomon's Wish* (AOT: Sixth Book, VII. GP: Part II, XLIV, 243. KHY: III, 59–60.)

2. *The Price of a Boiled Egg* (ICP: 65–68.)

3. *It Takes a Thief* (MR: Ruth, 69. LJ: IV, 132–134.)

4. *The Wise Are Not Proud* (OM: 534.)

5. *The Site of the Temple* (LJ: IV, 154.)

6. *The Building of the Temple* (TZ: I, 322–324. TZ: II, Song of Songs, 756.)

7. *What the Shomeer Was Like* (SH: I, 106–107. TZ: I, 324.)

8. *How Solomon Obtained the Shomeer* (MH: II, 117–118. T: Nashim-Gittin, 68. KHY: III, 64–69. ICP: 180–186.)

9. *What Happened to the Shomeer* (LJ: I, 34; V, 53; VI, 299.)

10. *The Throne of Solomon* (SH: I, 106–108. LJ: IV, 157–160. MH: II, 110. TZ: II, Targum Sheni, 731–734. KHY: III, 75–78.)

11. *The Great Hippodrome* (LJ: IV, 160–162; VI, 298.)

12. *The Report of the Mountain Cockerel* (SK: 122–125. TZ: II, Targum Sheni, 735. ET: 268 tells of Solomon's power over demons. See also KHY: III, 78–79.)

13. *The Queen of Sheba in Solomon's Court* (SH: I, 108–110. LJ: IV, 142–149. TZ: II, Targum Sheni, 736. MH: II, 111–113. KHY: III, 80–87.)

14. *The Woman of Sidon* (BTA: 174–178. MH: II, 126 gives another version.)

15. *The Three Brothers* (KHY: III, 101–106.)

16. *The Doctor and the Merchant* (OM: 536. *Tales of King Solomon,* by St. John D. Seymour, 42–43.)

17. *Solomon's Daughter* (MH: II, 123–124. ICP: 221–230.)

18. *Solomon the Beggar* (MH: II, 114–115. KHY: III, 131–135. ICP: 186.)

19. *A King Is Humbled* (BTA: 170–173. T: Moed-Shabbath, 107b.)

20. *Solomon's Many Names* (LJ: IV, 125; VI, 277.)

CHAPTER SIXTEEN: THE PROPHET ELIJAH

1. *The Reed in the Sea* (LJ: IV, 179. ET: 51. T: Nezikin-Sanhedrin, 21b.)

2. *A Kingdom Divided* (LJ: IV, 159–160. MR: Esther I.)

3. *Ahab Meets Elijah* (MH: II, 128. T: Moed-Taanith, 2. KHY: III, 149–152.)

4. *Four Signs in the Desert* (TZ: II, Haftorath Pinchos, 536–538.) KHY: III, 156–157.)

5. *Jezebel and the Prophets* (LJ: IV, 188–189. TZ: I, Haftorath Tisha, 352.)

6. *The Miracle of the Pitcher* (GP: Part II, XXIX, 210 on miracles. TZ: I, 92 attributes the miracle to Elisha, not Elijah; it is also attributed to Elisha in KHY: III, 165–167.)

7. *Elijah and the Informer* (LJ: IV, 213. MR: Gen. XCIV.)

8. *The Poor Man's Cow and the Rich Man's Treasure* (LJ: IV, 223–226.)

9. *Two Wishes That Came True* (LJ: IV, 206–207. BB: 277–283.)

10. *A Share in the World to Come* (T: Moed-Taanith, 22a.)

11. *Elijah and the Angel of Death* (LJ: IV, 200–201. VI, 322–323. ET: 73. MR: Lev. XXVII.)

12. *A Good Wife Is a Good Home* (LJ: IV, 206–207. TZ: II, Ruth, 770–771.)

13. *Miracles Are Not for the Wicked* (LJ: IV, 327. UN: 226–237.)

14. *Who is Elijah?* (LJ: IV, 201–203; VI, 325.)

CHAPTER SEVENTEEN: THE AGE OF PROPHETS

1. *Elisha Heals a Spring* (MH: II, 129–130. GP: Part II, XXXVI, 227 deals with causes for loss of prophetic powers. See also KHY: III, 160–162.)

2. *Shonamith of Shonem* (LJ: IV, 242–244. TZ: I, 93–94. KHY: III, 167–168.)

3. *Jonah ben Amittai* (OM: 219a. TZ: II, Haftoroth L'minchoh Shel Yom Kippur, 693–696.)

4. *The Curse of the Forty Colors* (BTA: 230–233.)

5. *Jonah Flees* (OM: 219a–220a. LJ: IV, 246–248. KHY: III, 172–173.)

6. *Jonah and the Whale* (OM: 218a–221a. LJ: IV, 249–250. KHY: III, 175.)

7. *The Wonders of the Deep* (OM: 218b. KHY: III, 176–178. BB: 284–293.)

8. *The Power of Repentance* (LJ: IV, 250–253. KHY: III, 181–182.)

9. *Jonah in the Desert* (LJ: IV, 252. KHY: III, 181–182.)

10. *The Prophet of Consolation* (LJ: IV, 263; VI, 358–359.)

11. *The Eye of the Mind* (BB: 302–306.)

12. *The Battle of the Gnats* (KHY: III, 366; LJ: VI, 263. BB: 294–301.)

13. *Whiter Than Milk* (UN: 254–266.)

PART V: *The Unconquered*

CHAPTER EIGHTEEN: THE TEN LOST TRIBES

The Great Mystery (See the Book of Mormon, First Book of Nephi. The literature on the fate of the Ten Lost Tribes is extensive. Practically every distant race or nation has been accounted for, at one time or another, by the claim that they were the descendants of the Ten Lost Tribes. In his *Epitome of the Ancient History of Japan*, N. McLeod advances the theory that the Japanese Shindai are descended from the Ten Lost Tribes. J. Adair, in his *History of the American Indians*, published in London in 1775, expresses the belief that the Indians were of Israelite origin. And until recently, large numbers of people held tenaciously to the conviction that the British are direct descendants of the Lost Tribes, proof being offered scripturally, historically and philologically. One book on the topic, the *Identification of the British Nation with Lost Israel*, by Edward Hines, published as late as 1871, sold over a quarter of a million copies, mostly to people who held his views. In the Book of Mormon, the First Book of Nephi, we find the statement, based on revelation, that the inhabitants of America were, in part, descendants of the Lost Tribes.)

1. *Beyond the Mountains of Darkness* (MH: III, 153–154.)

2. *The Great Alexander* (The Story of Ahikar, VII, 15–21. SK: 129–130.)

3. *Alexander and the Eagle* (KHY: IV, 180–182.)

4. *Water from Paradise* (FJ: 176.)

5. *The Restless Sambatyon* (UO: II, 162–169.)

6. *Alexander and Simon* (UO: II, 145–147, 158–159. KHY: IV, 159–161, 174–176.)

7. *Alexander and the Ten Tribes* (KHY: III, 150–180 for entire Alexander cycle of stories.)

8. *Gold for Dinner* (ET: 207. T: Nezikin-Baba Metzia, 8. KHY: IV, 171–173.)

CHAPTER NINETEEN: BABYLON IS TAKEN

1. *Prophet of Lamentation* (OM: 247a. TZ: I, 238–239. LJ: IV, 294.)

2. *Capture of Jerusalem* (LJ: IV, 300–304.)

3. *David's Tomb* (TZ: II, Targum Sheni, 736.)

4. *Blood of the Prophet* (LJ: IV, 305. TZ: II, Targum Sheni, 637. FJ: 69. UO: II, 24–25. KHY: III, 256–258.)

5. *The Road into Captivity* (LJ: IV, 313–316. KHY: III, 278–279.)

6. *The Three Pillars* (SH: I, 130. OM: 98b. TZ: II, 674. UO: II, 46–51. MH: III, 147. KHY: III, 208–209.)

7. *The Miracle in the Valley of Dura* (SH: I, 129–130. UO: II, 51–53. TZ: I, 92.)

8. *Susanna and the Elders* (AOT: Book X. UO: II, 38–43.)

9. *Nebuchadnezzar's Dream* (TZ: II, Targum Sheni, 730. GP: Part III, XLIV, 243.)

10. *Daniel Becomes Governor* (OM: 98b. KHY: IV, 10. BB: 325–333.)

11. *Daniel and the Lions* (AOT: BOOK XI. MH: III, 148–149. TZ: I, 260. UO: II, 69–79. KHY: IV, 11–16.)

CHAPTER TWENTY: IN THE DAYS OF AHASUERUS

1. *The Feast in Shushan* (OM: 52a. TZ: II, Targum Sheni, 738. UO: II, 97–99. MR: Esther is devoted to the Megillah dealing with all phases of the material in this chapter. See also TZ: II, Targum Sheni, 739.)

2. *Contest for a Queen* (TZ: II, Targum Sheni, 741. MF: 52–56.)

3. *Esther's Beauty* (LJ: IV, 383–386. KHY: IV, 68–69.)

4. *How Esther Remembered the Sabbath* (LJ: IV, 386–387.)

5. *Why Haman Hated Jews* (LJ: IV, 379–399; VI, 464. KHY: IV, 75–78.)

6. *Haman Complains to the King* (SH: I, 134. KHY: IV, 78–79.)

7. *The Queen's Prayer* (LJ: IV, 423–427. TZ: II, Targum Sheni, 745. UO: II, 116–117. KHY: IV, 101–102, 115.)

8. *Whom the King Wishes to Honor* (TZ: II, Targum Sheni, 745. KHY: IV, 127–132.)

9. *The Fate of the Wicked* (SH: I, 138–141. TZ: II, Targum Sheni, 747. LJ: IV, 435–440.)

CHAPTER TWENTY-ONE: THE WALLS OF JERUSALEM

1. *Mightier Than the King* (I Esdras, III and IV. UO: II, 80–87. KHY: IV, 35–38.)

2. *Builder of the Walls* (MH: III, 150. UN: 43–50.)

3. *Seed of the Olive* (KHY: II.)

4. *The Three Precepts* (UN: 217–225.)

5. *Heaven is Not "Up"* (UN: 246–253.)

6. *Judith and Holofernes* (AOT: Book IV. OM: 204b–209a. UO: II, 267–285. KHY: IV, 252–262.)

7. *The Bride at the Wedding* (Josephus, *Antiquities:* XI, 5.)

8. *Builder of Imperishable Walls* (ET: Introduction, XVII.)

Reading List with Notes

BIBLES, APOCRYPHA AND BIBLE STUDIES

THE MODERN READER'S BIBLE, by Richard G. Moulton; first
published in 1895; The Macmillan Company, New York.
   Contains both the Old and New Testament, with three books of
the Apocrypha: Tobit, The Wisdom of Solomon and Ecclesiasticus;
presented in modern literary form, with a veritable treasury of
acute commentary in the literary introductions and notes. The first
attempt to present the Bible as literature, and still the best.

THE TWENTY-FOUR BOOKS OF THE OLD TESTAMENT,
edited and revised by Alexander Harkavy; in 3 volumes; The Jewish Publication Society of America, Philadelphia, 1916.
   In the Harkavy edition of the Old Testament (which divides
the thirty-nine Books into the traditional division of twenty-four)
the Hebrew is given on the right-hand page and the English translation on the left. The Authorized Version is used, but revised by
the editor in many places for greater translation accuracy — but,
regrettably, with no improvement in the text as literature.

THE BIBLE: DESIGNED TO BE READ AS LIVING LITERATURE, edited by
Ernest Sutherland Bates; Simon and Schuster, New York, 1936.
   This includes the Old and New Testament as well as some of
the Apocrypha; arranged as literature, using both the Authorized
and Revised Versions. Some of the editing may be questioned;
otherwise a very good collection.

THE BIBLE FOR TODAY, edited by John Stirling; Oxford University
Press, New York, 1941.
   The best part of this version of the Bible is the Introduction by
the late William Lyon Phelps.

THE OLD TESTAMENT: AN AMERICAN TRANSLATION, edited by
J. M. Powis-Smith; The University of Chicago Press, Chicago,
1927.

The intention behind this version is excellent; the execution, however, is inedequate. This edition eliminated the "thees," the "thous" and the "thys" — and along with them also some of the finest poetry in the Books.

HAMISHE HUMSHE TORAH IM HAMISHE MEGILLOTH, edited by Rabbi Yitchok Krinsky; Vilna, 1923.

There are numerous editions of the Old Testament in the original Hebrew; and an even greater number of different editions of the Pentateuch. This Krinsky edition of the Five Books of Moses and the Five Megilloth, or Scrolls, is one of the best. It carries in parallel columns the Aramaic translation, the *Targum Onkelos*, running commentaries by Rashi, and Eben Ezra, and prolific notes under the headings of "The Tent of Light" and "The Rays of Light."

TZENOH-U-RENOH, in Yiddish, by Jacob ben Isaac Ashkenazi; in two volumes; first published in 1620; Matza Press, Vilna, 1906.

A work rich in folklore. This edition contains the usual commentaries gathered from Midrashic and Talmudic sources, as well as "words of moral wisdom from the Holy Zohar."

TANACH (The Old Testament) in Yiddish, translated by the well-known poet, Yehoash; in 2 volumes; *Jewish Journal* Edition, New York, 1941.

Hebrew text with excellent Yiddish translation in parallel columns; all songs and poetic works of the Bible rendered in verse.

THE APOCRYPHA AND THE PSEUDEPIGRAPHA OF THE OLD TESTAMENT, edited by R. H. Charles; The Clarendon Press, Oxford, 1913.

This work is in two volumes, one devoted to the Apocrypha and the second to the Pseudepigrapha. Those wishing to look into the strange and magnificent hall of "the Disputed Books" are advised to read these two volumes; excellent in format and print, in order of works and in clarity of notes.

THE KORAN, translated from the Arabic by J. M. Rodwell; Bernard Queritch, London, 1876. (More recent editions of this work are available in Everyman's Library.)

This, or any other translation, will indicate how much of the Old Testament and its folklore is incorporated in Mohammed's Suras.

THE SHORT KORAN, in English, edited by George M. Lamsa; Ziff-Davis Publishing Company, Chicago, 1949.

Though this book is insufficient to give a fair idea of the Koran as the Sacred Scriptures of the Moslems, it does, by arrangement of the material, indicate the role played by Old Testament characters in Mohammedanism.

THE STORY OF BIBLE TRANSLATIONS, by Max L. Margolis; Jewish Publication Society of America, Philadelphia, 1917.

A good essay on the translations of the Old Testament, from the earliest Targum to the present day; and the problems the original Hebrew presents to all translators.

AN INTRODUCTION TO THE LITERATURE OF THE OLD TESTAMENT, by S. R. Driver; T. & T. Clark, Edinburgh, 1891.

A scholar's discussion of the Old Testament as literature; old, but rewarding.

THE BIBLE AND THE COMMON READER, by Mary Ellen Chase; The Macmillan Co., New York, 1949.

A lively and penetrating discussion of the poetic wealth to be found in the Bible, written with passion and excitement; reads like a novel; and it is hard to believe that anyone reading this book would fail to wish to read or reread many parts of the Bible.

THE MISHNAH, THE TALMUD AND THE MIDRASHIM

MISHNAYOTH (also known as SHAAS, being the first letters of the Hebrew words meaning "The Six Books"), compiled by Rabbi Judah ben Simeon; in 6 books or Orders, with Introductions to two of the Orders by Moses Maimonides; Romm Press, Vilna, 1908.

The Mishnah is divided into 6 Orders; they, in turn, are divided into 63 Treatises or Tractates, covering regulations from those dealing with the labor prohibited on the Sabbath to laws pertaining to infidelity and divorce. The Mishnah is primarily religious law. The various editions differ only in the commentaries and notes by successive editors. In Hebrew the Six Books of the Mishnah are also called by the plural name *Mishnayoth*.

SAYINGS OF THE FATHERS, in Hebrew, with parallel translation into English and a commentary by Dr. Joseph H. Hertz; Behrman House, New York, 1945.

The most widely known of the treatises of the Mishnah is given here by the late Chief Rabbi of the British Empire, in faithful translation and with notes which make the Sayings comprehensible within the context of Judaism. (Strangely enough, "The Sayings of the Fathers" are also included in the Pseudepigrapha.)

TALMUD BAVLI, collected and edited by Rabbi Ashe and Rabina; edited by the Conference of Rabbis of the United States and Canada; The Eagle Publishing Company, Montreal, Canada, 1919.

This work in eighteen volumes covers the Commentary (called Gemara) of thirty-seven of the Mishnaic Tractates; one third devoted to Haggadah. There are many older editions of the Babylonian Talmud and they are all alike, excepting for the notes by the editors and the added commentaries.

THE BABYLONIAN TALMUD, edited by Isidore Epstein; Soncino Press, London, 1935–1950.

The complete and unabridged Babylonian Talmud in English, presented in thirty-four volumes, with copious commentaries, notes, and glossaries. The most ambitious and most successful single undertaking in Judaica studies in our century.

EVERYMAN'S TALMUD, by A. Cohen; new American edition: E. P. Dutton and Co., 1949.

A comprehensive summary of the basic teachings of the Talmud intended for the layman. Organized under such headings as: "The Doctrine of God"; "God and the Universe"; "The Doctrine of Man"; "Revelation." The brief Introduction explaining the historical background of the Talmud is, in itself, an excellent introduction to the whole topic.

MIDRASH RABAH, in Hebrew; in 3 volumes; Grossman Press, Stettin, 1860.

This work covers the commentaries and legends pertaining to the Five Books of Moses and the Five Scrolls (Megiloth); Song of Songs; Ruth; Lamentations; Ecclesiastes; and Esther. Rich in Biblical folklore.

BERESHIT RABAH, edited by J. Theodor; 100 chapters in 3 volumes; Itzkowski Press, Berlin, 1902–1932.

This is the first part of the Midrash Rabah, devoted to Genesis and attributed to Rabbi Hoshaiah (who lived in the 3rd century A.D.) because the Midrash begins with his name, although numerous other Rabbinic names are mentioned throughout all of the Midrashim; this Midrash, like the rest of the Midrash Rabah, is a collective work.

MIDRASH RABAH, translated into English by Maurice Simon and edited by H. Freedman; in 10 volumes; Soncino Press, London, 1939.

This translation of the Midrash Rabah, with introductions and commentaries for the contemporary student, is another of the splendid undertakings of the Soncino Press.

SEPHER HA'ZOHAR AL HA'TORAH, issued by Moses ben Shem Tov de Leon and attributed to Rabbi Shimon ben Yohai; in 3 volumes; Goldman Press, Warsaw, 1867.

The Zohar first appeared in 13th-century Spain and the controversy about its authorship created a stir that lasted many decades. In all likelihood this is not the work of one man but a compilation which was changed and edited for centuries before Moses de Leon revealed his manuscript. The contents of the Zohar, like the work of many mystics (like the Tao Teh King, the Sacred Book of the Taoist mystics) is an extraordinary mixture of brilliant observation and perceptive thinking with a substantial amount of antics in semantics.

INTRODUCTION TO THE TALMUD AND THE MIDRASH, by Herman L. Strack, translated from the German (name of translator not given); Jewish Publication Society of America, 1931.

A scholar's book on the history of the Talmud, the contents of the Mishnah and the elaborations in the Gemara; as well as the historical significance and contents of the Midrashim; with an extensive bibliography, primarily for the scholar.

THE ZOHAR, attributed to Shimon ben Yohai, translated into English by Harry Stirling and Maurice Simon; in 5 volumes; Soncino Press, London, 1931–1934.

Considering the wide interest in the mysticism of the Zohar outside the Jewish fold, it is surprising that there had not been an English translation earlier. This Soncino edition is a good, if too literal, translation; contains Prefaces, Appendices, and Glossaries. But unfortunately it lacks an Index.

ENCYCLOPEDIAS AND BIBLICAL DICTIONARIES

THE JEWISH ENCYCLOPEDIA, in 12 volumes; Funk & Wagnalls, New York, 1916.

The most comprehensive and reliable source on the folklore of the Old Testament in English; in fact; the only comprehensive Encyclopedia in English on any topic pertaining to Jewish life and history.

VALENTINE'S JEWISH ENCYCLOPEDIA, edited by A. M. Hyamson and A. M. Silvermann; Shapiro, Valentine & Company, London, 1938.
Excellent one-volume work; compact, well written, with fine illustrations.

OTZAR YISHROEL, edited by J. D. Eisenstein; in 10 volumes; *Hebrew Encyclopedia* Publishing Company, New York, 1906–1913.
As a source of folklore of the Old Testament, topically arranged, it is as good as any available; not as expansive as *The Jewish Encyclopedia* in English.

A DICTIONARY OF THE BIBLE, by James Hastings; in 5 volumes; American Edition, Charles Scribner's Sons, 1902. (Also available in condensed form in one volume.)
This is a good reference work on all topics pertaining to the Bible — inclusive, succinct, objective.

THE ENCYCLOPEDIA OF ISLAM, edited by M. T. Houtman and Associates; in 4 volumes, with a supplementary volume; Luzac & Company, London, 1913–1938.
The best single source for Islamic legends and beliefs related to Old Testament characters and events.

OTZAR MIDRASHIM, edited by J. D. Eisenstein; in 2 volumes; Eisenstein Publishers, New York, 1915.
This treasury of the Midrashim is arranged in dictionary form and contains all the important legends in the Midrash Rabah as well as all the minor Midrashim.

COLLECTIONS

KOL HAGGODOTH YISROEL, in Hebrew, edited by J. B. Levner; 5 books bound in 4 volumes; Toshia Press, Warsaw, 1902.
The best collection of all the legends of the Jews in Hebrew; concise and authoritative; the sources of each selected story given after the title in the Table of Contents.

THE LEGENDS OF ISRAEL, edited by J. B. Levner, and translated into English by Joel Snowman; James Clarke and Company, London, 1946.

This translation of the first volume of Kol Haggodoth Yisroel covers from Creation to the Death of Joseph.

M'OTZAR HA'HAGGADAH, in Hebrew, edited by Micah J. Berdyczewski (Bin Gurion); 8 books in 2 slender volumes; Itzkowski Press, Berlin and Warsaw, 1913.

Another excellent collection of legends, with sources indicated. The first half of this work is devoted to the legends from Creation to the formation of the Talmud, and the rest covers Jewish folklore from the third century A.D. to the Chassidim.

SEPHER HA'HAGGADAH, in Hebrew, edited by J. D. Ravnitzki and C. N. Bialik; 6 books in 3 volumes; Moriah Press, Jerusalem, 1922; Dvir Publishing Company, Tel Aviv, 1936.

This collection is of greater interest to the student than to the general reader, both in arrangement and presentation.

AND IT CAME TO PASS, by C. N. Bialik, translated by Herbert Danby; Hebrew Publishing Company, New York, 1935.

Legends and stories about King David and King Solomon.

THE LEGENDS OF THE JEWS, by Louis Ginzberg, translated from the German manuscript by Henrietta Szold; in 7 volumes; Jewish Publication Society of America, Philadelphia, 1909–1938.

The most comprehensive collection of Midrashic and Talmudic legends available in English; one half of the work devoted to notes on sources and the detailed and complete index; a monumental work.

FON UNSER OTZAR, in Yiddish; in 2 volumes: Volume I, From Creation to Joseph's Death, edited by Chaim Shauss; Volume II, From the Babylonian Captivity to the Roman Conquest, edited by B. J. Bialostovsky; Central Yiddish Culture Organization, New York, 1945–1949.

The historical notes by Dr. Shauss in both volumes are particularly interesting; sources are given; according to the announced plan, this series will consist of 10 volumes when completed, and cover the entire range of Jewish folklore.

OTZAR M'AMOREY TANACH, in Hebrew, by J. D. Eisenstein; a Concordance of words, phrases and idioms in the Old Testament; Bloch Publishing Company, New York, 1925.

Contains most of the homonyms of the Old Testament, alphabetically arranged, with critical and explanatory notes.

BIBLE TALES IN ARAB FOLK-LORE, by Joseph Meyouhas, translated from the Hebrew by Victor N. Levi; Alfred A. Knopf, London, 1928.

Contains legends from Creation to Jonah; mostly Midrashic stories in Arabic garb.

MISCELLANEOUS WORKS

MOREH NEBOCHIM, in Hebrew, by Moses Maimonides (generally known as Rambam, which stands for: "Our Teacher Moses the Son of Maimon"); Om Publishing Company, American Edition, New York, 1946.

Maimonides, a great metaphysician of the Middle Ages who tried to reconcile Aristotelian philosophy with Judaic doctrine, is one of the most revered of scholars among the Jews. His work is voluminous but his *Moreh Nebochim* (The Guide for the Perplexed) is best known; in it he deals with the propositions employed to prove the Existence of God. Of greater interest to the folklore student is his long discussion in this book on the homonyms of the Old Testament and the symbolical language of the prophets.

THE GUIDE FOR THE PERPLEXED, by Moses Maimonides; translated into English by M. Friedländer; Pardes Publishing House, New York; American Edition, 1946.

(See note above.)

A GUIDE TO THE PROPHETS, by Sidney B. Hoenig and Samuel H. Rosenberg; Bloch Publishing Company, New York, 1942.

Good résumés of the contents of the Books of the Prophets; good bibliography; should prove of value to teachers and ministers.

THE FOLKLORE OF THE OLD TESTAMENT, by Sir James George Frazer; 3 volumes; The Macmillan Company, London, 1918.

Comparative folklore studies on the most important concepts and beliefs in the Old Testament by the great folklorist and author of *The Golden Bough*.

THE FOLKLORE OF THE JEWS, by Angelo S. Rappoport; Soncino Press, London, 1937.

Good discussion on Jewish folklore, explaining its characteristics and influence on Judaism; with many examples arranged topically; and containing a good bibliography for the student who wishes to explore the subject more fully.

THE ANTIQUITIES OF THE JEWS, by Flavius Josephus; Standard Edition, translated by William Whiston; first published in 93 A.D.; John C. Winston Company, Philadelphia, 1823.

This great work gives inadvertantly a clear picture of how early the Haggadah was established and accepted by the Jews; particularly in the first ten books, covering from Creation to Cyrus the First.

A HISTORY OF THE JEWISH PEOPLE, by Max L. Margolis and Alexander Marx; Jewish Publication Society of America, Philadelphia, 1927.

To understand the folklore of the Old Testament it is helpful to know its historical background; for this purpose the one-volume scholarly work by Margolis and Marx could be read with profit.

A HISTORY OF THE JEWS, by A. L. Sachar, Revised Edition, Alfred A. Knopf, New York, 1940.

Covers thirty centuries of Judaism and Jewish history; one of the few really excellent books on this topic, so difficult to present in a single volume.

FROM THE STONE AGE TO CHRISTIANITY, by William Foxwell Albright; The Johns Hopkins Press, Baltimore, 1940.

A splendid presentation of the Old Testament times in proper historical perspective.

Acknowledgments

I am indebted beyond repayment to all the rich sources of Biblical lore consulted — those few mentioned in the Bibliography and the many not included. And to an even greater extent I am indebted to my maternal grandmother, whose oral knowledge of Biblical lore exceeded any single written record; and to it she imparted in the telling an exultation and warmth no written source can equal.

It also gives me great pleasure to record my indebtness to the following people who read this book before its publication and made many valuable suggestions: Prof. James Muilenburg of the the Union Theological Seminary; Dr. David Petegorsky, Director of the American Jewish Congress; Dr. Guy Emery Shipler, Editor of *The Churchman;* Dr. Algernon D. Black, Director of the Ethical Culture Society; Dr. Ben Botkin, Dr. R. Duncan Luce, Rabbi Louis I. Newman of Temple Rodeph Sholom, Rev. Dwight J. Bradley, Prof. John Paterson of the Drew Theological Seminary, and Dr. Joseph M. Dawson of the Baptist Joint Committee on Public Affairs. But, of course, for the weaknesses and shortcomings of this book the author alone must be held responsible.

To Miss Leah Weitman of the Jewish Theological Seminary and Mrs. H. Knox Bickford of the Norway (Maine) Memorial Library I am thankful for the graciousness with which they made their library facilities available to me while this book was in preparation.

J. G.

Index